The American Civil War and the Hollywood War Film

The American Civil War and the Hollywood War Film

John Trafton

palgrave
macmillan

First published 2016 by
PALGRAVE MACMILLAN

The authors have asserted their rights to be identified as the authors of this work in accordance with the Copyright, Designs and Patents Act 1988.

Palgrave Macmillan in the UK is an imprint of Macmillan Publishers Limited, registered in England, company number 785998, of Houndmills, Basingstoke, Hampshire, RG21 6XS.

Palgrave Macmillan in the US is a division of Nature America, Inc., One New York Plaza, Suite 4500, New York, NY 10004-1562.

Palgrave Macmillan is the global academic imprint of the above companies and has companies and representatives throughout the world.

Hardback ISBN: 978-1-137-50318-3
E-PUB ISBN: 978-1-137-49701-7
E-PDF ISBN: 978-1-137-49702-4
DOI: '10.1057/9781137497024

Distribution in the UK, Europe and the rest of the world is by Palgrave Macmillan®, a division of Macmillan Publishers Limited, registered in England, company number 785998, of Houndmills, Basingstoke, Hampshire RG21 6XS.

Library of Congress Cataloging-in-Publication Data

Trafton, John, 1982-
    The American Civil War and the Hollywood war film / John Trafton.
    pages cm
    Includes bibliographical references and index.
    ISBN 978–1-137–50318–3 (alk. paper)
    1. War films—United States—History and criticism. 2. United States—History—Civil War, 1861–1865—Motion pictures and the war. 3. History in motion pictures. I. Title.
    PN1995.9.W3T83 2015
    791.43'658737—dc23   2015021051

A catalogue record for the book is available from the British Library.

Contents

List of Figures   vii

Acknowledgments   ix

Introduction: The Civil War, Pathos
    Formula, and Genre Memory   1

1   Civil War Paintings and the War Panorama   27

2   Panorama, Phantasmagoria, and Subjective
    Vision in War Cinema   49

3   War Photography   71

4   Photography and the War Film   93

5   The Soldier Diary   123

6   Civil War Epistolary and the Hollywood War Film   143

Coda: The Civil War, the American War Film,
    and Cultural Memory   159

Notes   167

Chronology of Events   175

Filmography   179

Bibliography   181

Index   189

Figures

Figure 1.1 *Prisoners from the Front* by Winslow Homer (1866)   37

Figure 1.2 A painted cyclorama view of the
Battle of Gettysburg, recently reconditioned   44

Figure 2.1 Willard's two-thousand-yard stare in *Apocalypse
Now* (United Artists, 1979)   57

Figure 3.1 *Field Where General Reynolds Fell, Gettysburg*,
by Timothy H. O'Sullivan (1863)   80

Figure 3.2 A Union soldier lies dead at Cold Harbor, Virginia,
in 1864, in Ken Burns's *The Civil War* (1990)   82

Figure 3.3 A GI convulses in death throes in a Vietnamese
forest in *In the Year of the Pig* (1968)   82

Figure 4.1 Mike Deerfield (Jonathan Tucker) photographs
a war atrocity on his cell phone in Paul Haggis's
In the Valley of Elah (2007)   117

Figure 4.2 The shell-shocked face of the War on Terror:
Maya (Jessica Chastain) in the final shot of
Kathryn Bigelow's *Zero Dark Thirty* (2012)   120

Figure 6.1 Correspondence of the Civil War: the Cameron
family in D. W. Griffith's *The Birth of a
Nation* (1915)   147

Figure 6.2 Specialist Misha "Pemble" Pemble-Belkin
providing testimony in *Restrepo* (2010)   151

Acknowledgments

It is with admiration and gratitude that I acknowledge Robert Burgoyne for his invaluable guidance and wisdom. My thanks to Leshu Torchin, Elisabeth Bronfen, Ian Christie, Robert Rosenstone, Hermann Kappelhoff, Eileen Rositzka, Debra Ramsey, Katherine Hawley, and Garrett Stewart for their influence and encouragement. I would also like to thank all my colleagues at the University of St. Andrews Center for Film Studies for their friendship and all the help that they have provided over the years. Lastly, I would like to thank my wonderful wife, Fiona, and my family for their generous love and support.

Acknowledgments

Introduction

The Civil War, Pathos Formula, and Genre Memory

In the Ken Burns's documentary *The Civil War*, historian Shelby Foote described what he saw as the importance of the war in American national identity and cultural memory: "Before the war, it was said 'the United States are.' Grammatically, it was spoken that way and thought of as a collection of independent states. And after the war, it was always 'the United States is,' as we say today without being self-conscious at all. And that's the sum of what the war accomplished. It made us an 'is'" (Burns 1990).

Twenty-three years later, on the one hundred and fiftieth anniversary of The Gettysburg Address, *The New York Times* featured a text-to-text column contrasting two articles on the legacy of the American Civil War. In "Why the Civil War Still Matters," Robert Hicks argues that the radical difference between contemporary America and the America at the time of the war's centennial is reflected in the cultural engagement with the war during its sesquicentennial: "Everything that has come about since the war is linked to that bloody mess and its outcome and aftermath," he says, citing subsequent struggles for a more diverse, tolerant, and increasingly progressive United States as a result of the war's "unfinished work" (Hicks 2013). By contrast, Charles M. Blow argues in "Lincoln, Liberty, and Two Americas" that contemporary America is not only fiercely divided but also divided along "geographic contours . . . It is ever more clear that red states are becoming ideologically strident and creating a regional quasi country within a greater one" (Blow 2013). Regardless of how one views the Civil War's legacy today, it is clear that Civil War memory continues to provide a useful framework for interpreting American generational change. In July of 2013, an estimated 200,000 visitors (including 10,000 dedicated reenactors) descended upon Gettysburg National Military Park.[1] Months later, thousands were drawn to the same site for the sesquicentennial of Lincoln's famous speech, which included a live naturalization ceremony for sixteen new immigrants.[2] In April of 2015, a restored train traveled from Washington, DC, to Springfield, Illinois, a reenactment of the Lincoln funeral train traveling the same route and stops.[3] It is clear from these events and debates that a historical and cultural memory of the Civil War remains an essential component of understanding the American present and possible future.

The Civil War continues to have a strong presence in film and television more than a century after the war became a popular topic in early cinema. The recently concluded *HBO* series *True Blood* (2008–14) featured a Confederate veteran as a principle character. Steven Spielberg's *Lincoln* (2012) was met with critical and commercial acclaim, riding a wave of new considerations on Lincoln's legacy in the twenty-first century. Anthony Minghella's academy-award-nominated *Cold Mountain* (2003) revised many of the familiar Civil War combat film conventions in response to the recently launched Iraq War and larger "War on Terror." And 2016 will see the release of the Gary Ross (*The Hunger Games*) directed *The Free State of Jones*, the true story of a band of Confederate defectors' efforts to secede from the Confederacy. Whether in historical cinema, war cinema, or as a backdrop for other genres, memory of the Civil War is informed by generational change and thus reflected in new filmic narratives. A question then emerges for film scholars and historians interested in how cinema engages with the past: How do we categorize Civil War movies? Are they "historical films" or are they "war films"? Most would agree that *Lincoln*, though featuring scenes of carnage and its aftermath, is not a war film. *Cold Mountain* contains many tropes, visuals, and narrative strategies of war films, though many would be hesitant to categorize it as such. When we start to dig beneath the surface and look further into the past, however, a relationship between Civil War films and the broader war film genre becomes clear.

Sergeant Amos Humiston, months before his death at Gettysburg in 1863, wrote, "You have put the little ones to bed, dear wife, and covered them over with care. My Frankey, Alley, and Fred, and they have said their evening prayer" (Martin 2013). One hundred and forty-eight years later, Humiston's words would feature in the History Channel television film *Gettysburg* (2011) produced by Ridley and Tony Scott. What is striking about this film is that both the History Channel's marketing campaign and the film itself suggest a historical memory of the Civil War that is largely informed by the aesthetics of the Hollywood War film. The trailer opens with an overhead close shot of a dying soldier, his body slumped against a tree, his skin ghostly gray in color, exhaling his final breaths—a thousand-yard stare upon his face, as if the totality of the destruction from that day is written in his eyes. Placebo's song "Running Up That Hill" plays over scenes of carnage, death presented in a montage of slow and fast motion. The lyrics, "So much hate for the ones we love / Tell me we both matter," play as the trailer's subtitles proclaim: "For three days in a small farm town, we faced our deadliest enemy yet: ourselves." The film contains scenes where the blood of color guards, sniped from afar, splatter across the camera lens. Hand-held camera shots place the spectator in the midst of the Midwestern Iron Brigade's charge on the battle's first day, where, under a hail of miniball fire, the voice-over of Lieutenant Colonel Rufus Dawes (1838–99) relates: "The whole field behind is streaming with men, plunging in agony, sinking to death in the ground." The action is intercut with both talking-head statements from military historians and white-text-over-black-screen title cards that inform the viewer of both the date and precise time of day that the events they are about to witness took place, presented in a typeface and fashion that one would expect from *Black Hawk Down* or an Iraq War film. In *Gettysburg*, a reimagining of a distant historical past is achieved with the tools for reimagining the conflicts of the not-so-distant past, and yet this approach does not feel out of place.

It should come as no surprise that the generic codes of twentieth- and twenty-first-century war films would be used to depict a war that predates the advent of cinema. Throughout cinema history, filmic depictions of war have been in dialogue with both past genre codes and contemporaneous debates and representational modes; war films remember previous war film cycles and draw on the resources of the present day to say something new about the nature of war. The Civil War, a conflict that took place three decades before the Lumière film exhibitions and Edison's kinetoscope and vitascope inventions, was viscerally documented through large-scale panorama paintings, still photography, and soldier testimonials, leaving behind representational principles that would later inform the development of war film genre codes. The haunting images of no-man's-land in Lewis Milestone's *All Quiet on the Western Front* (1930) recall the scope and vision of war panorama paintings. Images of dead soldiers on Omaha Beach, rocked back and forth by blood-colored waves, in Steven Spielberg's *Saving Private Ryan* (1998) recall Mathew Brady, Alexander Gardner, and Timothy O'Sullivan's photographs of death harvests from Antietam, Cold Harbor, and other horrific battles. Captain Benjamin Willard's narration in Francis Ford Coppola's psychedelic Vietnam War film *Apocalypse Now* (1979) drew heavily from veteran Michael Herr's memoir *Dispatches* (1977), a haunting account of the Vietnam experience with prose that uncannily echoes the journals and letters of Civil War soldiers. These precinema modes for representing warfare can be seen as rehearsals for the war film in different ways. This book will explore how each of these representational modes cemented different formulas for providing war stories with pathos—formulas that have a distinct presence in war cinema throughout film history.

As theorists, such as Elisabeth Bronfen and Hermann Kappelhoff, have observed, depictions of war are constructed through their use of "pathos formulas" the way that works of art are aesthetically organized to mobilize emotions and to provide the spectator with a vantage point to experience chaos and take part in remembrance. This book will consider three precinematic modes of representation used to depict the Civil War, the pathos formulas encoded in these forms, and how the resulting aesthetic and narrative codes were employed by filmmakers since the advent of cinema. It will cover large-scale panorama paintings, still photography, and epistolary forms (soldier diaries and letter anthologies that left behind a record of eye-witnesses). The narrative codes and audiovisual strategies found in war films throughout cinema history can be read as a continued application of the pathos formulas found in these precinematic modes, combining art with the act of witnessing.

The large-scale panorama paintings produced in the wake of the Civil War, with Paul Philippoteaux's *Gettysburg Cyclorama* (1883) being a notable example, allowed the viewer a poetic sense of involvement as a means to navigate chaotic battle scenes. Although panoramas first appeared in Europe during the late eighteenth century and had antecedents in large-scale paintings, cultural and technological changes in the nineteenth century informed the development of the panoramic form in the United States. Increasing speed of travel (the railroad) and an increased speed of information (the telegraph) brought the static, and distinctly European, panoramas of cityscapes and pastoral landscapes into conflict with the late-nineteenth-century American culture. These paintings, often placed around circular rotundas and sometimes in motion, contained vague or elusive vanishing points, the spectator's vision brought to focus on different points as if an invisible editor or director were present. War panoramas conveyed the fury of combat through a sense of scale and the appearance of deep focus; the figures appeared larger than life, and the viewer's eyes were able to navigate freely across an immense, and in-focus, battlefield that seemed to move in conjunction with the spectator's movements. War panoramas also appeared to compensate for the restricted vision of the battle's actual participants, using the wide space of the painting to allow the spectator to survey the scene in a way that had never existed. The effect is similar to what can be found in examples from early cinema, notably in Abel Gance's *Napoleon* triptych (1927), D. W. Griffith's *The Birth of a Nation* (1915), and in later war cinema, such as *The Longest Day* (1962) and *Saving Private Ryan* (1998). The war panoramas and large-scale paintings, therefore, appear to anticipate what Paul Virilio referred to as "panoramic telemetry" in pictorial form (Virilio 1989, 69). The war panoramas can be read as a protowidescreen (or IMAX) experience, producing representational principles highly adaptable to war cinema.

Civil War photography found its strength in its ability to preserve a micromoment in the war's history that spoke volumes about the larger history of the war. These iconic photographs broke the history of the war into thousands of small pieces from which the viewer could derive broader truths about the whole. The photography of Mathew

Brady and his cohorts are considered to be some of the most iconic and haunting images of the war because, according to Rich Lowry, they "helped the country to understand what it was looking at" (Lowry 2012, 1). The images were encoded with a series of signs that could be translated into discernable themes of the war. In the years that followed the Civil War, much of the work of Brady and others was believed to be lost, a repression of painful memories referred to by some historians as "the hibernation period" (Morris 2007, 138). The "hibernation period" ended in the mid-1890s, coinciding with the advent of cinema; Brady's photography reemerged around a time when writing history with images would soon be seen as a national tradition. In visualizing combat in the twentieth and twenty-first centuries, the pathos formulas found in early war photography—encapsulated micro histories that situate the viewer in world of shared sentiments—were used by filmmakers in varying ways. In later wars, advances in photographic technology, and the ability to photograph combat as it took place, can be seen as a corrective to Brady's cumbersome equipment and slow shutter speeds, while still retaining the transmission of emotion and poetic affect. In many twenty-first-century war films, the use of digital imagery and videos can be read as a continuation of the generic codes anticipated by Civil War photography, revised through contemporary war cinema's simultaneous engagement with past war film cycles and the new digital age.

The end of the "hibernation period" also coincided with the release of Stephen Crane's *The Red Badge of Courage* (1895), heralded as a graphic and compelling account of the Civil War, told through the eyes of a young Union private and based largely on accounts from veterans, historians, and a popular anthology *Battles and Leaders of the Civil War*. The writings of soldiers provide what could be considered counterhistories. The soldier witnesses become alternative historians through their writing, presenting authoritative accounts that either challenge or contribute to the record created by historians and war correspondents. As with war photography, soldier diaries and letters can be seen as providing microhistories and exhibiting various pathos formulas, providing war cinema with narrative strategies designed to complement the visual encoding of war. These strategies include positioning the soldier character as a counternarrator to traditional war reportage, crosscutting between the battlefront and the home front and, following the advent of sound in cinema, voiceover narration exemplified in World War II films (Terrence Malick's *The Thin Red Line*), Vietnam War films (*Apocalypse Now*, *Platoon*, and *Full Metal Jacket*), and films depicting contemporary combat scenarios (e.g., video soldier diaries in Brian De Palma's Iraq War film *Redacted* [2007], Paul Haggis's *In the Valley of Elah* [2007], and war documentaries such as Tim Hetherington and Sebastian Jünger's film *Restrepo* [2010]). The epistolary traditions of the Civil War provided the larger war story with pathos, a clear narrative thread for the spectator to navigate through the chaos of war.

There are several issues at stake that I need to address before I explore Civil War representations and their effect on war cinema in greater detail. First, it is important to have a clear understanding of pathos formula—where the idea originates from and how it operates in the visual and literary arts. In the following chapters, I will be mapping out some of the ways these pathos formulas are exhibited in nineteenth-century painting, photography, and literature, and in the war film, so it is vital that the reader has a firm grasp of this concept at the outset. As we will be looking at war cinema (in particular, recent war cinema), I will also provide a brief overview of the war film—what constitutes a war film and theoretical frameworks for studying war films. I am chiefly concerned with the notion of "genre memory" as a useful framework—that is, the process through which films revise their generic codes and find a voice that is unique to the moments they were produced. This overview will also include some of the debates surrounding recent war films, which are critical to the textual analyses performed throughout this book, and will discuss why it is important to consider the influence of Civil War representations when looking at these films' visual and narrative strategies, despite the fact that they depict conflicts that are so far removed from the Civil War in many ways. Lastly, I will turn to filmic representations of Civil War itself in order to show an indexical relationship between these films and other war films. If the history of war films is shown to be a constant response to generational change, so too is the history of Civil War films, as evolving modes of Civil War scholarship and cultural remembrance have informed how the war is presented on film.

This book is divided into three sections, each focusing on one of the three modes of Civil War representation. The first section concerns the influence of war panoramas and begins with a chapter on the history of Civil War paintings and how they generated new ways of interpreting the past and created a particular vision of battle. Though war panoramas are a critical component of my argument, it is also necessary touch upon how American landscape painters (Winslow Homer, Sanford Gifford, and others) and newspaper sketch artists responded to the war, as their works reveal issues that are relevant to discussing panoramas and other representational modes. Chapter 2 will show how this panoramic vision of battle has been used, altered, or dispensed with through the history of war cinema, with Kathryn Bigelow's Iraq War film *The Hurt Locker* and Francis Ford Coppola's *Apocalypse Now* serving as my primary examples. *The Hurt Locker* offers an updated version of war cinema's panoramic vision, informed by documentary filmmaking and contemporary demands for verisimilitude in combat depictions. *Apocalypse Now*, by contrast, performs a sharp critique on both US involvement in Indochina and previous Hollywood war films by dispensing with the traditional panoramic vision and instead turn on the influence of a different precinema spectacle: phantasmagoria—a theatrical performance originating in Europe at the end of the eighteenth century where ghostly images were projected through a magic lantern onto a screen. The second section will focus on war photography and its influence on war cinema. Chapter 3, though providing an overview of this history of war photography, will focus on the history and practices of Civil War photographers, emphasizing the pathos formulas present in the images they created. Chapter 4 will explore how war photography and their accompanying pathos formulas informed the strategies of various war films, including contemporary war films that feature digital imaging and documentary styles as part of their visual grammar. In this chapter, I will focus my attention on Emile de Antonio's Vietnam War documentary *In the Year of the Pig* (1968), Clint Eastwood's World War II film *Flags of Our Fathers* (2006), and two Iraq War films, Brian De Palma's *Redacted* and Paul Haggis's *In the Valley of Elah* (both 2007), to show how a new language for writing war with images has emerged over the last decade. Chapter 5 will look at Civil War epistolary traditions and how they drew upon the literary culture of their day to provide a pathos-laden war story to compete with the record of the war from journalists and historians. This chapter will also examine how written accounts of World War I, World War II, and the Vietnam War contain the same strategies. The final chapter will show how the writings of soldiers are exhibited in the narration of war films, both fictional and documentary films. This chapter will especially consider the Afghanistan War documentary *Restrepo* (2010) in showing how the influence of written soldier accounts can be felt in contemporary war cinema.

Pathos Formula

How Civil War photography and epistolary forms provide war narratives with pathos is essential to my overall analysis and arguments put forth in this book. Therefore, it is important to define what is meant by "pathos formula." Stemming from the work of German art historian Abraham Moritz "Aby" Warburg (1866–1929), pathos formula can be understood as the way a work of art is aesthetically organized so that the spectator can experience its subject matter and become emotionally involved from a safe vantage point. By extension, pathos formulas in war cinema are strategies by which the intensity of combat is transferred into a formalized aesthetic (Bronfen 2012, 20). My concept of pathos formulas in this book draws on the work of Elisabeth Bronfen, in particular her important book *Specters of War* (2012). Bronfen observes that the old adage that one cannot truly imagine war unless one has experienced it firsthand is formally addressed through pathos formulas. War narratives rely on pathos to transport the reader or spectator to a chaotic world where, according to André Bazin, "war, with its harvest of corpses, its immense destruction . . . leaves far behind it the art of imagination" (Bazin 1967, 31). Bronfen also notes that the pathos provided by the characters and formal elements of these films "[apprehend] the ungraspable intensity of war" because a balance is struck between "comprehending an intense emotion by tapping into one's own imaginative capacity and offering a conceptual presentation of it" (Bronfen 2012, 20). The spectator's ability to arrive at some level of understanding the human cost of war is based on the visual presentation of a human emotion that can be perceived without having physically experienced the depicted event personally (Bronfen 2012, 20).

Another essential component to my discussion of pathos formulas is the work of Hermann Kappelhoff and the Mobilization of Emotions

in War Films Project (hereafter cited as MEWFP) at the Freie Universität Berlin, an important project that breaks war film pathos formula
in a series of "pathos scenes" and analyses how these scenes situate the
spectator in world of shared sentiments in order to mobilize emotions
through audiovisual strategies. The project identifies many different categories of pathos scenes "assigned to different realms of affect."
These pathos scenes are designed to create a sense of shared memory
and shared suffering, and each of these scenes has a distinct presence in
nineteenth-century Civil War representations.[4]

I would like to like to briefly catalog these scenes of pathos described
by the project, as they will be essential to my discussions later in the
book. In short, they are as follows:

1. **Transition between two social systems.** These are scenes that
   emphasize the differences between civilian life and soldiering life
   and the journey the soldier makes from one to the other. If we contrast the photographs of soldiers before and after the Civil War, we
   can see this transition through the face (and other visual signs within
   the frame), and in many cases in the photograph/display/exhibition
   process requested by soldiers before and after the war. In the writings of soldiers, we can see this process played out in many striking
   ways, as the journal of Elisha Hunt Rhodes demonstrates (discussed
   in Chapter 5). Painters such as Winslow Homer captured the effects
   of the war on the homeland in a way that shows an overlap between
   the two systems.

2. **Formation of a group body.** This is the relationship between the
   individual soldier, his military unit, and military institution. War
   stories abound with the forging of friendship and camaraderie, and
   thus they were captured in photographs and written war narratives.
   In the next chapter, we will also see how in Homer's *Prisoners from
   the Front* (1866) exhibits this bonding and sense of unity even in the
   face of defeat.

3. **Battle and nature.** In these scenes, a battle against nature "replaces
   the battle against the enemy and acts as a form of the experience
   of battle" (MEWFP). The immobilized wounded that lay in *The
   Wilderness* near Chancellorsville, Virginia, in 1864 were consumed
   by a forest fire started by the heat of shells and miniballs against
   dried leaves and dead trees; this incident was described in written
   accounts from survivors, and photographs of skeletal remains tell

this grim story of nature displacing Lee's armies as the agents of Union battlefield death.

4. **Battle and technology.** These scenes place technology at the center of the war story. The Civil War is an important moment of history to see the emergence of this pathos scene, as the conflict can be seen as a terrible consequence of a clash between modern technology and outdated military tactics and notions of battlefield heroics.

5. **Homeland, woman, home.** These are moments that depart from martial life and focus on a return to a home life, even if only in the soldier's imagination. Memories of home and loved ones exist in the form of flashbacks in war films and they have a distinct presence in Civil War epistolary, acknowledged directly in films such as Edward Zwick's *Glory* (1989).

6. **Suffering, victim, sacrifice.** These are scenes that focus on "bodily pain, vulnerability, and dying." The death harvest photographs from the Civil War, which I will describe in greater detail in Chapter 3, are prime examples of this. In soldier writings, we can see the influence of these scenes greatly in World War I narratives.

7. **Injustice and humiliation/moral self-assertion.** These are scenes of reflection; the soldier critically examines his war experience and morally evaluates the war itself. The writings of soldiers are rife with these pathos scenes (and they have a strong presence in Vietnam War films), but war photography, as encapsulated memories of war, are noted for their power to provoke this emotional response in the spectator.

8. **A sense of community as the shared filmic remembrance of shared suffering.** This is a pathos scene that crystalizes the emotive power of all the others and can be seen as the overriding purpose of pathos formula in war representation, whether it is painting, photography, or written soldier testimonies. The spectator is invited to take part in a communal remembrance by sharing in the suffering of those who survived and those who did not. In this form of pathos, we can see a connection between the photographs of the dead on battlefields (such as Gettysburg or Antietam) and films that memorialize those who fought, whether for noble or inglorious causes.

How do pathos formulas in operate in the three precinematic forms? Psychologically speaking, pathos formulas, according to Adi Efal, rely on "the situation in which the human being is able to bear the existence of chaotic power without being hurt" (Efal 2001, 221). Pathos formula "expresses this traumatic encounter between man and the world, [resulting from] a visual fixation, the source of which is a mimicry of some of the bearable qualities of the threatening force, that then becomes petrified and fixed as an image" (221). In large-scale paintings, panorama paintings in particular, the sheer terror of battle—one that exceeds the everyday human consciousness and threatens its security—is petrified in a fixed image through which the spectator can experience (and, by virtue of their size, explore) this chaotic power without being hurt. In Civil War photography, the aftermath of the carnage, shown through scorched-earth landscapes littered with corpses, also exceed the everyday human experience, carrying traces of the traumatic encounter. The soldier diary contains the following two forms memory found in pathos formula: (1) memory of the traumatic event, and (2) memory of a defensive consciousness of the recipient in relation to the encounter (222). Overall, pathos formulas, regardless of the representational modes that contain them, are "cultural products" according to Efal. Like film genre codes, they develop over history, producing different content in response to generational shifts.

In motion pictures, the psychological process behind pathos formulas plays a big role in how images are arranged and orchestrated to strike emotional chords, in not just war films but other genres as well. Horror stories, as Stanley Kubrick states, "show us the archetypes of the unconsciousness: we can see the dark side without having to confront it directly" (Kroll 1980). Here, Kubrick is describing the horror genre's use of pathos formula—an experience outside of one's daily consciousness such as an encounter with death and the supernatural is presented in a way that can be felt, in all its intensity, without the spectator being directly involved in it. This notion is touched upon in the work of Linda Ruth Williams, wherein she describes horror films, melodramas, and pornography as "body genres"—genres that derive their emotive power from eliciting physical reactions from the spectator at a distance.[5] Robert Burgoyne goes further in his description of the war film as a body genre; war films place the body of the soldier at the center of the narrative, the body as a "national symbol" that brings history to life "in a way that foregrounds corporeal experience" (Burgoyne 2012, 8). Paintings and photographs of soldiers, viewed alongside the soldiers' written testimonies, provide a somatic vision of the past. Here we can see a convergence of the pathos formulas found in Civil War–era representations in the figure of the soldier character as a "body at risk," providing the viewer with an experience of the past thorough bodily sensations that are both familiar and disturbing.

This simultaneous feeling of familiarity and repulsion found in representations of war echoes what Sigmund Freud called *das unheimliche*, or "the uncanny." As with pathos formulas, the uncanny operates on an aesthetic level and a psychological level, where, as Stephen F. Eisenman writes, "primal thoughts and fears" are invoked and the familiar is made strange (Eisenman 2007, 16). At first glance, this appears to be the opposite of what pathos formula aims for: an unfamiliar experienced rendered familiar and accessible through aesthetic strategy. The uncanny in battle, however, has been used in war films as a way of defamiliarizing the genre—the film plays on expectations created by previous films and finds its critical edge in making strange a film genre once familiar. This practice is linked to several war films that seek to challenge previous representations of war. In Chapter 2, I will show how Francis Ford Coppola's *Apocalypse Now* and Kathryn Bigelow's *The Hurt Locker* deployed instances of the uncanny as a way of challenging the traditional panoramic vision of war first exhibited in nineteenth-century American and European panorama paintings. Coppola, Bigelow, and other filmmakers draw upon or subvert traditional pathos formulas in order to produce new images of war that are relevant to the historical moment, a process referred to as "genre memory," which is a defining component in the history of the war film.

The War Film and Genre Memory

Of all the cinematic genres, the war film is one of the oldest and most celebrated. War films have performed many tasks throughout film history in varying ways. War films envision war's impact on culture and social space, they refashion ideas about racial and national identity, they reimagine war's rewriting of the human psyche, and they present a traumatic past has historical haunting, as a reminder of war's unfinished business. Each of these key elements of war cinema offers many teachable moments about a nation's progression in relation to a memory of its historical past, a memory that is culturally renegotiated through each successive generation.

As the nineteenth century drew to a close, actualities (short, nonfiction exhibition films) of the Spanish-American conflict (1898) glorified US military exploits in Cuba. During the 1910s, early silent cinema depicted the Civil War and soon set its sights on the Great War, with Griffith's propaganda film *Hearts of the World* (1918) and Charles Chaplin's dark comedy *Shoulder Arms* (1918) as early examples. Films from the 1920s and 1930s featured aerial dogfights (Howard Hawks's *The Dawn Patrol* [1930] and Howard Hughes's *Hell's Angels* [1930]), trench warfare (Lewis Milestone's *All Quiet on the Western Front* [1930]), and the lasting aftershock of trauma (King Vidor's *The Big Parade*, 1925). World War II found its way onto the big screen with incredible speed, the World War II combat film shaping a cultural understanding of the war and playing a propagandist, morale-boosting role in the war effort. The Korean War and Vietnam War would become enduring film topics, though direct depictions of the latter did not appear until years after that war's conclusion.[6] Post–Cold War conflicts also received cinematic treatments, the Persian Gulf War in particular being the setting for several films. On the surface, these various cycles of war films appear to stand in stark contrast to one another (the World War II–era combat films and the antiwar Vietnam War films, for example). The common thread through these war film cycles, however, is that war cinema, according to Robert Burgoyne, serves as "an index of generational change" and their generic codes are revised in response to generational change (Burgoyne 2013, 349). The history of the war film is marked by historical remembrance and revisions to cultural attitudes toward war, and both can be seen in the narrative and audiovisual strategies employed in these films.

Here we must pause and ask ourselves by what process are war films revised through each successive cycle? Also, how do war films retain a connection with the Civil War–era representational modes, even in ones depicting twenty-first-century combat? War films reinvent themselves through "genre memory," a notion described by Mikhail Bakhtin: genres change slightly with each use, remembering past usage while at the same time acquiring new modes of expression drawn from the present.[7] Twenty-first-century war films, for example, simultaneously remember past war film codes and incorporate contemporary discourse and new aesthetic codes in order to distinguish themselves from previous war film cycles and ground themselves in cultural relevance. An important component of Bakhtin's theory of genre memory, one that is central my readings of films in this book, is the concept of "double-voicing." When a film is double-voiced, it simultaneously depends on and violates genre norms. *Saving Private Ryan*, for example, is double-voiced through "filtering the events of World War II through the lens of Holocaust remembrance" (brought to prominence during the 1990s, notably through the reception of Spielberg's *Schindler's List*) and through a memory of the Vietnam War and Vietnam War films (Burgoyne 2008, 50). Genre memory and the process of double-voicing—"the adapting of an older genre to a new context"—provides an essential framework for highlighting the influence of nineteenth-century Civil War representations on the war film genre, and this book will place the Civil War as the central origin of this genre memory (58).

How genre memory operates in contemporary war cinema reveals a lot about the nature of America's cultural relationship with the past. At the start of the twenty-first century, a reinvigorated cultural memory of World War II's "Greatest Generation," profoundly shaped by Steven Spielberg's *Saving Private Ryan* (1998), informed a sense of American triumphalism in both war cinema and a post-9/11 America awash with patriotic fervor (Auster 2005, 205). Yet this generational memory of World War II would soon turn to a generational memory of the Vietnam War after the Iraq War was launched in 2003, and it soon became clear that films dealing with contemporary conflicts would be measured against the Vietnam War films. Two articles, one appearing in 2006 and another in 2008, appeared to confirm this, signaling the role that the memory of the Vietnam War films would play in the construction of the Iraq War films. Richard Corliss' 2006 *Time* article, "Where Are the War Movies?" and Peter Biskind's article, "The Vietnam Oscars," appearing in the March 2008 issue of *Vanity Fair*, both enquired into the apparent lack of Iraq War films. Corliss made a premature claim that "movies mean less than they did" at the time of the Vietnam War, and that the Iraq War has not "touched" Americans in the same way as Vietnam did (Corliss 2006).[8] His article also drew a parallel between the lack of Iraq War films and the lateness of the Vietnam War films—a decade of silence between John Wayne's jingoist film *The Green Berets* (1968) and the more thoughtful, penetrative films of 1978 (notably *The Deer Hunter* and *Go Tell the Spartans*). Biskind's article chronicled the production histories of Hal Ashby's *Coming Home* and Michael Cimino's *The Deer Hunter*, and closed with the argument that these two films "retain the power to provoke and divide," as "Vietnam remains an open wound" even amid US involvement in Iraq and Afghanistan (Biskind 2008). Both articles appear to suggest that the effectiveness of films concerning the Iraq and Afghanistan Wars would be measured against the Vietnam War films and the new subjectivities ushered in by the September 11 terrorist attacks.

The effectiveness of the visual style of contemporary war films has drawn much critical discussion. Surveillance technology used to wage modern war, the digital video and Internet technology used by soldiers, and on-the-ground witnesses capturing the war experience are integral to the visual language of contemporary war films. Additionally, the increased popularity and consumption of documentary films about contemporary conflicts also informs the visual coding and narrative strategies of many twenty-first-century war films. Yet what has not received attention is how the search by these contemporary war films for a rhetorical container can be linked to the representational principles and technological advances that emerged from the Civil War. As common thread found in all three Civil War representational modes is their ability to shape and reorient the spectator's perception of combat, I will link large-scale paintings, photography, and soldier testimony to a continually evolving filmic grammar informed by surveillance technology and targeting capabilities.

The work of Friedrich Kittler and Paul Virilio is essential to understanding the history of war cinema and how their "logistics of perception" have developed over the twentieth and twenty-first centuries. In his work *War and Cinema* (first released in 1984), Virilio highlights the ways in which war technology and cinema technology have developed in conjunction with one another, as both technologies are centered on perception and movement. From Etienne-Jules Marey's 1882 chronophotographic rife—a "precursor of the Lumiére brothers' camera and a direct descendent of the Colt revolvers and cylindrical guns"—to the strategic missile defense initiative of the Reagan era (dubbed "Star

Wars"), there exists an interdependency between the strategies for waging war and the strategies for representing war (Virilio 1989, 68). Virilio also acknowledges the challenge of providing verisimilitude in representations of battlefields that have been emptied of the capacity for art and imagination ever since the early attempts by American filmmakers to document the First World War.

Friedrich Kittler, taking his taking his cue from Paul Virilio's observation that there is "no war without representation" and that weapons are "tools not just of destruction but of perception," wrote that the history of the motion picture camera "coincides with the history of automatic weapons" (Kittler 1999, 6, 124). According to Kittler, "The transport of pictures only repeats the transport of bullets. In order to focus on and fix objects moving through space, such as people, there are two procedures: to shoot and to film. In the principle of cinema resides mechanized death as it was invented in the nineteenth century: the death no longer of one's immediate opponent but of serial non-humans" (124). Throughout this book, especially in Chapter 3 where I discuss photography, the work of both Virilio and Kittler will be used to bolster our understanding of how the aesthetic and narrative codes that emerged from the Civil War remained a key component of war film genre memory even as the logistics of perception in war changed dramatically.

As reflected in the sesquicentennial events, the Civil War plays an important role in the (ongoing) discourse on US national identity and, by extension, war films continue to provide a unique site for exploring competing national narratives. War, according to Anthony D. Smith, intensifies popular social nationalisms (Smith 2001, 120). Much of American war cinema, including many Civil War films, can be viewed as a hegemonic nationalist discourse par excellence, although many films appearing at the end of the twentieth century appear to acknowledge multiple forms of nationalism within a broad American narrative. In war films, the combat group embodies varying notions of national identity and in many instances provides a means for cinematically rendering debates on war mythology and narratives of nation. Additionally, Fredric Jameson writes, "American war films, taking class difference for granted and only gradually absorbing racial difference, found their originality . . . in the typology of personalities thrown together in a group (war machine)" (Jameson 2009, 1534). This book will take to task Jameson's argument that all war films are essentially alike through bridging a connection between the aesthetic and narrative strategies found in Civil War paintings, photography, and soldier writings, and will examine how varying concepts of national identity are renegotiated in the war film.

An enduring subgenre of the war film is the veteran film, in which the tortured mental state of the veteran is a discernable narrative device. As the condition of PTSD has become widely recognized and understood, contemporary war films have readily addressed the social issues surrounding traumatized veterans. I will explore at great length how Paul Haggis's *In the Valley of Elah*, a film that features both a Vietnam War veteran and an Iraq War veteran (and contains echoes of Michael Cimino's iconic Vietnam War film *The Deer Hunter* [1978]), repurposes the influence of war photography in war films in an attempt to mobilize antiwar sentiment. Additionally, there are other notable veteran films of the twenty-first century that exhibit themes from earlier veteran films. Jim Sheridan's film *Brothers* (2009), based on Susanne Brier's 2004 Danish film of the same name, is an Afghanistan War film that parallels Hal Ashby's Vietnam veteran film *Coming Home* (1978). Kimberly Pierce's *Stop-Loss* (2008) follows the moral decline of Iraq War veteran friends. Even popular US television contains traumatized veteran characters, notably the PTSD-afflicted Iraq War veteran Terry Bellefleur (Todd Lowe) in the HBO series *True Blood* (2008–14). The contemporary veteran film can be seen as a continuing chapter in the broad history of the war film and, at the same time, contrasts with previous war film cycles in how veteran characters and war trauma are portrayed on screen through its use of genre memory.

The concept of battlefield haunting is another critical component of war film studies, especially in recent years (the work of Robert Burgoyne and Elisabeth Bronfen being notable examples). In the war film, haunting renders real-world notions of trauma into poetic meditation. Newly understood symptoms of PTSD have been understood through aesthetic forms and literary tropes pertaining to the supernatural. This cinematic form enables the traumatic effects of battle to be conveyed viscerally and to adopt a deeper cultural meaning than what is implied by war reportage. As Burgoyne and I have written, historical haunting can be understood as the traumatic past still continuing to trouble a nation (Burgoyne and Trafton 2015, 11) and, in the case of war films, haunting as an aesthetic device serves as a constant reminder of war's unfinished business (Bronfen 2012, 5). This book will also consider battlefield haunting and an emerging form of scholarship referred to as "hauntology" in fleshing out the ways that formulas of pathos, found in Civil War representations, resonate in war cinema.

To summarize, there are five important features of war films that this book will read in relation to Civil War paintings, photography, and epistolary traditions:

1. War films reinvent themselves through genre memory.
2. War films rewrite their visual grammar in response to new "logistics of perception" in war.
3. War films bring into relief a discourse on national narratives.
4. War films are equally concerned with the lives of soldiers on the battlefield and away from the battlefield through domestic landscapes and social order altered by war trauma.
5. War films portray the battle zones of the past (and in some cases, the present) as haunted sites, an aesthetic rendering of war trauma.

The Civil War on Film

Filmic depictions of the Civil War, though often considered separate from the larger war film genre, have evolved through the same generational changes throughout film history that have contributed to the rise and fall of different war film cycles. It is important to consider the shifts in Civil War scholarship throughout the twentieth century, as these forms of scholarship engage with Civil War mythology in varying ways. Gary W. Gallagher identifies the following four successive forms of Civil War scholarly traditions: (1) the Lost Cause tradition, (2) the Union Cause tradition, (3) the Emancipation Cause tradition, and (4) the Reconciliation Cause tradition (Gallagher 2008, 2). From the silent era to the twenty-first century, Civil War films have been informed by each of these scholarly traditions in varying ways, providing a record for film scholars and historians of generational engagements with Civil War history and mythology. In examining a brief history of Civil War films, we can see how these films were tuned into these scholarly traditions at the times that they were produced.

The Lost Cause tradition "offered a loose group of arguments that cast the South's experiment in nation-building as an admirable struggle against hopeless odds" (2). As one of the earliest Civil War films, Griffith's *The Birth of a Nation* exemplifies the Lost Cause tradition in several striking ways, notably in it unambiguous sympathy for the Southern cause, its critique of the Reconstruction period, and its explicit endorsement of the Ku Klux Klan. The film's legacy as an overtly racist portrait of American history and Civil War remembrance provides both a starting point for scholarship on American Civil War films and as a stark contrast with Civil War films appearing toward the end of the century, films that would largely lean toward the other three traditions in varying ways.

The Union Cause tradition attempted to reframe the Civil War as an effort to preserve the union "in the face of secessionist actions that threatened both the work of the Founders and, by extension, the future of democracy in a world that had yet to embrace self-rule by a free people" (2). Between the unquestionably Lost Cause film *Gone with the Wind* (1939) and the 1960s, many films would come to depict the Civil War in ways that oscillated between the Lost Cause tradition and the burgeoning Union Cause tradition in the wake of Nazi Germany's demise. Some of these films depicted the war directly (such as John Huston's 1951 adaptation of Stephen Crane's *The Red Badge of Courage*) and some Westerns used war trauma as a character background story. It was not until the mid-1960s, however, that Civil War films interrogated the conflict with a more explicit antiwar slant—Andrew V. McLaglen's *Shenandoah* (1965) as an early example of such a film, and later Don Sielgel's *The Beguiled* (1971). Civil War films began to taper off during this period for the same reason that was behind their thematic shift: opposition to the Vietnam War was dramatically changing the American landscape as well as public attitudes toward war and war films. Civil War films, however, would return nearly a decade later alongside Vietnam War films and, in conjunction with the Civil Rights Movement, the Emancipation Cause tradition began to assert itself.

The Emancipation Cause returned the issue of slavery to the forefront of the discussion, reframing the war as a crusade to "remove a cancerous influence on American society and politics" (2). An exemplar of the Emancipation Cause in Civil War cinema is Edward's Zwick's *Glory* (1989), a film chronicling the history of the ill-fated 54th Massachusetts regiment, the first black regiment of the Civil War, led by abolitionist Colonel Robert Gould Shaw. A voice-over of Shaw reading a letter to his mother as the film's opening dialogue signals to the spectator that it will be Shaw who will narrate the Civil War; Kevin Jarre's screenplay is based on Colonel Robert Gould Shaw's personal letters, one of which describes his experiences at the Battle of Antietam (Canby 1989). The Battle of Antietam featured in the film's first act and the assault on Battery Wagner in the film's third act employ a panoramic vision of battle that appear lifted from the large-scale paintings and cycloramas. The death harvests after these battles, fields and beaches strewn with corpses, eerily echo the photography of Brady and his cohorts. The film, like both Civil War photography and epistolary forms, offers a history within the history—the historical significance of the Civil War and the meaning its historical memory holds for Americans is compressed into a story of a fraction of its participants. The sense of shared suffering and sacrifice, whether explicit or implied, operates in scenes of pathos used to make a story of brutal combat in a distant past accessible to an audience generations removed. As Robert Brent Toplin observed, "As a consequence of [late twentieth-century] homogenization, northerners and southerners were less contemptuous towards each other than they had been before. Yankees could study the Civil War and relate more empathetically to the hardship the southern people suffered in the years of conflict, and southerners could examine the history with less bitterness about the 'Damned Yankees' than their ancestors expressed. The Civil War seemed less a question of 'them' against 'us'" (Toplin 1997).

Lastly, the Reconciliation Cause attempted to highlight the American virtues embodied by soldiers on both sides of the conflict (Gallagher 2008, 2). The reconciliation cause would be articulated exceptionally in Ken Burns's critically acclaimed PBS documentary *The Civil War* (1990), a sprawling nine-part series running more than 11 hours. Narrated by author and historian David McCullough, *The Civil War* features several notable actors and actresses portraying the voices of the war's salient figures (Morgan Freeman, Jason Robards, Jeremy Irons,

Arthur Miller, and Julie Harris, to name a few). The soundtrack, containing some of the most popular songs of the war, is most famous for an original composition: *Ashokan Farewell*, written by Jay Unger in the style of a Scottish lament and later viewed as documentary's signature piece, as well as part of a soundtrack to the larger cultural memory of the war. The film's visual composition, however, is perhaps one of the most important contributions to twentieth-century Civil War cultural memory. The majority of the story is told through photographs from the war (and occasionally paintings) using a process that would later be known as "the Ken Burns effect," where the camera pans across photographs and zooms in or out at varying speeds (often to the rhythm of the music) to produce the illusion of motion within the pictures, as if the microhistories encapsulated in these photographs were coming to life. The images and epistolary are orchestrated in the film to make their subjects appear to move within the frame, and the emotional content often dictates how the Ken Burns Effect operates when looking at certain images. Burns's film also affirms Burgoyne's view of the soldier as an agent of history, presenting the past as a "corporeal experience." The Civil War becomes, for the viewer, a past that can be felt with recognizable bodily sensations and emotions. As such, I will refer to this film at several points throughout this book, as it provides a perfect example of what kind of war cinema can be created when all three Civil War–era representational modes are crystalized, and in Burns' film, this is the case.

While the influence of Civil War photography can be felt in documentary war films, another mode of historical inscription from the Civil War provided a template for narration in recent films concerning conflicts in Iraq and Afghanistan: the writings of Civil War soldiers. In the run-up to the Persian Gulf War, General Norman Schwarzkopf advised his staff to watch Ken Burns's PBS documentary series *The Civil War* (1990). "[Schwarzkopf] thought that, if anything, the series had reminded him that the soldiers were real human beings on both sides and not just arrows on a general's map," recalled Burns more than a decade later (Burns 1990). Burns's documentary, which begins with an Oliver Wendell Holmes quote stating that the war's participants had shared an "incommunicable experience," employs both Civil War photography and testimonials from soldiers, generals, slaves, politicians, civilians, and a host of others to provide an organic and contemporary relation to the past through the form of the traditional historical documentary. The use of letters and journal entries is critical to Burns's documentary, as they provide what he describes as history from both "the bottom up" and "the top down" in order to humanize an event so distant to a contemporary audience. Grunt documentaries, such as *Restrepo* and the award-winning Danish Afghanistan War documentary *Armadillo* (directed by Janus Metz, 2010) evoke the humanizing effect of soldier testimonials in a way that is comparable with the use of soldier diaries in Ken Burns's film.

A wave of made-for-television films followed in the wake of *The Civil War*'s success. *The Class of '61* (1993), for example, told the story of three friends, West Point graduates, who found themselves on opposing sides during the war. The film's cinematographer, Janusz Kaminski, caught the attention of Steven Spielberg, and henceforth became Spielberg's faithful collaborator. Media mogul Ted Turner also took a keen interest in a resurging interest in Civil War history and produced *Ironclads* (1991) with A&E, the story of the naval showdown between the *USS Monitor* and the *CSS Merrimack*. Among these films, Ronald Maxwell's *Gettysburg* (1993), also produced by Turner, stands out by being clearly in dialogue with Ken Burns's film and previous Civil War film cycles. Based on Michael Shaara's 1974 novel *The Killer Angels*, *Gettysburg* presents the events surrounding the battle (June 30–July 3, 1863) on an epic scale. The film was originally conceived as a television miniseries but the scope of the film and its cast (featuring Martin Sheen, Tom Berenger, and Jeff Daniels) inspired Turner to push for a theatrical release. *Gettysburg* differs from *Glory*'s post-Vietnam reappraisal of Civil War mythology in that it does not express the same antiwar sentiments or interrogate the issues of race surrounding the conflict. The film contains only a few brief discussions of slavery and only one short scene featuring an African American, a runaway slave named John Henry given shelter by the Twentieth Maine, early in the film. As a result, *Gettysburg* appears to affirm the Reconciliation Cause and acknowledges the important role that Burns's film played in the cultural reevaluation of the Civil War at the end of the Cold War. *Gettysburg*, however, may have been an early indication that there were flaws in the Reconciliation Cause, and it was in Maxwell's follow-up,

Gods and Generals (2003), were we can see that this may have been the case and that there was a need for a revised Civil War cultural tradition.

Gods and Generals chronicles the rise and fall of General Thomas J. "Stonewall" Jackson from the war's beginning to his death at the Battle of Chancellorsville in 1863, with many of *Gettysburg* cast members reprising their roles. The film was a critical and commercial failure, but an examination of the film's failure helps highlight the nature of contemporary Civil War discourse, especially when framed against the more successful Anthony Minghella Civil War film *Cold Mountain* released later that year. The film's careless appropriation of the Lost Cause tradition within a broader Reconciliation tradition proved to be a crucial error on the part of the filmmakers and a gross miscalculation. An uncritical stance on the Southern cause and a side-stepping of the brutality of slavery placed *Gods and Generals* under a shadow of irrelevance. "Here's a movie that Trent Lott might enjoy," wrote Roger Ebert in his review of the film. "Less enlightened than *Gone with the Wind*, obsessed with military strategy, impartial between South and North, religiously devout, it waits 70 minutes before introducing the first of its two speaking roles for African Americans" (Ebert 2002). In a scene between Stonewall Jackson (Stephen Lang) and his black servant Jim (Frankie Faison), Jackson proclaims that one day "your people will be free . . . and in so doing seal a bond of enduring friendship between us," perpetuating the myth of the nobility of the white Southerner and obscuring attempts to place slavery at the center of Civil War cultural memory.

Cold Mountain, on the other hand, evokes the war film genre codes in a way that is relevant to the post-Vietnam (and Iraq War) generation. The film begins at the Siege of Petersburg (late 1864) with a recounting of the attempt by the Union Army to dig a tunnel under the Confederate trenches, packing it with explosives, in order to blow a crater in the Southern lines for a Union attack. Famed Civil War historian Shelby Foote notes that the Civil War was a dress rehearsal for the trench warfare of World War I, exemplified by the Sieges of Vicksburg and Petersburg, and the opening sequence of *Cold Mountain* reflects this observation. The failed Union attack that follows in the film is reminiscent of both the attack on Fort Wagner scene in *Glory* and World War I films featuring trench warfare, such as both versions of *All Quiet on the Western Front* (1930 and 1979) and Stanley Kubrick's *Paths of Glory* (1957). The disillusionment felt by the film's central character, Confederate soldier Inman (Jude Law), also places the film more in dialogue with a cultural memory of the Civil War framed by a memory of US involvement in Vietnam. Inman sees no nobility in the Southern cause, only an American landscaped stripped of humanity, and thus choses to desert and make the long trek to his loved one, Ada (Nicole Kidman), residing at Cold Mountain, North Carolina—pathos scenes of "injustice and humiliation/moral self-assertion" (MEWFP). The journey is fraught with treacherous people, as well as allegories to Homer's *Odyssey*, that further complicates a memory of the Civil War framed in the Reconciliation Tradition.

   Cold Mountain and Martin Scorsese's *Gangs of New York* (2002)—a film that does not directly depict the war but nevertheless plays on the threat of conscription that loomed over New York's Irish immigrant community as caskets containing dead soldiers are unloaded at the same harbor they arrived at—signaled a new cycle of cinematic considerations on the role that the Civil War plays in American cultural identity. This can be read as a fifth mode of Civil War scholarship that fuses together elements from the Reconciliation Cause and the Emancipation Cause. Steven Spielberg's *Lincoln* (2012), for example, has at its heart a vision of an American identity that is wedded to sacrifice against the injustice of slavery. In an article for *The New Republic*, Sean Wilenz describes the film's dialogue with previous Civil War films: "Steven Spielberg set out to make a film about Abraham Lincoln. What he produced ought to remove, once and for all, the lingering strain of the Lost Cause mythology, at least in respectable cinema. It ought to render ridiculous depictions of the Civil War as anything other than a struggle over American slavery and its future. It ought to serve as a second Lincoln memorial, the one in which the hero is not chiseled out of stone" (Wilenz 2002).

   The film opens with a graphic depiction of The Battle of Jenkins Ferry in Arkansas (1864), emptied of any heroics or sense of triumphalism, and later features real photographs taken of slaves, attributed to Civil War photographer Alexander Gardner. Spielberg dispenses with the mythology found in earlier Lincoln portraits and draws upon the emotional language of *Saving Private Ryan* and *Amistad* in presenting the Civil War as a haunted site whose ghosts continue to stalk the American consciousness (Burgoyne and Trafton 2015, 24). Whatever we may call this new mode of Civil War cultural remembrance exemplified in *Lincoln*, it simultaneously affirms and challenges Robert Hicks and Charles M. Blows's arguments made at the Gettysburg Address sesquicentennial; Shelby Foote's view that The Civil War made America an "is" rather than an "are" is an articulation of the central argument put forward by Burns's film—what the Reconciliation Clause aims to do—and is reflected in new Civil War films. At the same time, however, these new films are turned into an urgent call to filter Civil War remembrance through atonement for slavery and a confrontation with the historical ghosts still haunting the American landscape.

1

Civil War Paintings and the War Panorama

If the nineteenth century was dreaming of cinema, as it has so often been said, then its paintings are some of the most lucid expressions of this dream. The Civil War paintings anticipated war cinema in many striking ways, notably in their ability to provide the memory of the war with emotional context. On the one hand, if pathos formulas aim to create within the spectator an encounter with death and destruction that is outside their everyday consciousness, yet at the same time tap into familiar sensations, then we can see plenty of overlap between paintings, war photography, and soldier writings. Regardless of whether it was combat, camp life, or an altered home front that was being depicted, paintings reduced the overwhelming chaos and inhumanity of the bloody affair into an identifiable moral and political message, just as Timothy O'Sullivan's "death harvest" photographs and Rhode Island soldier Elisha Hunt Rhodes's war diary would do. Large-scale panorama paintings would place the viewer into the thick of battle, making it a navigable experience, drawing upon photographs and sketches of battlefields for inspiration. On the other hand, these paintings can also be seen as a rehearsal of the war film independent of photography and epistolary traditions. The panorama paintings, for example, anticipated the role of telemetry and surveillance in future combat scenarios, providing a field of vision that has been replicated in many war films (and challenged in many others), as we will see in the following chapter. Although this chapter will primarily consider the influence of the war panorama painting and its development in the United States during the mid-nineteenth century, it is also important to discuss other paintings that responded to the Civil War and the many changes in the American experience that lead up to the war. The paintings of the American romantics and luminists—members of the Hudson River School and those inspired by it (Frederic Church, Sanford Robinson Gifford, Conrad Wise Chapman, and others)—and the paintings of Winslow Homer provided the history of the war with an emotional meaning that was rooted in concepts of American destiny. The panorama paintings, by contrast, were derived from a rich European tradition of large-scale painting, depicting battles on an epic scale, and whose production was fueled by exhibition practices in European capital cities that resemble a form of protocinematic theatrics. When the panorama was introduced to the United States, their subjects and exhibition practices were reshaped by American history and uniquely American conditions. This chapter will chronicle this history and focus on Paul Philippoteaux's *Gettysburg Cyclorama* (1883), the most famous panorama painting of the Civil War, as a prime example of American war panoramas. If the advent of cinema in the United States is the product of motion picture science and the aesthetic and narrative practices of the nineteenth century, what Tom Gunning refers to as a "historical succession of styles" (Gunning 1991, 5), then my examination of Civil War paintings and panoramas will also show that the rise of cinema can be linked to explorations of the American landscape, the rise of travel technology (namely, the railroad), and military targeting technology.

A crucial thing to take into consideration at the outset is the role that news media played in covering the war. Later I will discuss how war photography contested the sketch illustrations in newspapers and how soldier testimonials challenged war reportage, but for this chapter it is important to note how these journalistic illustrations also informed the response to the war by painters; both painters and newspaper sketch artists attempted to provide the story of the war with an emotional content beyond the written word. There are many instances of painters taking their cues from sketches, as well as photographs and eye-witness testimonies (as we will see specifically in the creation of the *Gettysburg*

Cyclorama), constituting a marriage between the three representational modes, wedded to a desire to provide the war story from history books and newspaper articles with pathos. This is due in part because the history of sketch illustration and painting during the Civil War are so intertwined. Winslow Homer, perhaps one of the most famous American painters of the era, was a regular contributor of sketches to *Harper's Weekly*, a staunchly pro-Union publication; other painters, such as Frederic Church and Eastman Johnson, worked in conjunction to promote patriotic support of the Union as a national ideal. Painters like Sanford Gifford and John Ferguson Weir served in the Union army, and all the aforementioned painters produced images that "explored new ideas about race, American identity, and the nature of [the] human experience" (Goodheart 2013, xvii). The paintings of the war (and their effect on the home front) produced by these painters, as well as the commemorative war panorama paintings produced after the war, provide the memory of the war with deeper meaning beyond a chronology of events and lists of casualty figures—a transmission of chaos and intense suffering, yet at the same time a sense of moral ascendency.

By 1850, sketch illustrations were popular in Europe and began to find their way into American publications. Frank Leslie, the illustrator for the *Illustrated Times of London*, was hired in 1852 by P. T. Barnum to supervise illustrations for the New York version of *The Illustrated Times*. In 1855, Leslie created an illustrated publication of his own: *Frank Leslie's Illustrated Newspaper*. Coupled with new methods in the engraving process and the ability for the sketchers to make quick pencil sketches on the spot while interviewing people who could contribute useful information, *Frank Leslie's Illustrated News* was able to make a huge turnover of more than half a million dollars a year. In 1857, the publishing firm of Harper and Brothers established *Harper's Weekly*, run by Fletcher Harper, and soon incorporated illustrations in their reportage. By 1860, *Harper's Weekly* was the strongest of these publishers, followed closely by John King's *New York Illustrated News* (founded in 1859). During the war, each of these publications had correspondence artists in the field that would send back illustrations at incredible speed. The South, by contrast, did not have the same success with publishing illustrated newspapers[1] due to a shortage of ink, paper, engravers and, most importantly, sketch artists (although one notable publication was the *Southern Illustrated News,* run out of Richmond by Ayers and Wade, but this folded in 1864). The sketches were transferred to wood engraving blocks where they were etched into the block using wood carving tools, creating a relief image in a size appropriate for the page.[2] The engraving was then filled with ink and pressed onto the page, bringing images of combat to the home front in a way that eerily anticipated the war correspondence of the twentieth century. Sketch illustrations would continue after the war and, although later displaced by photography, they would retain their emotive power and ability to narrate events beyond the capacity of imagination.

Though we can see plenty of evidence of the influence of sketch illustration on Civil War paintings, a curious sketch would appear after the war in an 1875 issue of *Harper's Weekly* that illustrates the relationship between Civil War paintings and newspaper illustrations in striking ways. An article on the centenary of the Battle of Bunker Hill featured Winslow Homer's sketch *The Battle of Bunker Hill—Watching the Fighting from Copp's Hill, in Boston.* The battle itself is not clearly depicted; citizens of Boston, seated on their rooftops, watch the battle from afar—billowing clouds of black smoke from the distant hills across the Charles River fill the skyline as if they are from a volcanic eruption. In a departure from usual form, Homer clearly shows the expressive faces of some of the battle's spectators. In several of his Civil War paintings, by contrast, Homer obscured the faces of soldiers—these witnesses of combat horrors were anonymous everymen with their eyes either cloaked in shadow or out of focus.[3] This mode for depicting Civil War soldiers was also practiced by many of Homer's contemporaries, notably veteran Conrad Wise Chapman (1842–1910) and Gilbert Gaul (1855–1919), painters who combined art with historical memory. One needs to ask why Homer shifted his style on this occasion of remembrance of a battle that took place nearly a century before the Civil War only to return to and expand on his previous aesthetic strategies and experimentations in his art throughout the remainder of his life. It could be that, to Homer, the Bostonians were a stand-in for Americans whose nation had been defined within the span of a century by two wars—a look of shock and horror upon their faces that invites the viewer to simultaneously take part in remembrance and confront traumatic historical memory. It could also be that Homer is anticipating a new mode of spectatorship, a generational looking-back, facilitated by constantly evolving art forms and strategies. In viewing the relationship between nineteenth-century painting and the development of generic codes in the cinema of the twentieth century, we should consider both explanations to be the case. How pathos is conveyed through painted depictions of war is essential to understanding how the war film codes evolved throughout cinema history. At the same time, it is important to consider how successive generations revise their relationship with the past through aesthetic forms, and historical films—war films among them—would provide salient examples of this process in the twentieth and twenty-first centuries.

Though photography, at first glance, appears to be the obvious forerunner of motion pictures, it is very important to start with nineteenth-century paintings in our examination of how and why war film codes developed. Pathos formulas, as discussed the in the introduction, can be read as strategies for orchestrating an emotional content, and understanding the various categories of pathos formulae and how they operate is essential to understanding the war film aesthetic. The paintings that depicted the war exhibit many of these pathos formulas, providing ways of reconsidering how these paintings anticipated the arrival of pictures in motion. First, I would like to discuss how some of the nineteenth-century American philosophical and literary movements influenced how artists responded to the war—the words of Ralph Waldo Emerson, Nathaniel Hawthorne, Henry David Thoreau, Louisa May Alcott, and Herman Melville framing the impending war as the inevitable fulfillment of America's destiny. This is crucial to take into consideration, as many of these ideas will reemerge in my discussion of Civil War epistolary traditions in Chapter 5. Then I will explore the work of the American painters—focusing on Winslow Homer—and how, steeped in the words of Emerson and his contemporaries, they visually provided the story of a nation at war with pathos. Lastly, I will turn to war panoramas and how their response to the Civil War turned memory into spectacles of remembrance and national mourning. The aim here is to understand the aesthetic formulas contained in these paintings, visual strategies that were later repurposed in war cinema.

The Meteor of the War: The Ideological Underpinnings of American Art

Before the Civil War, America's imagination of war was rooted in the highly popular paintings and portraits from John Trumbull (1756–1843) and Charles Willson Peale (1741–1827), paintings of the American Revolution (e.g., *The Surrender of Cornwallis at Yorktown* and *The Signing of the Declaration of Independence*, which is shown on the back of a two dollar bill) that emphasized heroism and a type of history commonly referred to as "grand manner history"—a form of classical art laden with metaphors and inspired by the style of the Renaissance masters. Prints of these paintings were made using fast printing and coloring techniques, and before the start of the Civil War, there were several hundred commercial art publishing houses in the United States providing prints that were a popular feature of parlor rooms across the country. While the popularity of these paintings is indicative of a public desire to take part in remembrance, they were considered by many Civil War veterans to be gross misrepresentations of "the real nature of war" (Thompson 1960, 16); these paintings merely commemorated historical moments and, while imparting a sense of pathos in some respect, concealed the trauma that those who endured the war were painfully aware of. The Civil War, nevertheless, provided artists with inspiration for paintings that would continue to play a strong role in preserving a cultural and historical memory after the war, though in a different way than the paintings of Trumbull and Peale. These paintings exhibited moral messages deeply rooted in nineteenth-century American religiosity and philosophy, much in the way that we will see with written war narratives.

In looking at nineteenth-century American painting, I draw upon the important work of Eleanor Jones Harvey, as she provides an effective framework for interpreting the response of American artists to seismic historical change. She places the conflict, in artistic terms, from 1859 (when war was immanent) to 1876 (the centennial, in which "America found closure"), which, given the grim predictions of conflict embedded in earlier American landscapes and the work of many of the great American writers and thinkers of the century, seems like appropriate contours.[4] In an interview for *The Modern Art Notes*, Harvey described Civil War paintings as beauty combined with the gruesome.[5] Harvey places these paintings into three different categories—literal, metaphorical, and psychological—and touches upon an important sense of pessimism and moral outrage that they impart through visual metaphors. For Hermann Kappelhoff, this sense of moral outrage is combined with feelings of remembrance, and although images of death, destruction, and shell-shocked faces commonly associated with these types of pathos scenes are largely obscured in paintings, these emotions are still transmitted through a relationship with the American landscape (Kappelhoff 2001, 4). The paintings produced in the wake of the Civil War allowed the viewer a poetic sense of involvement as a means to navigate through an American landscape divided by war and to understand, viscerally, what was happening to the nation.

The Hudson River School was an American art movement during the nineteenth century, influenced by the European Romanticism movement, which envisioned the American landscape in a way that exuded the Enlightenment principles upon which the country was founded and emphasized idealistic and poetic notions about what America meant. Frederic Edwin Church, Sanford Robinson Gifford, Albert Bierstadt, and Thomas Cole were some of the notable artists of this movement, and although Winslow Homer was not a part of this movement (in many ways, his work strongly contrasts with the movement), his work was nevertheless motivated by similar ideals (abolitionism and the work of Ralph Waldo Emerson, for example). The Hudson River School, according to Eleanor Jones Harvey, painted "America as a place, a concept, and spiritual state of mind," exhibiting a "primal experience in nature" linked to the American transcendentalism of Emerson and Thoreau (Harvey 2013, 17). The paintings from the Hudson River School and, by extension, Homer, would serve as an outlet for emotion, whether a sense of awe, grave foreboding, or even a sense of moral outrage. Their works would dominate the exhibition halls of New York City, and it is clear from many reviews in *The New York Times* that the metaphors layered within the frame were identifiable to those tuned into the national mood and anxieties. As Ralph Waldo Emerson said in his "The American Scholar" speech, "The first in time and the first in importance of influences upon the mind is that of nature. Every day, the sun; and after, the sunset, night and her stars. Ever the wind blows; ever the grass grows. Every day, men and women, conversing, beholding and beholden. The scholar is he of all men whom this spectacle most engages" (Emerson 1837).

By the 1850s, it became clear to the likes of Emerson, Hawthorn, Melville, Alcott, and Thoreau that war was not only inevitable but a "fulfillment of America's destiny to lead the world in moral perfection" (Fuller 2011, 38). Such prophesying did not feel out of place, as early tremors of a North and South conflict over the slavery question had been felt repeatedly for decades. Thomas Jefferson, in response to the Missouri Compromise of 1820, wrote that maintaining slavery was like holding a "wolf by the ears." Abolitionist and Presbyterian minister Elijah Lovejoy was murdered by a proslavery mob in 1837, a nation left stunned by the death of a white man over slave issues. Frederick Douglass escaped from slavery the following year and published his memoirs years later, well-received in both the United States and Europe, and the territory of Kansas exploded with violent clashes between proslavery and antislavery factions in 1854. The die was clearly cast, however, when the decade ended with John Brown's failed raid on Harper's Ferry in 1859, an attempt to seize a federal armory and start a slave revolt (Brown was captured by a force led by Colonel Robert E. Lee and subsequently hanged in the presence of students of the Virginia military institute lead by Thomas J. Jackson). Victor Hugo called for Brown to be pardoned, Emerson compared Brown's execution to Christ's crucifixion, and for Herman Melville, John Brown was the "Meteor of the War." For many, Brown represented a throwback to early American puritanical militarism, as Brown claimed that "without the shedding of blood, there is no remission of sins" (50). When one looks at the response to Brown's Harper's Ferry raid, as well as earlier events that anticipated the Civil War, it becomes clear that they are informed by the promise of a nation, the coming of what Emerson, who seemed to relish the possibility of war, described as the "New Canaan" (38). When one looks at the Hudson River School paintings before the Civil War, it is clear that this notion of a promised nation is embedded in the vastness of the landscapes, an American frontier presented as an Eden.

Pausing briefly for a moment, let us consider the following passage in order to illustrate the resonance the notion of a promised America carries in the American imaginary: "I have a dream that my four little children will one day live in a nation where they will not be judged by the color of their skin but by the content of their character" (King Jr. 1963).

The quote may be familiar to most US high school history students. It is, of course, from Martin Luther King Jr.'s "I Have a Dream" speech, delivered in Washington on August 28, 1963. What may not be so familiar are these words: "Five score years ago, a great American, in whose symbolic shadow we stand today, signed the Emancipation Proclamation. This momentous decree came as a beacon light of hope to millions of Negro slaves who had been seared in the flames of withering injustice" (King Jr. 1963).

While the second passage, which opens the speech, may not be as iconic as other portions of the speech, the words carry an air of familiarity through evoking the opening lines of Lincoln's Gettysburg Address. As David W. Blight notes, however, it is more than the wordage that connects the two speeches—they are both rooted in an American promise (Blight 2011, 2). This promise harkens back to the notion of America as the "New Canaan." Here we can see the persistence of this idea in American culture even as recently as the naturalization ceremony at the Gettysburg Address sesquicentennial. Though the atrocities that occurred under manifest destiny during the nineteenth century (and some of the more retrograde aspects of American exceptionalism in modern times) are examples of an ill purposing of the American promise, King's speech and American landscape art can both be viewed, by contrast, as acknowledgments of the progressive power of the American promise, layered in deeply spiritual meaning.

The idea of America's destiny and the fulfillment of prophesies appear as meteorological metaphors in the Hudson River School paintings. The metaphor of the approaching storm, popular with abolitionists in the decades leading up to the war, featured strongly in these works, with Martin Johnson Heade's *Approaching Thunder Storm* (1859) being a notable example. The aurora borealis can also be seen in several of these landscape paintings, interesting because the northern lights were visible along the Eastern seaboard at various points throughout the war, a rare occurrence. Depictions of exploding volcanoes and icebergs appear in the work of Frederic Edwin Church, metaphorical stand-ins for the dominant political discourse of the era. Also, South America and the tropics often stood in as a metaphor for the American

South, tropical paradises that were subtly infused with rivers of blood metaphors or ash-clouded skies (as seen in Church's depiction of Ecuador's Mount Cotopaxi erupting over a tropical Andean plateau, an 1862 reinterpretation of Church's earlier and more tranquil paintings of the same region). What is even more interesting is that many of these landscape paintings are accompanied by literary narration, written by poets and other writers who often accompanied landscape artists, providing an emotive narration to what was being depicted (Harvey 2013, 16). Of Church's *Cotopaxi*, his longtime friend and writer Louis Legrand Noble described the Andean plateau as a "great battlefield of nature's forces," an explicit comparison between a natural calamity and the ensuing national calamity.

It is also difficult to ignore the role that religion, in particular American Protestantism, played in providing an explanation of events, particularly in regards to the notion of an American promise. Though both Abraham Lincoln and Hawthorne warned against "the folly of pretending to understand the intent of an inscrutable divinity," the artistic response to the approaching war was colored by religious interpretation in many instances (Fuller 2011, 51). It is here that we can establish an interesting connection with the visual arts and the writing of the era, as American religiosity provided a framework for understanding, and writing about, death in corporeal terms (an idea that I will later return to). In the case of paintings, religious metaphors were employed to provide the images with a moral message, a pathos formula that invites the spectator to spiritually connect to the American natural landscape.

Winslow Homer's Soldiers and Manet's Battleships

Harvey observes that very few artists directly painted the war, as there was little market for "Americans killing one another" and it was difficult to identify heroes. Rather, they approached the war in a more elliptical manner, teasing out the layered war. She also cites Alexander Gardner's photography exhibition at Mathew Brady's New York gallery in the fall of 1862, which "brought the war to our doorstep" according to *The New York Times*, as the first time America saw the war's corpses, constituting a major challenge for artists responding to the war (Harvey 2013). In response, painters sought to restore empathy to the medium and tell a different story than the one provided by photography.

When not illustrating for *Harper's Weekly*, Winslow Homer painted soldiers and soldiering life, focusing on the nameless soldier—the soldier as the everyman. Even in paintings containing figures identifiable to historians, there remains a sense of both anonymity and a transmission of some of the war's overarching themes and effects on the national psyche. Consider Homer's painting *Prisoners from the Front* (Figure 1.1), released in 1866. This painting was considered a triumph of Homer's career, a depiction of Northern triumph and Southern disarray. Three Confederate prisoners of war are brought before a Union officer. The prisoners' clothes are ragged and not properly buttoned, their hands at their front or in-pocket, whereas the Union officer, whose face is more in focus, is immaculately dressed, his hands nonchalantly behind his back, with a dashing saber hanging at his side. And yet, the landscape is bleak, devoid of trees and plant life, a scorched earth. In *Prisoners from the Front*, Sarah Burns and Daniel Greene identify a connection to the death

Figure 1.1   *Prisoners from the Front* by Winslow Homer (1866). © Stephen St. John/National Geographic Creative/Corbis.

harvest photographs—images of corpses strewn across abandoned battlefields. Both Homer's painting and Timothy O'Sullivan's famous *Harvest of Death* photograph are seen as "canonical and authoritative" accounts of the war, as in these images the soldiers, landscapes and, by proxy, the spectator, are altered by the war in a single instance (Burns and Green 2013, 3). Here we can see a connection between painting and photography that would later manifest in war films—a micromoment in the war's history that, through a series of visual cues and signs, speaks volumes about the history existing outside of the frame. Harvey proposes that the larger story in *Prisoners from the Front* is more than just a "chivalric meeting of vanquisher and vanquished coming to an honorable truce" (Harvey 2013). Rather, the painting suggests a "lingering hostility" between the Confederates and the "clueless" Northerners, an early visual example of a recurring war film trope and a constant reminder that war is a nation's unfinished business (Harvey 2013, 171). This is also an eerie anticipation of Charles M. Blow's 2013 assertion in *The New York Times* that "we are moving toward two Americas with two contrasting—and increasingly codifying—concepts of liberty" (Blow 2013). An appropriate caption for Homer's painting could be the words of Confederate Brigadier General Henry A. Wise at the Appomattox surrender: "You may forgive us but we won't be forgiven. There is rancor in our hearts which you little dream of. We hate you sir" (Primono 2013, 168).

What is very interesting is how the paintings of Homer and the landscape painters intersect with the other two modes of Civil War representation in embedding meaning into their paintings. According to Diane Dillon, Sanford Gifford, who served in the war, may have turned toward the photographs of O'Sullivan and Alexander Gardner, in particular the death harvest photographs, as is reflected in Gifford's landscapes depicting scorched earth and uprooted trees (Dillon 2013, 155). Homer's *On Guard* painting (1864) contains striking similarities to Mathew Brady's photograph of the Union breastworks on Culps Hill, Gettysburg, and since Homer, as a *Harper's Weekly* sketch artist, was present at Gettysburg, it is likely that he would have seen Brady in action and the wood engraving made from the photography (Burns 2013, 178). Also, as I mentioned earlier, what is also interesting is that poets often accompanied landscape artists to provide an emotive narration to what was being depicted. Although my discussion of panorama paintings will focus on a pathos formula tied to perception in war and war strategies, Homer's Civil War paintings share with the panorama paintings an attempt to familiarize a seemingly ungraspable experience through evoking recognizable sensations. The landscape painters, in their use of meteorological metaphors and their presentation of the frontier as an affirmation of the literary philosophy and transcendentalism of the day, also accomplish what Paul Philippoteaux attempted to do with his *Gettysburg Cyclorama*: infusing a moral message into a distinctly American tableau.

A work of art appeared toward the end of the war that anticipated the appearance of these representational principles in the war panorama paintings. The curious thing was that this example was produced in Europe rather than the United States, though it is nevertheless worth examining, considering that the principle artists involved in late nineteenth-century American panorama paintings were European. In 1864, Èdouard Manet, often credited as the grandfather of the Impressionist movement, painted *The Battle of the Kearsarge and the Alabama* and *The Kearsarge at Boulonge*, depicting a navel engagement between the USS *Kearsarge* and the CSS *Alabama* off the coast of Cherbourg and its aftermath. Manet never witnessed the battle and instead drew upon testimonies from eye witnesses, sketches, and newspaper articles. Of his painting of the battle, Juliet Wilson-Bareau and David C. Degener note a "rich but narrow range of colors" and no "single, central focus" (Wilson-Bareau and Degener 2003, 41). This aesthetic strategy is very interesting, even when taking into consideration Manet's absence from the event (and by some accounts even visiting Cherbourg itself), as it points to a technique exemplified by in the panorama paintings: elusive or vague focal points and vanishing points—a reliance on the spectator to be the editor of the story unfolding before their eyes. What is also interesting is that Manet, in drawing upon testimony and sketches, foreshadowed Philippoteaux's survey of the Gettysburg battlefield later in the early 1880s (though Philippoteaux would also be aided by an additional supplement that was of crucial importance: photographs).

Panorama Paintings

In 1899, William W. Young, Marc Klaw, and A. L. Erlanger debuted their stage production of the Lew Wallace (a Civil War veteran) novel *Ben Hur: A Tale of Christ* (1880) on Broadway. The play featured spectacular sets and props, including chariots and real horses running along a treadmill controlled from beneath the stage, in a way that anticipated the cinematic form of the epic film. What was also interesting about this production was its use of a large painting that was "whipped across the back of the stage by two enormous rollers at a speed of thirty miles per hour" (Burgoyne 2008, 24). This painted backdrop makes use of the theatrical principles and exhibition practices of panorama paintings throughout the nineteenth century. Panorama paintings, often presented in circular rotundas—sometimes in motion, controlled by gear mechanisms under the floor—created an illusion of a real world in motion with constantly changing perspectives, a clear antecedent of motion pictures. Originating in Europe, the panorama began with spectacular cityscapes (Edinburgh, London, Paris, etc.) and pastoral landscapes, influenced by European Romanticism, but soon turned its attention toward war. The Battle of Waterloo, Napoleon's assault on Moscow, and the Siege of Sebastopol in the Crimea were some of the many subjects of war panoramas that adorned European exhibition halls. This art tradition proved to be very popular in the United States, starting with journeys across the American landscape and eventually turning toward the Civil War as a subject. The war panoramas, both European and American, offered a vision of battle that not only can be read as a precursor to the war film but also acknowledge the expanding technology of surveillance used in war, demonstrating a linkage between war representation and optical telemetry.

The panorama industry, in both Europe and the United States during the nineteenth century, appeared to anticipate the film industry in terms of production and exhibition practices. International companies were formed in the early 1800s, employing artists that could produce a panorama in less than a year (operating out of company-owned workshops built to the shape of exhibition rotundas where they would eventually be shown) and managing a network of these exhibition houses, in coordination with local businessmen, promotion agents, and financiers (Comment 1999, 18). In France, artist Jean-Charles Langlois, a former French officer during the Napoleonic Wars, painted battle sequences drawn from his own experiences (notably *The Battle for Moscow* [1834]), and later would commission the creation of exhibition rotundas (the most famous being one at the north end of the Champs-Elysées in cooperation with the famous architect Jacques Ignace Hittorff). In 1859 he formed his own limited company with its own exhibition space (48–50). In London, the Barker family's rotunda in Leicester Square featured battle scenes from the Napoleonic War's North African theater and from colonial India; Thomas Edward's Panorama Strand would soon rival the Leicester Square Rotunda, with *The Battle of Waterloo* (1826) being one of their most successful exhibitions (25). In the United States, John Banvard's moving panorama *Mississippi from the Mouth of the Missouri to New Orleans* toured Louisville, Boston, New York, and eventually London, accompanied by a speaker providing commentary (63–64). By the 1870s, moving panoramas were largely seen as not only a US innovation but also a popular US import, with, by Stephan Oettermann's estimation, more than one hundred million spectators visiting panoramas worldwide from 1870 to the end of the century (66).

In his study of panorama paintings, Oettermann argues that panoramas were the products of the nineteenth century with no precursors. The development of the panorama was not based on previous developments in the arts but rather on changes in culture (Oettermann 1997, 5). Though a dubious claim, as the first panoramas appeared in the late eighteenth century and had antecedents in large-scale paintings, cultural changes did inform the development of the panoramic form throughout the nineteenth century.[6] For Americans in the latter half of the nineteenth century, the traditional, static, circular panoramas were "visually inadequate to the situation in which they found themselves"; American moving panoramas "anticipated, in art, the speed of travel" and communication in response to the onset of railroad travel and the end of a war documented through haunting photographs (Oettermann, 1997, 323). As John Huddleston points out, "The steamboat, the railway, newspapers, and the telegraph enabled the United States to maintain an evolving unity" and, as consequence, the static panorama seemed out of step with the times (Huddleston 2002, 5). The European panoramas were primarily focused on cities and pastoral landscapes that were familiar to the European viewer, whereas the American moving panoramas paintings often depicted the rugged landscapes of the American West, still the primitive unknown in the minds of many eastern city dwellers. These paintings, moving around a circular rotunda, contained vague or elusive vanishing points, the spectator's vision brought to focus on different points as if an invisible director and editor were present.

Erikka Huhtamo writes that the Civil War "created a heated market for visual representations." Photography would prove to be highly effective at capturing the trauma in the aftermath of combat, "but most of the dramatic moments escaped the lens of the camera" (Huhtamo 2013, 264). The war years saw the rise in popularity of the moving panorama, often with musical accompaniment, with artists and theater proprietors reaping great benefits. As Banvard's *Mississippi from the Mouth of the Missouri to New Orleans* panorama demonstrated, touring moving panoramas and lantern shows were popular forms of mass entertainment, and the Civil War itself would become "a lucrative topic for touring panorama showmen" (19). Though a clear pathos formula can be gleaned from early war panoramas—the ability to partake, from a safe vantage point, in an encounter with death that exceeds the everyday human experience—it was not until after the war that panoramas found their potential in using this pathos formula as part of war remembrance that would anticipate war film strategies in easily discernable ways. What is also clear is how their scope and use of deep focus can be linked to advances in military surveillance technology and targeting capacities.

"People often ask me: what if they had machine guns in the Civil War?" muses Garry Adelman, historian for the Civil War Trust. "I always say: 'Forget all of that.' One set of walkie-talkies could have changed the outcome of the Civil War" (Moat 2011). In "The Traveling Shot over Eighty Years," Paul Virilio notes that the story of war and cinema could have started with the American Civil War, or perhaps the Crimean War, two plausible starting points considering that both wars were the earliest photographed conflicts. Virilio, however, choses to begin the story in 1904 with the Russo-Japanese War, which saw the first use of the searchlight in combat; conflicts that occurred before the Russo-Japanese War can be read as "fundamentally a game of hide-and-seek with the enemy"—surveillance and reconnaissance obtained through binoculars, on foot, or on horseback (Virilio 1989, 69). Though night attacks were a rare phenomenon in the Civil War, and clearly there were no electric lights with which to illuminate enemy entrenchment, binoculars (field glasses) and telescopes were widely used by officers and scouts, as were hot air balloons in which "aeronaut scouts" often transmitted their findings via telegraph.[7] This sense of vision, what Virilio describes as "the logistics of perception in war," offers a corrective to the restricted field of vision of a soldier taking cover under heavy fire, whether in the Peach Orchard at Gettysburg or on Omaha Beach on D-Day. The war panorama removes this restriction and broadens the level of spectatorship as if the viewer is placed into the thick of battle as an individual soldier through an invisible, omniscient narrator. The advent of widescreen and, by the 1950s, cinemascope, seems to be an extension of this and, according to Virilio, is linked to "the advance of panoramic telemetry," the means of surveillance and reconnaissance in battle (69).[8]

The large-scale paintings of the Civil War anticipates this "panoramic telemetry" in pictorial form and thus produced a representational strategy that was highly adaptable to war cinema—one that provides chaotic battle scenes with the sense that they can be easily navigated with the eye from a safe distance while at the same time participating in their intensity. This is the primary pathos formula contained in war panoramas, and it relies on an aesthetic device that Jonna Eagle calls "strenuous spectatorship"—a witness that provides the viewer with "a privileged vantage point on action alongside a fantasy of assault" (Eagle 2012, 19). The framing of soldiers, flags, fortresses, and battlefields in war panoramas constructs an engendered mode of engaging with the action and an ascendant screen culture; the viewer can witness cavalry charges, artillery barrages, and hand-to-hand combat, standing in for the war correspondents who were there that day (in war cinema, decades later, the camera would assume the role of strenuous spectator; 18). Strenuous spectatorship in war panoramas combine a war experience with the exhibition conventions that would later evolve into what Tom Gunning calls "the cinema of attractions" in order to create a mode for engaging with war as a spectacle (19). To show how this is exhibited in Civil War panoramas, I would like to turn to the creation of Philippoteaux's *Gettysburg Cyclorama* (Figure 1.2).

Paul Philippoteaux trained at the École des Beaux-Arts in Paris at age 16 and produced his first cyclorama with his father, Felix, in 1871—*The Defense of Fort D'Issy* (sometimes referred to as *The Siege of Paris*)—exhibited on the Champs-Elysees. He later traveled to America to take advantage of the new possibilities to be found in American panorama paintings, informed by the American landscape and rail travel, and contrasting with the European styles. It is not clear how Philippoteaux conceived of the idea to portray the Battle of Gettysburg as a cyclorama, though there is some evidence that suggests that he meet with famed Gettysburg veteran General Winfield Scott Hancock, through *New York Times* connections, who provided him with intimate details of the battle (Childress 2010, 103). Philippoteaux traveled to Gettysburg in the early 1880s, armed with sketches of the battle based on survivor descriptions and military maps provided by the War Department in Washington, DC, taking extensive photographs

Figure 1.2   A painted cyclorama view of the *Battle of Gettysburg*, recently reconditioned. © Stephen St. John/National Geographic Creative/Corbis.

on the landscape (103). It would take him more than two years to complete the panorama, which was subsequently toured and reproduced for display in Boston, Chicago, New York, and Philadelphia. Though not the largest, the second version of the *Gettysburg Cyclorama* (often referred to as "the Boston version") was purchased by the National Park Service for display at the visitor center at The Gettysburg National Military Park, where, after several years of constant conservation and renovation, the painting stands today. Depicting the disastrous Confederate offensive on the battle's third and final day, often referred to as "Pickett's Charge" or the "High Water Mark of the Confederacy," the *Gettysburg Cyclorama* (the Military Park's version) is 377 feet long, 42 feet high, and weighs 12.5 tons.[9] The cyclorama is accompanied by props—canons and broken fences—and sound effects, in keeping with the spirit of the original displays (as originally intended by Philippoteaux and the distributors). The scope of the painting suggests an anticipation of an IMAX experience and, as Bronfen points out, the *Gettysburg Cyclorama* turned "historical painting into mass entertainment" (Bronfen 2012, 113).

The combining of spectacle with art goes beyond the *Gettysburg Cyclorama* in depicting the Civil War. The creation of the American Panorama Company in 1883 foreshadowed the rise of film production companies at the turn of the century. Though folding in 1887, the American Panorama Company produced many successful works of art and is linked to a rich history of immigrant artists.[10] Perhaps the second most famous, though still influential, Civil War panorama is *The Battle of Atlanta*, painted in 1885–86 by a team of German panorama artists hired by The American Panorama Company in Milwaukee. The Atlanta cyclorama, currently housed at the Civil War Museum in Atlanta, offers a 360-degree experience as well, also accompanied by props, a recorded narration by veterans and their relatives (set to music), and is marketed as "the world's longest running show."[11] Additionally, *The Battle of Chattanooga* panorama, depicting the view from Lookout Mountain on the day of the battle, was also created by The American Panorama Company. As the United States had already proven itself as a successful market for moving panoramas before the war, and the Civil War panoramas that came after the war continued the fusion of art and entertainment in a way that seemed to anticipate cinematic spectacles.

American Painters, the Panorama Painting, and the Rise of Cinema

The paintings of Homer overlap with the Civil War panorama paintings through a particular pathos formula: both instruct the viewer on how to understand and remember the war, and they turn an indescribable experience, striped of humanity by bloody carnage, into an identifiable moral or political message (Bronfen 2012, 112). In Philippoteaux's *Gettysburg Cyclorama*, the chaos of battle is structured, organized, and choreographed in such a way that an overwhelming and disorientating experience is easily navigable, in a manner that anticipates film editing; whatever morals and politics that could be gleaned by soldiers in the sweltering July heat of 1863 are transformed into a message of patriotic remembrance, eulogy, immortalization, and a word of caution to the next generation. The *Gettysburg Cyclorama* and other Civil War panoramas also exhibit the pathos scenes of "battle and technology," "suffering, victim, and sacrifice," and "sense of shared suffering" (MEWFP). Homer's *Prisoners from the Front*, by contrast, uses a single moment after a battle to remind the spectator that the war was collectively fought by individuals rather than simply by towering figures like Lee, Grant, Jackson and others; we need not know the soldier's name, rank, age, state or county of origin, or family history—only that these were men among equals fighting for the Emersonian notion of a promised nation.

In looking at these paintings from the Civil War, we can see the emergence of aesthetic strategies and ideologies that seemed to anticipate the cinematic form. When Philippoteaux and his collaborators arrived at Gettysburg in 1881, their survey of the battlefield, along with testimonies from veterans and eyewitnesses, seemed to "anticipate Hollywood's reenactments" (Bronfen 2012, 253). Most of all, these paintings (along with the ascendant photography from the era) directly acknowledged a world of sounds, colors and, most importantly, motion that existed exterior to the pages of a journal or history book; as Robert Rosenstone observes, representations of the past are not "a real world . . . but then again, neither is that other historical world, the one conjured up for us in the text books" (Rosenstone 2006, 1). Civil War paintings and panoramas, like the war films of the following decade, would provide the past with rich complexity and sedimented emotions through an aesthetic formal engagement with historical memory. As we will see in the next chapter, Civil War paintings and panoramas were an important component of the genre memory that gave rise to the war film and still remain relevant to the discussion of how and why contemporary war films have radically revised their audiovisual codes: the panoramic field of vision found in the *Gettysburg* or *Atlanta* cycloramas would appear in the Civil War battles of Griffith's *The Birth of a Nation*, the Napoleonic Wars in Abel Gance's famous triptych, trench warfare in *All Quiet on the Western Front*, and D-Day in *The Longest Day* and *Saving Private Ryan*. Conversely, this genre memory would be altered or dispensed with to place the spectator in the haunted battle zones of Vietnam (*Apocalypse Now* and *The Deer Hunter*) and Iraq (*The Hurt Locker*) and to defamiliarize the war film genre itself. We will see how the influence of the precinema spectacle of phantasmagoria is used in *Apocalypse Now* to disrupt the panoramic field of vision and sense of involvement that was seen by Coppola as a part of built-in audience expectations from previous war movies. *The Hurt Locker*, by contrast, offers a revised panoramic war vision designed to meet a demand for verisimilitude in combat depiction and informed by documentary filmmaking.

2

Panorama, Phantasmagoria, and Subjective Vision in War Cinema

In 2008, the US military implemented a therapeutic virtual reality video game, developed at the University of Southern California, called *Virtual Iraq*, a simulation program used to treat Iraq and Afghanistan War veterans suffering from PTSD, a condition documented in nearly 20 percent of returning veterans at the time of the study.[1] The program was modeled on the landscapes and gameplay of popular war video games, such as *America's Army* and the *Call of Duty* series, but rather than presenting a subjective panoramic vision of the battlefield, a feature that made these games popular, *Virtual Iraq* provides the player with optical illusions and a series of randomly generated images and scenarios that are tailored to the specific case history of the patient. The participant dons 3D glasses and headphones and is transported to Iraq by the therapist to confront specific elements of the Iraq War experience in order to master his or her traumatic experience.

Virtual Iraq exhibits Jonna Eagle's notion of "strenuous spectatorship," an engendered mode of engaging with military action that provides the viewer with "a privileged vantage point on action alongside a fantasy of assault" (Eagle 2012, 19), and an aesthetic principle that underscores the nineteenth-century war panoramas. The war panorama, a precinema attraction that attempted to transport the viewer into the thick of battle, invited the eye to navigate the equally focused foreground and background action, an experience that attempted to mimic actual combat participation and one that war films would attempt to recreate—sweeping wide shots of Omaha Beach in *Saving Private Ryan* and *The Longest Day* (1962) and World War I trench warfare in *Paths of Glory* (1957) are but a few examples that exhibit the influence of the panorama on war cinema.

In *Virtual Iraq*, however, the spectator is not a stand-in for a war correspondent but rather a direct participant in the action, absorbed into a world that goes beyond a mere 360-degree cyclorama of war-torn Baghdad, complicating the traditional pathos formula of war panoramas—a defamiliarization of the classic war film panoramic vision. The experience *Virtual Iraq* highlights has a distinct presence in both Iraq War films and Vietnam War films, where the condition of the traumatized soldier is discernible as a narrative device. This is expressed in numerous scenes that detail the imprinting of war on the human psyche, scenes that convey the hallucinatory and subjective experience of war through a variety of visual strategies. Two films that are especially significant in this regard are *Apocalypse Now* and *The Hurt Locker*. Both films render this remapping of the human psyche through expressive visual design and employ a distinct mode of subjective representation.

"The Vietnam War," according to William Hagen, "was an intimate, loosely framed, on-the-run *cinéma vérité* experience," and a similar point could be made about the Iraq War. Representations of both wars can be seen as a competition of "war narrators," challenging the mainstream media's account of the war in more viscerally compelling ways (Hagen 1983, 230). Both *Apocalypse Now* and *The Hurt Locker* broach audience expectations of war already shaped by documentary films, photo journalism, embedded print and television journalism, and (in the case of the Iraq War) Internet videos. These media responses to war set the stage for Coppola and Bigelow to craft their films in a style that defamiliarized the war landscape viewers were accustomed to. At the time of *Apocalypse Now*'s production, "any film about Vietnam that followed the traditions of realistic narrative filmmaking (especially of war films) would be working against a collective sensibility that had arrived at different preconceptions of what was authentic," and as similar preconceptions about the Iraq War experience became evident, *The Hurt Locker* followed the same rhetorical project as *Apocalypse Now* (231). The styles of both films are intended to encourage the progression away from previous memories of the war experience toward deeper moral and philosophical debates. Although Coppola's and Bigelow's films employ different visual styles, the intentions of their authors are similar. In this chapter, I will show how *The Hurt Locker* borrows the narrative structure and the trope of battlefield haunting from *Apocalypse Now* in order to provide a critique of the way war rewrites the human psyche. Battlefield haunting in *The Hurt Locker* and *Apocalypse Now* is expressed through uncanny repetition and a constant return to the scene of trauma through an episodic narrative structure. I will also show how both films render the traumatic, interior space of battle through the rewriting of war film genre codes. Both films incorporate the influence of precinematic spectacle forms into their visual languages. *Apocalypse Now* radically departs from the influence of the panorama painting, a form with a strong presence in earlier war films, instead using phantasmagorical imagery of a haunted battle zone. By contrast, *The Hurt Locker* translates the new logistics of perception to the traditional panoramic vision of the battlefield and in doing so offers a new visual mode, the moving panorama war film.

The Panoramic War Film

Geoff King characterized *Apocalypse Now* as a spectacle of "authenticity" and "artistic imagination" (King 2006, 288). The key word here is *spectacle*, as war representations have been a form of spectacle since early cinema—as evidenced by the marketing of D. W. Griffith's film *The Birth of a Nation*—and the nineteenth-century battle panorama has long been recognized as an influence on war films. To better understand this influence, first consider the impact of a late twentieth-century battle panorama. *The October War Panorama*, housed in a museum located at the spot of Anwar Sadat's 1981 assassination in Cairo, depicts an Egyptian victory over Israeli forces during the October War (Yom Kippur War) of 1973. Built in 1989 by North Korean artists on Kim Jong Il's suggestion to then president Hosni Mubarak, the museum fails to mention the successful Israeli counteroffensives that followed and the UN-brokered ceasefire.[2] Additionally, a similar work, the *Tishreen Panorama*, exists in Damascus, Syria, also built by North

Koreans, depicting Syria's participation in the same war, much to the same effect. These panoramas essentially rewrite history for Egyptian and Syrian nationalist sensibilities. They both function in a way similar to Paul Philippoteaux's *Gettysburg Cyclorama*. Both old and new war panoramas promise (a selective) verisimilitude based on what Paul Virilio identifies as the link between optics and warfare.

The influence of nineteenth-century-panorama vision is present in early war films, such as Griffith's *The Birth of a Nation*, in which the Civil War battle sequences seems as if they could have been lifted straight from Philippoteaux's painting, as well as films from the 1920s that depict combat scenes in epic scale: Abel Gance's *Napoleon* (1927), for example, which was originally presented as a triptych projected onto three screens. The panoramic vision is present in the World War II combat film—in films produced during World War II and in later films about that conflict, such as *The Longest Day* (1962) or *Saving Private Ryan* (1998)—and thus, through the resulting visual codes, helped define the "panoramic war film."

The panoramic vision of battle notably serviced the antiwar critique of Lewis Milestone's *All Quiet on the Western Front*. The scope of warfare, in particular in sequences of German attacks on the French lines, is presented as a montage of wide shots of the battlefield—a seemingly endless sea of trenches and networks of barbed wire—and close shots of soldiers leaping down on their adversaries and engaging in hand-to-hand combat. The trenches are shown as a subterranean labyrinth directly opposed to the visible world of civilization, yet once the soldiers emerge, they find themselves engulfed in nightmare realm of mist, smoke, and flashes of artillery shells. *All Quiet on the Western Front* also contains one of the most extensive and brilliant uses of a moving camera in any sound film up to that date, effectively lending itself to its panoramic vision of World War I. Milestone, using a rotoambulator (a camera crane attached to a dolly with three wheels) for his panoramic tracking shots, combined the pathos formula contained in war cycloramas—the ability to experience the intensity of battle without being overwhelmed by it—with the realities of mechanized war, as his panning camera mimicked panning machine guns. The resulting experience is a revision of the aim of Philippoteaux's *Gettysburg Cyclorama*; the spectator does not take part in patriotic remembrance but rather they are made to feel that they have been caught up in a vast, impersonal, and meaningless disaster. How Civil War films exhibit the panoramic vision is also very revealing. *Gone with the Wind* (1939), though not directly depicting Civil War combat, should also be considered part of the canon of Civil War films for its sweeping portrayal of the war's impact on civilian life, a film shot in a scope reminiscent of war panoramas. Sherman's March to the Sea is briefly shown as the silhouettes of Union soldiers marching against a red background, illuminated by the flames of Atlanta and other Georgian towns destroyed in their wake. In one of the film's most iconic scenes, Scarlett O'Hara walks through the streets of Atlanta, littered with wounded and dying Confederate soldiers, the camera slowly pulling back to reveal the magnitude of the carnage and mass suffering, the shot ending on a panoramic image of Atlanta near a scale of the city's namesake war panorama painting. These moments aid in the film's support of the Lost Cause tradition, rendering the film as a highly problematic piece of Civil War remembrance from a contemporary standpoint, though it clearly exhibits the influence of the panorama in cultural memory of the war.

The panoramic vision of the war film is also explicitly felt in Ronald Maxwell's 1993 *Gettysburg*'s battle sequences. Copious tracking shots, crane shots, and shots filmed from remote-controlled miniature helicopters are used in the film to capture the scope of the battlefield and to provide a sense of scale, an aesthetic strategy found in other combat films that aim to place the spectator at the heart of the action. Additionally, *Gods and Generals* retains this panoramic vision of battle. Sweeping recreations of the First Battle of Bull Run, Fredericksburg, and Chancellorsville exemplify the connections between Civil War films and the broader war film genre, in particular earlier war films.

Apocalypse Now, however, radically departs from panoramic vision and instead draws upon another precinema spectacle art form: phantasmagoria, the use of optical illusions and juxtaposition of images to produce a distinctly haunting rendering of time, space, and events. Developed in Paris during the late eighteenth century, phantasmagoria was a spectacle form in which a lantern, placed behind a screen and mounted with a shutter containing painted slides, projected ghostly images upon the screen (Christie 1994, 111). The lantern projector would often be mounted on rails behind the screen so that these images appeared to move around the screen, perceived by the audience as revenants (Burgoyne 2010, 3). This form appears to have influenced subsequent movements in art, and war has often found itself to be the subject of these paintings, in particular those of the surrealists—Salvador Dalí, Antonio Gattorno, and others. But the aim of phantasmagoria is not authentic recreation but rather to suggest something ghostly, or unearthly, about the subject represented. By invoking this form, Coppola's film transports the Vietnam War itself to a haunted realm at the dark side of human nature.

By contrast, *The Hurt Locker* presents a new approach to the panoramic war vision, one that presents the battlefield through a 360-degree view from a series of identifiable and unidentifiable spectators; *The Hurt Locker* is what I will call a "moving panorama" war film, one in which the panoramic vision of battle is all encompassing and unrestrained. I am using the term "moving panorama" to signify a particular type of panoramic vision, one in which the viewer is surrounded on all sides by a 360-degree panorama field and experiences the event depicted as a montage of different perspectives. This experience not only exceeds the verisimilitude promised by the traditional panorama but also offers the illusion of being transported into the event. Like the *Virtual Iraq* video game, the war experience of *The Hurt Locker* reenacts a particular form of battlefield experience through this style, providing a new visual language for war. Beginning with the immediacy of observation-based material, Bigelow "experientializes" the rendering of war in a way that is "raw, immediate, and visceral" (Thompson 2009). Starting from a *cinéma vérité* approach reminiscent of Stanley Kubrick's *Full Metal Jacket* (1987), *The Hurt Locker* creates a montage of multiple perspectives—achieved through multiple cameras, varying film stock and camera speed, inconsistent angling, and so on—in order to mimic the manner in which the human brain records traumatic battlefield events.

Originating in Europe during the late eighteenth century, the phantasmagoria was a theatrical visual art form that relied on images projected from the magic lantern device over landscape art to suggest ghostly hauntings and to evoke the gothic. This effect was achieved, literally, through smoke and mirrors and also with the projection of images over paintings of a landscape or people—an optical illusion in which the uncanny clashes with the rational. This is what Tom Gunning describes as "the summoning of phantoms . . . while displaying the triumphs of the new sciences" (Gunning 2004, 5). This form was adopted into cinema by the likes of George Méliès and the German Expressionists, generating a visual style that Coppola drew upon for *Apocalypse Now* and much of his other work (for example, Coppola's 1992 horror film *Bram Stoker's Dracula*). *Apocalypse Now* can be characterized as a phantasmagorical war film based on its presentation of the battle zone as a place of haunting memories, incoherency and, most importantly, psychological degradation stemming from PTSD. Coppola himself even characterized the increasing surrealism during the film's progression as "phantasmagoric imagery."[3] This is achieved in two distinct ways: editor Walter Murch's use of dissolves and juxtaposition and cinematographer Vittorio Storaro's philosophy and use of color.

    Apocalypse Now also does not derive its approach to war trauma from a shared use of traditional fiction genre formulas. *Apocalypse Now*, according to John Hellmann, analyses the Vietnam War through "the specific ethos, imagery, and pattern of the hard-boiled detective formula" (Hellmann 1982, 429). The style of Willard's voice-over narration echoes that of Raymond Chandler and Dashiell Hammett's characters. Veronica Geng observes, "Willard talks in easy ironies, the sin city similes, the wary, laconic, why-am-I-even-bothering-to-tell-you language of the pulp private eye" (Geng 1979, 70). The symbolic use of ceiling fans and venetian blinds in Coppola's film is a borrowed trope as well. Even Willard's descent into the "heart of darkness" resembles the quest of the film noir antihero. In Willard's story, an actual jungle replaces the concrete one.

    The opening of Coppola's film immediately alerts the audience to the role of trauma and emotional battle wounds in the film's narrative by suggesting, through the use of visual and audio dissolves and juxtapositions, that not only Willard but America itself is haunted by the ghosts of the Vietnam War. A jungle set ablaze by napalm partially fades to an upside-down image of Willard giving what *Life Magazine*'s World War II artist and correspondent Tom Lea coined the "the two-thousand-yard stare"—an extension of Sophocles's term "one-thousand-yard stare" (specifically from *Ajax* and *Philocetes*) that was later used in Vietnam.[4] A cigarette with a long, cylindrical ash dangles from his mouth and fingers, an empty bottle of brandy sits on his nightstand along with a suspicious-looking spoon, and a pistol lies beside him on the bed sheets. In this sequence, Willard is doing what he will continue to do throughout the film—a constant return to war trauma—but the ambiguous temporality of the sequence calls into question exactly what the traumatic event was.[5] Is Willard recalling traumatic events that occurred prior to the film's central events, placing this sequence as the true beginning of the film's chronology? Does this sequence take place at the end of the film—Willard reliving the mission to kill Kurtz—as the images of flying helicopters from the napalm scene and shots of Kurtz's compound ablaze would suggest? Perhaps this sequence bears no relation to the narrative and rather acts alone as a visual essay on America's memory of Vietnam? In any case, Coppola never reveals what event is being remembered, but this sequence exemplifies the strength of one of the film's prominent motifs: war trauma elevated to the status of ghostly manifestations, haunting American mythology and national narratives.

In discussing *Apocalypse Now*'s use of phantasmagoria, let us use, for example, the image of Willard's two-thousand-yard stare from the film's opening (Figure 2.1). This shot is established through a partial-dissolve transition, starting with a shot of a burning jungle, then dissolving to a stationary shot of Willard looking upwards, then partially (not completely) dissolving back to the burning jungle so that the juxtaposed shot of Willard is in the foreground, and then bringing the burning jungle shot more into focus and Willard less into focus. The flaming jungle shot is a tracking shot that moves the images of flying helicopters and burning palm trees across Willard's face like an image from phantasmagoria theatre (Christie 2010). This shot in the opening sequence sets the expectation for the film's thematic content and visual rendering of war. The aim here is to establish a doubling between Willard and Kurtz that Coppola will revisit in the film's closing; Garrett Stewart notes that the film closes "upon its opening image," as if Willard's story is, by phantasmagoria, grafted onto Kurtz's story, both stories underlining the dark side of neocolonialism (Stewart 1981, 468). As Willard proceeds upriver to Kurtz's compound, the technique

Figure 2.1   Willard's two-thousand-yard stare in *Apocalypse Now* (United Artists, 1979).

of dissolve and juxtaposition continues with increasing intensity until the film's ending, a scene of Willard leaving Kurtz's compound upon completion of his mission, a shot composition that echoes the phantasmagoria in the opening scene.[6]

In Coppola's film, "a luminous presence is superimposed on a dark past," offering a link between Storaro's use of color and the presence of phantasmagoria in the film (Storaro 2001, 270). In a study of chromophobia—fear and anxiety aroused by the use of particular colors—David Batchelor writes, "Figuratively, color has always meant less-than-true and the not-quite-real" (Batchelor 2000, 52). Storaro's colors are designed to achieve precisely this. The use of orange, green, blue, and cloudy off-white colors pierce shadows and darkness to establish onscreen an otherness from the battle zone. The dark-light contrasts contribute to the film's thematic context. One of the few explicit appearances of the color white occurs when Kurtz's Montagnard guards are revealed: "Whitewashed, spectral natives who seem to travesty the pale Anglo villain come among them" (Stewart 1981, 458). In an interview with *The Guardian*, Storaro cites the illustrations from Burn Hogarth's *Tarzan* as an inspiration for the choice of colors in *Apocalypse Now*: "[Francis and I] didn't want to do anything naturalistic . . . I didn't want it to look like reportage. I put artificial color [and] artificial light next to real color [and] real light—to have the explosion of napalm next to a green palm tree, to have the fire of an explosion next to a sunset in order to represent the conflict between the cultural and the irrational" (Jones 2003). Storaro additionally characterizes the film's cinematography as representing "a discourse on the senses of civilizations"—the notion that light represents the civilized world and darkness represents the uncivilized (primeval) world is presented through "technological color's abuse of natural color forms . . . in cinematic terms, this is the conflict central to the film . . . it is the way artificial colour violates natural colour" (Storaro 2001, 280).

Willard's memories also shape the narrative structure by using genre formulas to defamiliarize both the story and the visual form, a disruption to the traditional panoramic vision of combat. In addition to borrowing tropes from the hard-boiled detective story and applying surrealist visual strokes, *Apocalypse Now* is in dialogue with the Gothic horror genre in its invocation of Sigmund Freud's *The Uncanny*. The uncanny clearly appears in the film through an increase of the unfamiliar, evoking feelings of dread, as Willard draws closer to Kurtz. An interesting example can be found in a deleted scene from the original John Milius script titled "The Monkey Sampan Scene," which takes place just before the death of The Chief. In this scene, the PBR Street Gang encounters an abandoned sampan, overrun by monkeys, floating downriver from Kurtz's compound. As the sampan passes, the sail whips around to reveal the nude body of one of Kurtz's Montagnards. Despite appearing in neither the theatrical nor the *Redux* version of the film, the scene represents a pinnacle of defamiliarization, building on the sense of dread that is present in both versions of the film— the psychedelic Do Long Bridge sequence with flares, soldiers jumping into the water with not army rucksacks but suitcases ("take me home"), blaring tuba notes, and Lance on LSD. Lance prancing around the PBR with a purple-smoke grenade just moments before Mr. Clean's death from gunfire that seems to materialize from the jungle as though by magic, the French colonialists appearing out of the fog like ghosts (in the *Redux* version), the shoreline decorated with corpses (Willard: "He was close. He was real close. I couldn't see him yet, but I could feel him"), and the arrow and spear attack by a hooting Montagnard mob resulting in the death of The Chief are other uncanny moments intended to disrupt any realist conception of the Vietnam experience. These are not images from *Life Magazine* or an Emile de Antonio documentary. The war ghosts that plague Willard are compounded through these moments, as they are unfamiliar even to him. Elisabeth Bronfen writes that this kind of haunting "feeds into and sustains the notion that war is an unfinished business." Coppola takes the viewer to the site where the Vietnam ghosts that plague American cultural memory emerge, "relentlessly haunting the present" (Bronfen 2011, 30 and 6).

In *Apocalypse Now*, war trauma is not conveyed simply through visual aesthetics. It is evoked through the episodic structure. *Apocalypse Now*, Cunningham writes, contains a "deliberately uneven push of [the] narrative's individual episodes . . . [that] progress towards a tangible climax . . . while the true development . . . takes the powerful form of commentary . . . on the shattered nature of the individual war experience" (Cunningham 2010). In *Apocalypse Now*, the uneven push is underscored through what Coppola calls "matching upwards"— adding details to successive scenes without too much concern whether these details match those in previous scenes (e.g., the sudden, unexplained appearance of a bandage on Willard's cheek just before the tiger sequence, and the disappearance of the puppy recovered from the sampan massacre scene; Coppola 2001). The progressive episodes in *Apocalypse Now*, experienced by PBR Street Gang during their journey up the river toward Kurtz, feel slightly jarring when examined against the main narrative thread (the quest to find and terminate Kurtz) and thus speak to the psychological degradation experienced by the characters.

In a 2010 interview for CNN, *Apocalypse Now* screenwriter John Milius was asked if he would "like to compare *Apocalypse Now* to *The Hurt Locker*," to which he responded, "They're very different. But . . . they don't really make any commentary on the war itself . . . The film is an examination of what people do within that experience."[7] This has been a repeated characterization of Bigelow's film—that it presents an apolitical or nonpartisan view of the Iraq War, a claim that has been contested on the ground that any treatment of the Iraq War is inherently political in nature.[8] This characterization mirrors, in many respects, Coppola's description of *Apocalypse Now* when the film was previewed at the Cannes Film Festival months before its official release: "My film is not a movie; it's not about Vietnam. It is Vietnam."

In an interview for the *Writer's Guild of America*, screenwriter Mark Boal commented that *The Hurt Locker* is not the first war film to use an episodic approach: "*Apocalypse Now* is told in chapters . . . and war is like that in that it does not have a neat little through line . . . [*The Hurt Locker*'s] structure came about in an attempt to be faithful to the reality of the situation" (Faye 2011). I contend that both films rely on the psychological deterioration of their central characters as the connective tissue for their episodic structures in service of their genre memory in relation to the influence of war panoramas on war cinema. *Apocalypse Now* dispenses with this panoramic vision and turns toward the influence of phantasmagoric theater, whereas *The Hurt Locker* revises the role of the spectator and traditional pathos formula of the war panorama.

The Hurt Locker and the Moving Panoramic War Film

A year after 9/11, Stephen Doherty wrote that the most successful films about the attack and the so-called War on Terror would be wrapped in disguise—nonwar films and nonhistorical films, steeped in allegory, would be seen as more suitable for addressing the geopolitical and cultural shifts in the wake of 9/11 (Doherty 2005, 221). Ten years after 9/11, Martin Barker examined the apparent commercial (and often critical) failure of War on Terror films in his book *A Toxic Genre*, a study of contemporary war films that first appears to confirm Doherty's prediction. "The issue of failure," Barker writes, "inevitably became linked to the summoning back of Vietnam, and Hollywood's failure to comment while the war continued."[9] The critical and popular success of Kathryn Bigelow's Oscar-winning Iraq War film *The Hurt Locker*, however, suggests that twenty-first-century war films had previously been in search of a cinematic grammar suitable enough to match the success of previous war film cycles in realistically portraying contemporary combat scenarios, and *The Hurt Locker* can be seen displaying a successful grasp of this new war film language. Additionally, Bigelow's film *Zero Dark Thirty* (2012) can be seen as a successful coda in the search for an effective visual language for contemporary warfare.

The Hurt Locker tells the story of an explosive disposal unit in Iraq (circa 2004), centering on danger-addicted Sergeant First Class William James (Jeremy Renner), and uses a montage of competing perspectives during scenes of bomb disarmament. Editors Chris Innis and Bob Murawski use cinematographer Barry Ackroyd's footage from four 16mm cameras in a way that disorientates the spectator while at the same time evokes a documentary approach to the war experience. The viewer is treated to cuts that do not match on action, cross the 180-degree axis (inherent to traditional rules of filmmaking), and oscillate between shot sizes and static and motion shots with no apparent connecting logic—the result being example of Eisenstein's concept of overtonal montage.[10] What is striking about this approach to the war film is how adaptable it has been to nonwar films. Gary Ross's science fiction blockbuster *The Hunger Games* (2012) utilizes a similar visual technique—a montage of handheld camera shots, according to Ross, brought a sense of urgency to a film that has been characterized by some as an antiwar parable.[11]

The Hurt Locker also provides a corrective to failings of previous Iraq War films by returning to encounters with self-endangerment and risk, which, according Michele Aaron, is central to the history of the moving image (Aaron 2014, 34). Robert Burgoyne also notes that the film acknowledges that the war film genre is a "body genre," deriving its "most intensive cultural meanings" by placing the body-at-risk at the center of the narrative; sacrifice and the body-at-risk situates *The Hurt Locker* in direct correlation with previous successful war films, such as *Saving Private Ryan* and *Flags of Our Fathers*.[12, 13] Similar to *Jarhead*, *The Hurt Locker* also turns on an engagement with the Vietnam War films. Bigelow herself has characterized the film as a combat film in tradition of Vietnam War films like *Full Metal Jacket*. Although *The Hurt Locker* has been characterized as a psychological drama (nearly confirming Doherty's assertion that successful War on Terror films will be "wrapped in disguise"), Bigelow has countered that Vietnam War films also carry this trait (Keough 2013, 142). The characters of Francis Ford Coppola's psychedelic Vietnam War film *Apocalypse Now* (1979), for example, are slowly sucked into the abyss of war's corruption of the psyche. *The Hurt Locker* speaks to this same psychological decline despite its use of a radically different filmic style and use of a radically different time and setting. *The Hurt Locker* also taps into *Apocalypse Now*'s constant at-risk status of the soldiers, transporting the jungles of Vietnam, with unseen danger lurking in the fog, to an urban Iraq combat setting. Both psychological drama and the somatic experience of war are therefore orchestrated in *The Hurt Locker* to enhance the realism it promises and to place the film as both something new to the genre and as a continuation of the visual and narrative traditions that have made the genre and enduring one.

If the moving panorama was a response to the increasingly irrelevant form of the static panorama, the moving panoramic vision of *The Hurt Locker* can be seen as a similar response to previous war films and changes in visual culture. If the panorama could not have developed without the Industrial Revolution, then the development of Bigelow and Barry Ackroyd's approach to *The Hurt Locker* may be linked to the digital revolution. The visual rendering of the battle zone in *The Hurt Locker* can be compared to the nineteenth-century tradition of the moving panorama, a form that was specifically developed as an alternative to the nineteenth-century European static panoramas. The moving panoramic vision is expressed in Bigelow's film through the cinematography and use of fast montage with varying points of view. In contrast to the static panorama, in which the audience is "in control of the spectacle" and "the visual experience of battle [is organized through] . . . several vantage points," the visuals work in conjunction with the war trauma and battlefield haunting central to the film's narration (Bronfen 2012, 193). The influence of the panorama paintings on war films is rewritten in *The Hurt Locker* to introduce a unique visual code, one chiefly inspired by the American tradition of the moving panorama. As great battles were often the subjects of nineteenth-century panorama paintings, a link can be drawn between the historical developments of the panorama painting and the war films of the twentieth and twenty-first centuries, one that includes the moving panorama and the visual approach taken in *The Hurt Locker*.

In *The Hurt Locker*, the uncanny is presented as a constant, psychological return to the opening scene of the film, even by characters not involved in the scene. This scene establishes the elements of the uncanny present in the film through conversation with Freud's view of "the dominance in the unconscious mind of a 'compulsion to repeat' . . . a compulsion powerful enough to overrule the pleasure principle" (Smith 2000, 3690–91). The film opens with the death of Staff Sergeant Thompson (Guy Pierce) by an IED. In conventional Hollywood screenwriting, this sequence would be considered part of the plant and payoff technique—grim foreshadowing—but screenwriter Mark Boal, formerly an embedded journalist in Iraq, uses this scene as a nightmare that slowly takes hold of its characters. If we accept the writer, director, and production team's characterization of the film as having a documentary approach, then this sequence contributes to the film as a metadocumentary, one where human, emotional depth—generally lacking in documentary films or in *cinéma vérité*—is restored to expand the narrative capacities without undermining verisimilitude. The central motif of the "hurt locker," which serves as both the title and suggests an ambiguous theme in the film itself, may be considered key to understanding the film's traumatic, psychological subject.

The definition of the term "hurt locker" is left unclear. The term itself is military slang for a state of severe physical or emotional pain and anxiety, particularly after a dangerous encounter, but it remains an elusive concept, open to redefinition by the viewer. An alternative definition can be found in the two boxes, or lockers, shown in the film, ones that connect characters to the opening scene. The first is a flag-draped white box containing the personal effects of Thompson. Sergeant J. T. Sanborn (Anthony Mackie) observes as Thompson's helmet and dog tags are placed in the locker next to a folded flag. For Sanborn, the closing of Thompson's hurt locker does not bring closure after he has witnessed Thompson's death in the opening scene. Rather, this ritual elevates Thompson's demise to the level of haunting, a ghost present in missions Sanborn will embark on throughout the remainder of the film. The ghostly haunting of Thompson's death is present in the *mise-en-scène* of the bomb-disposal sequences, a topic to which I will return. The second locker is one that James keeps under his bunk—a treasure chest of "trophies" from previous missions (detonators and wires)—a box that James describes as being "full of things that almost killed me." James is not haunted by the ghost of Thompson but rather by his own memories; the artifacts contained in James's hurt locker are reminders of his brushes with death on many occasions, a personal haunting in the making.

If we examine the *mise-en-scène* of the post-Thompson bomb-disposal scenes, we can locate many examples of repetitions that evoke a sense of traumatic haunting. Garbage, aluminum cans, cardboard boxes, and plastic bags litter the streets (could they be concealing an IED?), providing a labyrinthine maze for the main characters to navigate and reminding us of the pile of garbage that concealed the IED that killed Thompson. A car driven by a possible insurgent, who engages in a stare down with James, has green grass on the dashboard, recalling a conversation between Sanborn and Specialist Owen Eldridge (Brian Geraghty) during Thompson's death sequence (Eldridge: "What this place really needs is grass. We can start our own grass business . . . Sanborn and Sons"). The Pepsi logo is seen on a discarded soda can during Thompson's death and can also be found in the background of James's first bomb-disposal scene. Iraqi civilians flee from the site where a bomb was discovered in Thompson's death scene and, in one of James's scenes, human traffic slows down the explosive ordnance disposal (EOD) response and raises the tension. Most importantly, the composition and camera movements are consistent throughout all the bomb-disposal sequences: tracks, pans, tilts, and zooms occur at multiple angles and differing speeds without being connected through a discernable logic. The cinematography, along with the multidimensional sound mix, contributes to the film as a moving panorama and to the uncanny repetition of occurrences and details surrounding Thompson's death.

One critical example of traumatic repetition is found in the sequence in which military psychologist Lieutenant Colonel John Cambridge (Christian Camargo) visits a still-recovering Eldridge. Eldridge is playing a warfare video game, possibly as part of his therapy, and stops to speak to Cambridge, dismissing the doctor's credibility by saying, "Hey, it's Mr. Be-All-You-Can-Be." When Cambridge asks what he is thinking, Eldridge picks up his unloaded rifle, points it downward, and says, "Here's Thompson. He's dead." He then pulls the trigger and says, "He's alive." He repeats this twice, looking into Cambridge's eyes. Eldridge blames himself for Thompson's death, as he failed to shoot the man responsible for detonating the bomb that killed Thompson. During James's bomb-disposal sequences, Eldridge, still suffering from prior trauma, does not fire upon any potential threats to James's life, setting up a repetition of the original traumatizing event: the death of Thompson and Eldridge's own sense of guilt. It is only during an encounter with insurgents in the desert that Eldridge, through encouragement from James, is able to kill to save himself and his team.

Ironically cinematographer Barry Ackroyd addresses the digital revolution through nondigital means (the use of 16mm cameras). The role that documentaries and Internet videos play in the contemporary audience's relationship with the Iraq War informs this approach. This is due in part to the variety of methods by which we experience the moving image—the multitude of screens we encounter daily. Writing about large-scale paintings, Ian Christie asks whether "our ability to contemplate such vast acres of canvas with more equanimity [has] something to do with our expanded sense of image scale—from proliferating IMAX cinemas and giant plasma to the miniature screens of our smartphones" (Christie 2011) The approach taken in *The Hurt Locker* can be described as a moving panorama, the merging of two different cinematic traditions: montage and the moving frame. The moving panorama that is *The Hurt Locker* is a montage of competing gazes through multiple cameras that express their own consciousness. This new formulation of panoramic vision offers a novel way to analyze the visual score of *The Hurt Locker*, and it extends our understanding of the new logistics of perception in contemporary war films.

Barry Ackroyd's near documentary approach in Paul Greengrass's *United 93*—handheld tracking shots and low angel shots—appear in *The Hurt Locker* as well. Ackroyd, operating four Super 16mm cameras simultaneously, constantly crossing the 180-degree line, and "providing multiple points of view," intended to "make you feel like a participant" while providing the space for the actors to "do long takes with continuous action." A single scene could be captured through a combination of close shots—aerial shots, long shots, and medium shots—few of which are static. The images produce what Giles Deleuze refers to as "camera consciousness," in which "we are no longer faced with subjective and objective images" but rather a free-floating perception that amounts to an "emancipation of the viewpoint" (Deleuze 1986, 26). The copious footage from four 16mm cameras provided ample material for editors Chris Innis and Bob Murawski to use in a montage in the creation of the Iraq War zone as a moving panorama.

As discussed earlier, Walter Murch's editing in *Apocalypse Now* makes extensive use of partial dissolves, juxtaposed frames, and double exposure. By contrast, the editing of *The Hurt Locker*, particularly the bomb-disposal mission scenes, can be characterized as an overtonal or associational montage. The combination of tonal (cutting based on emotional or thematic content), metric (cutting based on time), and rhythmic (cutting based on both time and image) montage creates a psychologically complex narration—in the case of *The Hurt Locker*, a narrative flow not restricted to the perspective of the protagonists. Consider a series of shots in a sequence in which James disposes of a bomb in the trunk of a car at the UN building.

This series of 12 shots lasts approximately 25 seconds, covering several different angles and assuming multiple points of view (some of which are unidentified). Each shot is shaky and handheld, whether it acts as a tracking shot or a static shot. The traditional editing technique of matching on action is abandoned here, as is fidelity to the 180-degree-line rule. The scene proceeds in the following manner: the mission is interrupted by a terrorist's sniper bullet from a balcony across the street from and behind the EOD team. It is witnessed from the sniper's point of view, the soldiers' points of view, and undetermined points of view, the frequency of the cuts and the variety of angles and compositions increasing as the tension rises. After the terrorist is killed, tension grows again when it is revealed that the unidentified viewpoint from across the street is from a young Iraqi with a video camera, and the logic (or illogic) that determines the presentation and combination of shots and angles is again applied in the sequence.

The visual approach in *The Hurt Locker* suggests a break with the conventional influence of the panorama on war films, just as the visual approach in *Apocalypse Now* was also a departure from conventional form. Just as Coppola and Storaro wanted to take *Apocalypse Now* beyond the war journalism that invaded American television screens during the Vietnam War, Bigelow sought to distinguish her film from an even broader range of war coverage available to the Iraq War generation. The use of multiple cameras and montage suggests a competition of perspectives that, in some respects, comments on the contending video and photo journalism of the war itself (Internet videos from soldiers and Iraqi civilians, documentary films, and cable news coverage, both American and other). This is achieved through the editing scheme of *The Hurt Locker*, which can be compared more effectively to the nineteenth-century American tradition of the moving panorama than to the static panorama. The Iraq War battle zone, no matter how familiar it has become to us through other films and media, is rendered uncanny by editing that draws attention to undefined witnesses.

War as a Way of Thinking

Coppola's exaggerated portrayal of the battle zone as a haunting, phantasmagorical state and Bigelow's hyperrealistic battle zone, where the camera is a free-floating witness not restricted to the traditionally orchestrated war film experience, mark distinctly different visual approaches to the war film. The phantasmagorical imagery of *Apocalypse Now* offers an original visual representation of war. The otherworldliness of Coppola's Vietnam becomes a haunting hall of mirrors for the Western spectator, and the metaphysical journey to the cause of this haunting is aided by Storaro's nonnaturalistic colors and Walter Murch's juxtaposed frames, mimicking the magic lantern images of eighteenth- and nineteenth-century phantasmagoria. The film's narrative running along "the river, the liquid track that keeps the story moving despite [its] episodic interludes," according to Murch, allows the space for the "characters to break the frame" and, by extension, the ghosts of Vietnam as well (Ondaatje 2002, 70). The result is a Vietnam never seen by the likes of Walter Cronkite or the audiences of *Hearts and Minds* (Peter Davis 1974), but rather a Vietnam that may only exist in the minds of its traumatized veterans.

The Hurt Locker is a war film whose style can be compared to the therapeutic video game *Virtual Iraq*. Unlike other popular war video games like the *Call of Duty* series, *Virtual Iraq* and *The Hurt Locker* are devoid of the panoramic battlefield landscapes that are manifest in twentieth-century war films. *Virtual Iraq* and Bigelow's film also do not make use of the panoramic pathos formula; the spectator of *The Hurt Locker*, and the player of *Virtual Iraq*, are no longer in control of the spectacle. The visual approach in *The Hurt Locker* acts in counterpoint to James's acting out as a form of self-defense. The theatrical escapism promised by the rush of battle is a motivation for James, but the cinematography and editing are not in conjunction with this view, and as such, we, the spectators, are dragged along by James through the Iraq War experience with no relief from the encroaching war trauma.

Elisabeth Bronfen notes that in war films, "we implicitly take part in cultural haunting" (Bronfen 2012, 7). Both films discussed engage with this cultural haunting—the Vietnam films confronting the ghosts of Vietnam and the Iraq War films anticipating the ghosts of that war that have yet to enact their haunting on American culture. *Apocalypse Now* and *The Hurt Locker* are exceptional cases in this regard, as they offer up the battle zones of American wars as some of the most haunted sites in American history. It is in this approach that the uncanny functions as part of Bigelow and Coppola's "aesthetic formalization" of this cultural haunting. Rational human logic is subsumed by the otherworldliness of the combat zone. Where *The Hurt Locker* and *Apocalypse Now* also converge in this respect is in their presentation of warfare not as a place of battlefields (a series of towns to be conquered, fortresses to be overtaken, beaches to be stormed, etc.) but rather as a state of mind (or battle zone) in which the mind is invaded by a primitive warrior code. If the evolution of the war film is marked by addressing "war as a way of seeing," as Virilio remarked, then *Apocalypse Now* and *The Hurt Locker* delve deeper in their search for new modes of analyzing the impact of war. War, in these films, is a way of thinking, and the cultural haunting produced by war plays a formative role in shaping this way of thinking.

The Hurt Locker has been regarded by some as an end of the cycle of war film failures (Barker 2011, 156). For me, Bigelow's film also signaled a new turn for the genre; it was a film that future war cinema would be measured against, just as was the case with several late-twentieth-century war films such as *Apocalypse Now* and *Full Metal Jacket*. The Afghanistan War documentary *Restrepo*, for example, was constantly compared to *The Hurt Locker* in terms of verisimilitude and a depiction of the mind-set of the seasoned veteran.[14] Like *The Hurt Locker*, *Restrepo* enjoyed a modest box office success, but its continued and sustained success on DVD, television, and Internet downloads further cemented its legacy and the reputation of its filmmakers, Sebastian

Jünger and the late Tim Hetherington. Both *Restrepo* and *The Hurt Locker*, however, draw their strength on an engagement with both past war film forms and contemporaneous digital and documentary modes. Both films exemplify the process of genre memory and indicate their place in the broader history of the war film through their visual style and narrative strategies.

3

War Photography

In 2013, *The Guardian* ran a story on Ed Drew, a US aerial gunner serving in Afghanistan who had brought with him a field camera that used a wet plate collodion process.[1] This was the first time since the American Civil War that this process had been used to document soldiering life. The resulting photographs of his fellow soldiers were revealing: "I know all of my subjects well and fly with them on missions, and I felt it essential in telling their story that I connect with them at a close level. No photographic process can achieve this better than a wet plate."[2] The soldiers are positioned in ways that are eerily reminiscent of the Civil War photographs of Mathew Brady and his cohorts. There are solo portrait pictures of soldiers seated or standing against a canvas backdrop, rarely smiling, and emoting their combat experience through their facial features. Also, there are group photographs of soldiers posing in camp in front of helicopters or gunnery equipment. What these photographs have in common is that they project a sense of haunting. The presentation of wars as haunted sites in historical memory has been a persistent feature of war photography since the Civil War, and Ed Drew's photographs continue this tradition.

As mentioned earlier, prior to the Civil War, America's imagination of war was rooted in the popular "grand manner history" paintings and portraits of John Trumbull and Charles Willson Peale, for example. Although a key component of a pathos formula, inciting a desire to take part in remembrance, is reflected in these paintings, they were considered by many Civil War veterans, and indeed many civilians, to be gross misrepresentations of "the real nature of war" (Thompson 1960, 16).

Civil War photography can be viewed as a response to a desire to provide the story of a nation at war with verisimilitude. The invention of the daguerreotype in the 1830s by French artist and chemist Louis Jacques-Mandé Daguerre—photographs created on copper plate using light-sensitive, iodized silver crystals—may have posed little threat, at first, to the emotive power of an artist's brush and imagination, though it was clear that they would soon contend with a new representational language. At the start of the Civil War, the daguerreotype had largely been displaced by more cost-effective processes: the wet plate collodion process, created in 1851 by British photographer Frederick Scott Archer, for example. At the same time, however, new photographic technologies retained not only the ability to achieve a specific look and feel to what was being photographed but also the ability to tell stories that exceeded the time and space of the frame through a series of visual signs and codes that provided the story with pathos. This chapter will explore the history and legacy of Civil War photography and its accompanying photographic genres and pathos formulas.

The Rise of War Photography

One of the first photographers to capture war was Englishman Roger Fenton (1819–69), assigned by Queen Victoria to photograph the Crimean War (1853–56). As was the case with the Civil War, slow shutter speed and cumbersome equipment did not allow for actual combat to be photographed. Rather, the resulting photographs were of encampments, cities under siege, and haunted landscapes scorched by bloody carnage. What these images reveal—the stories they tell—are microhistories that provide the history of the war with pathos. Of one of Fenton's images of camp life, French critic and photographer Ernest Lacan wrote, "Mr. Fenton ... has taken us into the camps and shown us the life of a soldier in the Crimea ... This group, lit by rays of the rising sun on one side, forms an admirable tableau, full of truth, movement and life" (Bolloch 2004, 11). What is curious about Lacan's statement is that he felt a sense of movement in still images. The images he saw captured an experience and range of emotions that exceeded the frame, experiences and emotions that were outside of his daily consciousness yet at the same time seemed familiar to him—a quintessential example of pathos formula in action. For Hermann Kappelhoff, these emotions, often transmitted through the face, constitute a type of movement, a "dynamic play of thickly assembled microimpulses" (Kappelhoff 2012, 2). The reception of Fenton's photography suggests an interesting historical link between this sense of movement in war photography and war panorama paintings. French panorama painter Jean-Charles Langlois (mentioned in Chapter 1), inspired by the Paris exhibitions of Fenton's photographs, traveled to Crimea with French photographer Léon-Eugène Méhédin and subsequently produced the *Panorama of Sebastopol*, displayed in a rotunda on the Champs-Élysées from 1860 to 1865, which incorporated scenes from Méhédin's photography in the massive tableau (Bolloch 2004, 12). Though Crimean War photography may have set the stage for one particular expression of pathos formula, it was in the year after the war's conclusion that war photography turned toward a subject absent from Fenton's photographs but that would be a critical feature of Civil War photography: death.

Photographs from the Crimean War relied on romantic iconography, echoed in Tennyson's poetry, whereas Civil War photographs showed images of the dead and wounded on the battlefield. It was four years before the Civil War, however, that the world was introduced to battlefield death through photography. Italian-born British photographer Felice Beato, who had also photographed the Crimean War, was assigned to travel with the British army through India in 1857. In a controversial move, Beato photographed the aftermath of storming of the Secunda Bagh in Lucknow, Northern India, and the resulting photographs showed a battlefield littered with corpses. It was the first time battlefield dead had been captured on camera, evidence of war's brutality that would manifest in Civil War photography and photographs of wars that followed (Anderson 2005, 21). Beato's Lucknow photographs utilize pathos formulas in a similar way as Fenton and Méhédin's Crimea photography but strike a different traumatic chord. Death photography, according to Kappelhoff, relies on a "paradoxical sensation of one's own death" and an experience "beyond one's own perception"—the fear of death condensed into a microepisode (Kappelhoff 2012, 3). These images act as historical hauntings by transmitting a sense of shared suffering; a conflict between notions of "meaningful death" (heroic sacrifice in service of God and country) and "meaningless death" (soldiers killed by the arrogance of a nation and the leaders who put them in harm's way) is reconciled through pathos formula allowing a spectatorial identification with the deceased (3). Five years later, when Mathew Brady exhibited Alexander Gardner and James Gibson's photographs *The Dead of Antietam*, the *New York Times* wrote, "Of all objects of horror one would think that the battlefield should stand preeminent, that it should bear away the palm of repulsiveness. But, on the contrary, there is a terrible fascination about it that draws one near these pictures, and makes him loth to leave them."[3] The *Times* recognized in this instance this pathos formula encoded in these images, in action. The history of war photography that ensued would be defined by both a reliance on this formula and a sense of historical haunting encapsulated in these images.

Before the Civil War began, Mathew Brady was already a recognized brand name in the United States and Europe. His daguerreotypes were a consistent feature in *Harper's Weekly*, and he was a favorite of leaders who wanted portraits (Horan 1955, 14). In the early stages of his career, Brady marketed himself as a visual historian, having an acute awareness of how history would be preserved by his photographs. Brady knew at the start of the war, before the First Battle of Bull Run, that to photograph the Civil War was to serve as its historian. In 1861, he proposed a plan to President Lincoln, Alan Pinkerton, and Secretary of War Simon Cameron to create a photographic history of the war for its duration (13). The US government declined to support Brady's plan. Had the plan been approved, the resulting volumes and exhibitions could have been read as an early template for documentary war cinema. A determined Brady went into the field anyway, supported by colleagues with military connections, and found himself in silent competition with other documentarians: newspaper sketch artists practicing an established craft that rose to popularity in the United States and Europe during the 1840s and 1850s.

As mentioned earlier, sketch illustrations played an enormous role in documenting the Civil War and shaping public perception of the war. At the outbreak of the war, only one illustrator, Thomas Nast of *The New York Illustrated News*, had sketched in the midst of combat in Italy during Garibaldi's campaign. After the fall of Fort Sumter in April 1861, illustrators converged on Washington, often accompanying recently formed military units to the capital, waiting for deployment. What followed can be seen as one of the earliest forms of war correspondence producing visual images—a proto-news-media network. Field correspondents for *Frank Leslie's Illustrated Newspaper* (some estimates claim there were around one hundred men at any given time) sent back hundreds of illustrations; likewise with *Harper's Weekly*, one of the most widely read during the war, with a strong pro-Union bent. The wood engraving process provided the illustrated news with a quick turnaround time, and how quickly the issues were sold, read, and discarded—in conjunction with the ability of the images to agitate and muster emotions—could be read as a harbinger of war reportage in the twentieth century. In May and June of 1861, just before the first Union invasion of the Confederacy and the First Battle of Bull Run, illustrators who had come to Washington to embed themselves into the army encountered Mathew Brady staying at the Willard Hotel. Brady, who had also come to the capital with the intention of following the Union army wherever it went, exchanged ideas with the illustrators he met, notably Alfred Waud of the *New York Illustrative News* (later *Harper's Weekly*).[4] As the Union army crossed the Potomac on July 16, 1861, so did Brady, with the blessing of General Irvin McDowell and the support of General Winfield Scott Hancock, accompanied by many of the illustrators he had met in Washington.

An article in the May 2012 issue of *National Geographic* describes a problem with Civil War–era sketches, one that set the photography of Brady and others apart from the illustrators' work, providing him with a representational advantage. Illustrations were subject to manipulation in the engraving process, "censoring images considered too negative or graphic and altering drawings to make them more stirring or upbeat" (Katz 2012, 54). By contrast, photographs could not be manipulated in the same way as sketch illustrations. It is true that Brady and his cohorts often staged their photographs. Soldiers, both dead and alive, were posed in a manner to achieve a certain emotional effect, and other photographic techniques, such as double exposure, were employed, resulting in a form of photography known as "spirit photography."[5] Nevertheless, photographers could only stage the what was in front of the camera before the shutter closed, and the result was a facsimile of real life, one whose meaning at the time the picture was taken could not be significantly manipulated in post. As a result, it was not a coincidence that the Copyright Act Amendment, which extended copyright protection to photographs, was passed at the war's end in 1865; war photography was "based on mechanical skill . . . [and was] a creative field of original authorship" and thus served as a precinema paradigm for the blending of artistic and documentary representations of war (Bolloch 2004, 9).

Throughout the twentieth century, much of the discussion of Civil War photography centered on Mathew Brady, his legacy (exhibited strongly in Ken Burns's *The Civil War*) eclipsing those who worked with him. In recent years, Alexander Gardner, a Scottish immigrant who produced some of the most moving photographs of the war (including several iconic portraits of Abraham Lincoln), has received well-deserved attention, notably in the 2012 BBC documentary *The Scot Who Shot the American Civil War* (coinciding with the sesquicentennial of the Battle of Antietam) and in Steven Spielberg's *Lincoln* (also 2012). The photographs of Alexander Gardner are considered to be some of the most iconic and haunting images of the Civil War because they "helped the country to understand what it was looking at." Gardner understood that he was introducing the country "to a new way of seeing war" and that his images contained a series of signs that could be translated into discernable themes of the war (Lowry 2013, 12). Gardner also distinguished himself from Brady by crediting those who worked with him, notably his principle field photographer, Timothy O'Sullivan, who photographed the dead at Antietam. It is here that I would like to turn to the recent work of Jeff Rosenheim on Alexander Gardner, illustrating how Gardner's approach to photography and the marketing practices of his studios appear to foreshadow both cinematography and film production in many striking ways: "The Civil War photographers were very good at converting photographs that were made in one format to multiple formats, which were sold almost immediately. For ten or fifteen or twenty-five cents, you could get stunning views, you put them into a stereopticon viewer, and a . . . cinematic scope of the war comes to life" (Rosenheim 2012).

Gardner's studios, which bore a sign advertising "Views of War," offered many different types of photography and photographic processing, often embellished with India ink and other forms of watercolor.

These coloring processes anticipate what film scholars like Joshua Yumibe and others have observed about that early cinema: so-called black and white film was never completely black and white, and color plates and color stenciling was a common practice in early cinema.[6] The most requested photograph types, according to Rosenheim, were the following:

- *Carte-de-visite.* Small photographs comparable to trading cards.
- *Stereographs.* A forbearer to 3D photographs that were viewed through special lenses.
- *Imperial photography.* Large photographs touched up with India ink.
- *Ambrotypes.* Photographs made on glass plates (rather than the copper plates that daguerreotypes used), deliberately underexposed in the camera—a process similar to Polaroid photography—and placed over a colored background (usually black) in the glass frame.
- *Hallotypes.* Two glass plate photographs bound together.
- *Ivory types.* A photograph on gold-tone paper placed over a colored, untoned paper, allowing the colors to shine through (Rosenheim 2012).

While covering the war, *The Times of London* noted, "America swarms with the members of the mighty tribe of cameristas, and the civil war has developed their business in the same way that it has given impetus to the manufacturers of metallic air-tight coffins and embalmers of the dead."[7] Picture gallery tents followed the armies around, servicing soldiers with photographs during downtime. The photographs most popular with soldiers were the ambrotypes and the carte-de-visite. If a soldier had enough cash to spend, he generally chose the ambrotype. Named after its 1854 inventor, James Ambrose Cutting, the ambrotype was a negative placed over a black background inside a fixed frame, the glass varying in thickness to achieve different optical effects (and sometimes different colored backgrounds or glass plates were used to achieve a particular look). Ambrotypes, according to Rosenheim, seemed to anticipate "Hollywood perfection" in their subjects and also framed the figures in a classical structure, exemplified in portraits of soldiers and famous leaders of the war (Rosenheim 2013). This classical structure would be one of the many aesthetic strategies that would be challenged by the war, much in the way that late eighteenth-century and early nineteenth-century historical paintings would be challenged by artists and photographers during the Civil War.[8]

A soldier that did not have enough money for an ambrotype would purchase a carte-de-visite. Carte-de-visites were printed on thin paper that was then mounted onto thicker paper and were generally about 2.5 by 4 inches in size. Soldiers found the carte-de-visites easy to use for their own purposes in a way that eerily foreshadows the video diaries of soldiers in Iraq and Afghanistan (which I will explore further in the next chapter). Soldiers used them as keepsakes and gifts to send to loved ones or for portrait albums, including "field albums" for army units to document their military history. What is even more striking about carte-de-visites was how they were used journalistically and for antislavery propaganda. Photographs of slave children and workers with flayed skin from brutal whippings—some of which appear as ambrotypes and ivory types in Spielberg's *Lincoln* (inaccurately suggesting Gardner as the photographer)—were printed on carte-de-visites by abolitionist groups to hand out at meetings and to the press. Subsequently, carte-de-visites were made of former slaves serving in the Union army and documented efforts to educate formerly illiterate slave families, again to the same effect (Rosenheim 2012). The carte-de-visites can be seen as a forerunner to cinema on the grounds that they could easily be mass produced for public consumption and their distribution was also aimed at provoking an emotional response or call to action.

Civil War photographers also pioneered new genres of photography. John Huddleston identifies the following three photographic genres that are critical to the discussion of war photography and war cinema: (1) the sequential picture story, (2) socially concerned photography, and (3) depictions of scorched earth (Huddleston 2002, 14). Sequential picture stories were a series of photographs taken throughout the duration of a particular event—selected and presented so as to give the illusion of something being documented close to real time. This process is exemplified by a series of photographs titled *The Federals Execute a Spy in Mississippi*, one of the earliest forms of sequential picture stories during the war. In the first photograph—a long, wide shot—a spy (in the right side of the frame) stands before a Union firing squad (on the left side of the frame), his own coffin at his side. In the closer shot that follows, the spy lies dead beside his coffin in the foreground and the Union men leave on horseback in the background. This was a process that seemed to anticipate Eadweard Muybridge's work with motion photography. Socially concerned photography was intended to provoke an emotional response in the viewer, the photographer clearly aware of the pathos formula at work within the frame. These pictures tended to be photos of slaves and ex-slaves, often as carte-de-visites carried by abolitionists or reprinted in antislavery publications. Scorched-earth photography, while not originating during the Civil War (Roger Fenton's Crimean War photograph *The Valley of the Shadow Death* being a notable early example), displays landscapes touched by war— sometimes littered with corpses, sometimes showing bombed-out buildings or deserted cities, but always featuring an "American ideal pastoral landscape" disturbed (14). These photographs expanded on the relationship between humanity and nature, a popular subject for artists and writers of the era.

Perhaps the most striking and haunting examples from the scorched earth genre were the death harvest photographs. Rows of Union corpses at Gettysburg, arranged by Timothy O'Sullivan at Gettysburg (Figure 3.1), and Confederate and Union dead, side-by-side, in front of the pacifist Dunker Church at Antietam, photographed by Gardner, would change the reality of war in the public imagination, shifting the view of the conflict away from pageantry to fact. As with Felice Beato's Lucknow photographs, and indeed even in photos of death and atrocities in Iraq, notions of battlefield glory (meaningful death) are demythologized and a sense of shared suffering is generated by the image, which relies on a pathos formula that creates an identification between the spectator and the dead.

In death harvest photographs, we can see a connection between the visual language used by photographers and that used by painters, as seen in Eleanor Harvey's work on harvest metaphors in paintings (Harvey 2013). Gardner framed the territory in a similar way as landscape painters had done previously, yet he populated these familiar spaces with the dead and the bereaved as a disruption to "the terrain of everyday life" (Lowry 2012, 3). These photographs can also be read as many of the pathos scenes described by Herman Kappelhoff and the Mobilization of Emotions in War Films Project at the Freie Universität Berlin;

Figure 3.1   *Field Where General Reynolds Fell, Gettysburg,* by Timothy H. O'Sullivan (1863). © Stephen St. John/National Geographic Creative/Corbis.

scenes of suffering and sacrifice—scenes that focus on "bodily pain, vulnerability, and dying"—and scenes of injustice and humiliation instruct the viewer to take part in a communal remembrance by sharing in the suffering of those in the photograph, strewn across the battlefield or disinterred from hastily dug graves. In this sense, the death harvest photographs crystalize the emotive power of other pathos scenes and are themselves a pathos scenes par excellence.

The photographic strategies, genres, technologies, and processes developed by Brady, Gardner, O'Sullivan, and others placed photography in contrast with the battlefield sketch illustrations of *Harper's Weekly* through their ability to explicitly present images as moments out of time. Civil War photography (and other war photography that followed) drew its power, according to Alan Trachtenberg, from its ability to portray the war "as an event in real space and time" by presenting its subjects as only fragments of a larger history with no connection to the overriding political rationale for war (Trachtenberg 1989, 74–75).

The same can be argued of motion picture moments in war cinema. The flag raising on Mt. Suribachi, photographed by Joe Rosenthal in 1945 and featured live in Allan Dwan's *Sands of Iwo Jima* (1949), is a moment that generates meaning "without connecting syntax" (Hairman and Lucaites 2007, 177). John Miller's (Tom Hanks) shell-shocked gaze into the camera in *Saving Private Ryan* performs a similar task. Photography breaks the history of a war into thousands of small pieces from which the viewer can derive broader truths about the whole.

To illustrate how formulas of pathos operate in war photography, consider Figures 3.2 and 3.3. The viewer may not know the names of either soldier, but what cannot be described in a June 1864 edition of *Harper's Weekly* or in a *New York Times* article circa 1965–68 is transcribed through these images. In both images, the brutality of combat is worn on the face, where, according to Hermann Kappelhoff, "the moment of blinding horror is stretched out in time as a finely graded play of sensation." The emotion becomes an image and the image becomes an emotion (Kappelhoff 2011, 2). Elisabeth Bronfen adds that the pathos provided by these figures "[apprehends] the ungraspable intensity of war" because a balance is struck between "comprehending an intense emotion by tapping into one's own imaginative capacity and offering a conceptual presentation of it" (Bronfen 2012, 20). The old adage that one cannot truly imagine war unless one has experienced it firsthand is formally addressed through pathos; the spectator's ability to arrive at some level of understanding of the human cost of war is based on the visual presentation of a human emotion that can be perceived without having physically experienced the depicted event personally. The emotions transmitted by both images are not informed by time or place and yet they feel familiar to us.

In an interview for *Modern Art Notes*, Jeff Rosenheim, the curator for the 2013 "Photography and the American Civil War" exhibition at New York's Metropolitan Museum of Modern Art, notes a striking difference between soldier photographs taken at the beginning and at the end of the Civil War. The soldiers photographed at the end of the war had, in the parlance of the time, "seen the elephant"; their faces did not show fear or pain but rather a hollowness (Rosenheim 2013). In these photographs, we can see the emergence of another type of photographic genre, one that would be seen especially in the "two-thousand-yard

Figure 3.2 A Union soldier lies dead at Cold Harbor, Virginia, in 1864, in Ken Burns's *The Civil War* (1990).

Figure 3.3 A GI convulses in death throes in a Vietnamese forest in *In the Year of the Pig* (1968).

stare" photographs of shell-shocked troops from World War II and Vietnam. In these photographs, war trauma—what would be later known as post-traumatic stress disorder (PTSD)—is a discernable narrative device, a scene of pathos that elicits feelings of both moral outrage and remembrance, a shared sense of suffering. As we will later see, this particular photographic genre will have a distinct presence in war cinema owing to the persistence of war films drawing their emotive power from the soldier's traumatized state.

Although Civil War photography can be seen as providing verisimilitude in contrast to sketch illustrations, it must be understood that photography is still a practice in which representation is shaped by personal politics, and this was just as true during the Civil War as it is now in the digital age. Joel Snyder writes, "[While] Civil War photographs have been considered non-mediated copies of the facts they are supposed to represent," the photographs are, in fact, "both representations and presentations . . . made by men who worked with definable attitudes and goals to satisfy the needs and expectations of the broad but determinate audiences" (Snyder 1976, 17). The imagination and sentimentality of the photographer provided an organizing principle for the composition and subject matter contained in the photographs, and in this regard, Brady and his cohorts can be seen as prototypical documentarians.

Photography after the Civil War and the Rise of the War Documentary

In the years that followed, much of Brady's work was believed to have been lost, a repression of painful memories referred to by Civil War historians as "the hibernation" (Morris 2007, 138). This hibernation ended around the mid-1890s with a rediscovery of Brady's photographs alongside the emergence of motion picture (Klingsporn 2006, 33). Writing history with images came to be seen as a national tradition to which a new generation of image makers could claim a connection (Corwin 2010, 4). Further advances in war photography, however, would involve attempting to photograph actual combat as it took place, an impossible task for the cumbersome equipment and slow shutter speeds of Civil War photographers. These advancements would be aided by the longstanding link between photographic technology and military technology, which theorists Friedrich Kittler and Paul Virilio have discussed at great length.[9] "The history of the movie camera coincides with the history of automatic weapons," writes Kittler, for example. "The transport of pictures only repeats the transport of bullets. In order to focus on and fix objects moving through space, such as people, there are two procedures: to shoot and to film. In the principle of cinema resides mechanized death as it was invented in the nineteenth century: the death no longer of one's immediate opponent but of serial non-humans" (Kittler 1999, 124). In the history of photography that followed the Civil War, we can see a clear emergence of a relationship between military targeting technology and image making, a relationship that can still be felt in the present.

The years after the Civil War saw the rise of the instantaneous photography movement, a type of protocinema in which multiple cameras are used to capture moving objects in a series of successive still images. At the forefront of this movement was Eadweard Muybridge, an English photographer who had spent a considerable amount of time working in the United States photographing the landscape of the American West and pioneering advances in stereoscopic and panoramic photography. Muybridge became most famous for his studies of motion in California during the 1870s—notably, successive photographs of a galloping racehorse—aimed at learning things about the physical universe that the human eye could not detect. His discoveries and technological breakthroughs are also credited with influencing later developments in motion picture technology by the likes of Thomas Edison and William Dickson.[10] Of Muybridge, Tom Gunning writes, "His discoveries rely upon a modern rational and scientific mastery of space and time in which each has been calculated and charted in relation to the other . . . Muybridge's photography . . . makes visible a drama that would otherwise remain invisible: the physical body navigating this modern space of calculation" (Gunning 2003, 225). In this sense, Muybridge, and other pioneers of instantaneous photography, paved the way for the pathos formulas contained in war photography to expand their register. If the photographs of the dead at Antietam, for example, project the traumatic experience of battle contained in images of the aftermath and use a pathos formula that provides the viewer with an encounter with death from a safe vantage point, then through capturing motion, the parameters of the pathos formula could be expanded while still retaining its qualities. It is also no surprise that Muybridge and French photographer Étienne-Jules Marey influenced one another, and therein lies a connection between the Civil War and Virilio and Kittler's work on the war and cinema. In 1882, Marey invented the chronophotographic gun—a camera modeled on the Gatling gun (first used by the Union army during the Civil War)—that was able to take several photographs in rapid succession, furthering and complimenting Muybridge's work in instantaneous photography. By the end of the nineteenth century, photography, military technology, and telemetry, as well as a desire to bring narratives of the past and present to life, appeared to be fully cemented together.

The end of the nineteenth century also saw the rise of the photojournalist. Sketch illustrations were still used journalistically at the outbreak of the Spanish-American War, but they were soon displaced by photography. By 1897, the year before US involvement in the war, *New York Times* articles featured photographs daily (Anderson 2005, 58). In 1896, *Leslie's Illustrated News* began to use photographs to document atrocities in Cuba, part of a campaign of provocative journalism that is credited with drawing America into the conflict (59). The advent of the half-tone process, the printing of photographs directly on paper, during the 1870s and 1880s can be seen as a logical extension of the paper-printing techniques used by the Gardner studios (such as with carte-de-visites) and as a response to an increased demand for realism in reporting as a result of Civil War photography. The "yellow" newspapers, however, found themselves in competition with a new form of photojournalism whose technology originated through a marriage of traditional photography and military technology (Marey's camera gun): actuality films—short, nonfiction films documenting a single place or event. Like Civil War photography, the Spanish-American War actualities were reconstructed after the fighting took place—the raising of the American flag over Morro Castle or the daring raids of the Rough Riders, for example. Guy Westwell identifies a specific expression of pathos formula manifest in these actualities—a conflict between the insistence that a war film be read as a realistic representation and the infusion of "high melodrama" into the form (Westwell 2006, 12). The actualities were made to meet the demands of photojournalism—providing the story of war and presenting it to the public with verisimilitude—and yet, at the same time, a premium was placed on bringing human drama into the story.

The Great War saw a continuation of both the link between advances in military targeting technology and the pathos formulas of Civil War photography and Spanish-American War actualities. In World War I, smaller and more portable cameras "allowed the photographer's eye to be more intrusive than ever before" (Brewer 2005, 91). Military units assigned with the task of photographing the war for propaganda purposes were established, and lightweight Kodak cameras were carried into battle by soldiers for personal use (producing pictures so evocative that state war departments sought them out to supplement the images created by the photography units). Also, military operations (such as bomb disposals) were photographed as they occurred (Bolloch 2004, 15–16). Perhaps one of the major defining features of the First World War, however, was the use of aircraft for attack and surveillance purposes. In a *New York Times* article on the Museum of Fine Arts, Houston's 2012 exhibition "War/Photography: Images of Armed Conflict and Its Aftermath," Carol Kino describes how, in World War I, the British military used "semiautomatic aerial cameras affixed to planes," demonstrated in the photographs of Captain Alfred Buckham.[11] What is interesting is the use of the word "semiautomatic" in the camera's description. To "shoot" with a camera and to "shoot" with a gun become one and the same.

The end of World War I ushered in what some have termed the "Golden Age of Photography" (approximately 1919–40), described by Sharon Corwin and Ron Tyler as a new generation of photographers advancing photographic technology by embracing the art form as a national tradition (Corwin 2010, 3). Two ideas of what a photographer should be were merged during this period. First, the photographer "should provide an image of a social fact that is far away or otherwise hidden from view," and second, the photographer should provide images that "can reflect and document a social investigation, most often [involving] the vexed issues of class, labor, race, and ethnicity" (3). Photographs such as Dorothea Lange's "Migrant Mother" (1936), a haunting image where the impact of the Dust Bowl and the Great Depression is written on the face of a mother holding her children, are some of the prime examples from the Golden Era of Photography that exhibit these principles. It is no accident that this new generation of photographers were influenced by Parisian photographer Eugène Atget[12] and Civil War photographer Mathew Brady, because their work contained prime examples of early forms of documentary practices and "allowed artists to claim a connection to an established . . . national tradition" (4). Photography as historiography, therefore, was a reliable national tradition to connect the audience to a history that was largely hidden from them.

In World War II, military technology continued to inform advances in photographic technology. The Contax rangefinder, for example, used extensively to photograph World War II, featured an M42 lens mount, known as a "bayonet mount," which allowed the user to quickly photograph without removing their eye from the eyepiece, the camera now akin to an infantrymen's rifle. Famed war photographer Robert Capa's "D-Day Landing" (1944), for example, was shot using a Contax camera at a slightly canted angle, creating images that would be echoed in *Saving Private Ryan*. The image of soldiers, their backs to the camera, rushing into an abyss, places the spectator in the midst of the charge and narrates the fear and chaos of the day. Here we have a coalescence of the pathos formula found in Civil War photography and the Civil War panorama painting; the spectator is placed into the thick of hellish combat and yet is able to take part in patriotic remembrance from a safe distance.

Among the countless photos, documentary films, and newsreels, there is one photograph in particular that I would like to discuss that serves as a convergence point for the pathos formulas found in Civil War and World War I photography, an image not of combat but merely of a soldier's face. Tom Lea's "That 2,000-Yard Stare,"[13] sketched from a photograph taken on the Pacific island of Peleliu, appeared in *Life Magazine* in June 1945. The image is a raw, aesthetic rendering of PTSD, imparting a narrative of war experience that exceeds the frame. The soldier has "seen the elephant" in the same sense as Civil War veterans—the totality of the war, and indeed the story of the war, is written on his face and interpreted through a series of discernable signs. In images such as these, Robert Hariman and John Louis Lucaites assert that "emotions are construed as the outward expression of internal forces," creating their emotional power "by situating an outcry within its compositional structure," expressing what is not otherwise being expressed (Hariman and Lucaites 2007, 145). An image, still or moving, possesses the power to tell a story beyond what is simply captured in the frame.

The term *post-traumatic stress disorder* was not coined until years after the Vietnam War. Until then, the term *post-Vietnam syndrome* was more commonly used to describe symptoms akin to "battle fatigue" (World War II), "shell shock" (World War I), or "soldier's heart" (the Civil War). Later the term "Gulf War syndrome" would be added to the lexicon. Battle trauma is rendered in war photography and war cinema as battlefield haunting, suggesting a lasting cultural memory of war as a nation's "unfinished business" (Bronfen 2012, 20). The Vietnam War saw a continuance of the war trauma captured in photographs of "thousand-yard stares," notably in the photography of Don McCullin, some of which bare an uncanny resemblance to Tom Lea's *Life* picture. Vietnam War photography, both motion picture and still, found its strength in the photographic principles from the Golden Era of Photography, providing social fact to what is often hidden from view.

Documentary filmmaking in Vietnam can be seen as a logical extension of these principles, motion pictures that derived their strength from the pathos formulas of war photography. In 1967, Eugene Jones released *A Face of War*, perhaps the first critical American documentary on the Vietnam War. Jones's film impressed radical documentarian Emile de Antonio as it attempted to counter US Department of Defense documentaries, but de Antonio was concerned that the film failed to address the viewpoint of the Vietnamese.[14] For his Vietnam War documentary, *In the Year of the Pig*, which I will discuss at greater length in the following chapter, de Antonio found more inspiration in foreign documentaries like Pierre Schoendorffer's *The Anderson Platoon* (1966), Joris Ivens's *Le 17e parallèle: La guerre du people* (The Seventeenth Parallel: Vietnam in War [1967]), and Ivens's collaboration with Chris Marker, Jean-Luc Godard, and others in *Loin de Vietnam* (Far From Vietnam [1967]; Lewis, 2000, 79). The influence of these films, particularly Ivens's *Le 17e parallèle*, can be felt in de Antonio's film, as these films offer portraits of the Vietnam War through the eyes of the Vietnamese. The convergence point of Jones, Ivens, and de Antonio's documentaries are a retention of the principles found in the Golden Age of Photography and the Civil War: an attempt to reveal what is hidden from mainstream war reportage and preserve a graphic history of the war for future generations, one which would counter the history provided by the networks and the mainstream media. If the technology introduced during the Civil War not only furthered the development of mechanized war but also influenced the strategies used to document war (illustrated by the work of Virilio and Kittler), then we can say this relationship continued in documentary filmmaking in Vietnam and beyond.

Digital Fatigue: The Afghanistan and Iraq Wars and Contemporary War Photography

Although I will be discussing this more in greater length in the following chapter, I would like to briefly touch on photography in contemporary combat theaters and how it can be viewed as both a technological development along the lines of Virilio and Kittler's theories and as a continuation of the pathos formulas embedded in Civil War photography and beyond. The digital videos from soldiers in Iraq and Afghanistan, which feature in-war documentaries and inform the narrative strategies of several contemporary war films, provide a particular form of pathos and offer a variety of histories—fragments that contribute to the larger war story. Visualizing combat in the twenty-first century can also be seen as a continuation of the relationship between targeting and photography. The visual codes of the Iraq War and "War on Terror" films, for example, are informed by digital media on a small scale and contemporary surveillance and targeting technology on a large scale, what Garrett Stewart describes as "narrative agency subsumed to technology at every level, from aerial tracking . . . to eye-level confrontations" (Stewart 2009, 45). Satellite imaging, missile targeting computers, CCTV camera security footage, and Internet video chat appear in films such as *Syriana* (2005), *Lions for Lambs* (2007), *Body of Lies* (2008), and *Zero Dark Thirty* (2012) both as depictions of contemporary warfare and as a means to place the spectator in the midst of a new digital war—a repurposing of the pathos formulas contained in the war photographs of Capra and Philippoteaux's panorama. War communication technology, according to Patricia Pisters, has become democratized, "no longer organized from the top down" (Pisters 2010, 242). The soldier's photos and videos serve as time capsules and provide pathos in varying ways; they do not overtly instruct the viewer on the broader history of the wars in Iraq and Afghanistan, but rather they offer ways of reading this larger history.

Garrett Stewart argues that the use of digital technology in framing the action feels cumbersome rather than minimalist. The "very programing of the genre," according to Stewart, "may seem to have crashed—and in part from the electronic overload at the plot level itself" (Stewart 2009, 47). The result is what Stewart refers to as "digital fatigue": contemporary war films that feel just as staged as previous war films and contemporary mainstream media coverage, an irony when one considers that the aim of this new representational mode is to contest previous war cinema and mainstream media coverage. The term *digital fatigue* can be read as an allusion to *compassion fatigue*, a critique of this new logistics of perception coupled with a critique of how modern war is conducted (i.e., drone attacks, satellite targeting, depleted uranium).

I would like to offer an additional reading of the term *digital fatigue* and how it pertains to contemporary war cinema. *Fatigue* can also imply a soldier's combat fatigue (uniform). Digital technology is not only being used to wage war and represent it but also being used by soldiers to carve out a soldier identity. Twenty-first-century American war cinema appears to acknowledge that the post-9/11 era is the first time in history when the soldier is literally a filmmaker, and how the soldiers distinguish themselves as individuals can be based on how they film themselves. Increased access to digital motion picture cameras by the public at large—cheaper, lighter, and easily portable—has replaced the traditional soldier diary and epistolary tradition and recast the soldier as a documentarian of his own war.

By contrast, Patricia Pisters argues that Iraq War films, and other contemporary war films, stand alongside Baudrillard in denouncing the presentation of "virtual war[s] without human targets" (Pisters 2010, 238). The influence of war technology upon cinematic representations of war does not actually strip war cinema of human agency, a feature of war films since the Silent Era. Rather, the logistics of perception in war, both in waging war and in representing it, are contested in order to humanize the war experience and to provide a critique of the war. Pisters's view is that twentieth-century war cinema, in particular the Iraq War films, constitutes a "Logistics of Perception 2.0." To me, this appears to be a natural cycle, reoccurring at various points in the history of the war film. The new logistics of perception that Pisters identifies in the Iraq War films is genre memory operating as it did since early cinema, using the generic resources that have been made available (genre memory) and employing filmmaking techniques shaped by war technology.

At first glance, "Logistics of Perception 2.0" appears to be a far cry from Civil War era photography. The *Life Magazine* photographs of World War II and the Vietnam War feel painfully antiquated by comparison, and consequently Brady's photographs appear as antiques from a primitive age. Contemporary war films also appear to be wholly distinct from any previous war film cycles, and yet this is not the case; twenty-first-century war films are a continuing chapter in the broader history of war cinema, as there are underlying principles behind Civil War photography that are retained in contemporary war films. In post-9/11 combat scenarios, many soldiers assume the role of war photographer under the auspice of digital video and photography technology becoming cheaper, lighter, and more mobile.

No War without Representation: Civil War Photography and Beyond

In his essay on the role of photography in the development of the war film form, Geoffrey Klingsporn provides an addendum to Paul Virilio's view that "there is no war . . . without representation." Klingsporn takes Virilio further back before World War I to the American Civil War, citing the importance of battlefield photographs thought to have been lost after the war that reemerged during the 1890s, thereby coinciding with early cinema (Klingsporn 2006, 33). It is on this basis that I argue that the Civil War was a conflict that provided the blueprints for the war film, as it was the site where Napoleonic tactics gruesomely collided with technological innovation. Civil War historian Shelby Foote argues that the Civil War was a rehearsal for World War I and the conflicts that followed, as shown by the use of trench warfare, Gatling guns, repeating rifles, and troop deployment by train (Burns 1990).

The photographs that survived the Civil War found their emotive power in the pathos they transmitted. The living and dead featured in these photographs provide human agency to an untold story and invite the spectator to take part in remembrance from a safe distance. For Elisabeth Bronfen, the pathos provided by the figures in these photographs "[apprehend] the ungraspable intensity of war" because a balance is struck between "comprehending an intense emotion by tapping into one's own imaginative capacity and offering a conceptual presentation of it." This formula of pathos is used to the same effect in war films, both fictional narrative and documentary, as it allows for the audience to navigate through the chaos of battle spaces that have been stripped of the capacity for imagination.

4

Photography and the War Film

I would like to start with documentary war films before broadening the discussion to fictional narrative accounts of war. I find this to be a critical starting point because there is a connection between documentary war films and fictional war films in how their images are orchestrated to mobilize an emotional response. This connection can be strongly felt in contemporary war films, as many of these films acknowledge a direct influence of the war documentary form. Kathryn Bigelow's *The Hurt Locker* (2008) was shot by Barry Ackroyd, a longtime Nick Broomfield collaborator, his documentary credentials reflected in the film's use of zooms and handheld camera shots; likewise, a similar visual aesthetic is present in Paul Greengrass's *Green Zone* (2010), which Ackroyd also shot. Brian De Palma's polemical Iraq War film *Redacted* (2007) is presented in documentary form, recalling actual Iraq War documentaries from previous years, such as Petra Epperlein and Michael Tucker's *Gunner Palace* (2004). This chapter will consider how the influence of photography can be felt in both the documentary and narrative war film form, starting with a reading of Emile de Antonio's Vietnam War documentary *In the Year of the Pig*. What makes the documentary film form such a reliable intertext in this film cycle is the orchestration of fact and emotion in war documentaries, rooted in a historical tradition of combing reportage and direct testimony. This tradition, I argue, has antecedents in precinema history, exhibited in nineteenth-century documentation of the American Civil War—namely, in photography and the writings of soldiers. Both of these precinematic modes of witnessing are aimed at provoking strong emotions through the use of fact-based documentation, and their influence can be felt in war cinema in both the twentieth and twenty-first century.

De Antonio's *In the Year of the Pig* was a polemical challenge to the official discourse concerning the Vietnam War promoted through television. It relied heavily on the power of images not shown by the media, offering a competing set of images that provide a counterhistory of the Vietnam War; at the time of the film, images of the war were either distorted, sanitized, or not shown by the mainstream media.[1] De Antonio rearranged and presented these early photographs of the war in a way that recalls the role of surviving Civil War photographs, preserving a graphic history of the war for future generations, one which would counter the history provided by the networks and the mainstream media.

Next I will turn to Clint Eastwood's World War II film *Flags of Our Fathers* (2006), a film that explicitly draws upon war photography's power to provide the story of war with a moral message captured in a micromoment. *Flags of Our Fathers*, chronicling the lives of the Iwo Jima flag raisers from Joe Rosenthal's iconic photograph, also expanded on the visual codes of previous war films. Gruesome combat scenes were shot on desaturated film stock, a technique used by cinematographer Janusz Kaminski in Spielberg's *Saving Private Ryan* (1998), and handheld camera shots were also abundant in these sequences. *Flags of Our Fathers*, according to Robert Eberwein, thematized the issue of historical reality and critiqued the process by which heroism and war legendry is engendered in the public imagination, a process still felt in the radically different culture of the present day (Eberwein 2010, 139). The film's narrators also make explicit comparisons between World War II and the Vietnam War. In this instance, the generational memory of the Vietnam War serves as a reference point for the construction of a twenty-first-century look back at World War II.

Flags of Our Fathers advances the argument that photography, as a component of cultural memory, can renegotiate notions of national identity, engaging with what Alison Landsberg calls "prosthetic memory"—memories that are experienced as "a result of an engagement with a wide range of cultural technologies" and "become part of one's personal archive of experience" even though that memory does not actually belong to that person (Landsberg 2004, 26). Eastwood's film reconsiders the American war hero mythology from a post-9/11 perspective, a generational glance back at World War II that is clearly informed by the social and cultural changes of the twenty-first century—an example of genre memory and an updated generational memory. My reading of the film will show that one of the critical things that separates the cycle of twenty-first-century war films from previous cycles is in how ideas of national and ethnic identity are explored through an interrogation of American exceptionalism, and the representational principles contained in Joe Rosenthal's iconic photograph *Raising the Flag on Iwo Jima* (1945), which inform how Eastwood strategically engages with this interrogation, echo the photographic genres and pathos scenes of Brady and his cohorts.

Lastly, I will exam how two Iraq War films, Brian De Palma's *Redacted* and Paul Haggis's *In the Valley of Elah* repurpose the influence of war photography through Garrett Stewart's notion of "digital fatigue" and what Patricia Pisters calls "logistics of perception 2.0." *Redacted* employs a fragmented, episodic narrative structure rather than a fluid and linear one and a visual style dependent on multimedia interfaces, taking us closer to the heart of the action in a way that 35mm cinematography cannot. De Palma's film also underlines the incapacity of earlier film modes to represent contemporary combat experiences. *In the Valley of Elah* draws upon a similar visual grammar as *Redacted* to service its antiwar critique; a cell phone video from a missing Iraq War veteran may help solve a murder in Haggis's film. The film conveys an altered social landscape without the physical modification of the landscape in the production design, a contemporary vision of the Civil War photography scorched earth genre. There is a sense of social urgency in both *In the Valley of Elah* and *Redacted*, reinforced by the recognition that they were addressing a living history rather than a distant historical memory.

In the Year of the Pig

In the 1920s, two ideas were introduced that bolstered the need for documentary moving images. Walter Benjamin argued that it was important for writers to take up photography in order to provide images—ones encountered daily by the public—with narrative and context.[2] In his *Kino-Eye Manifesto*, Dziga Vertov argued for a form that would replace *mise-en-scène* with documentary to create an "'unplayed film' over the 'played film.'"[3] Both of these ideas are manifest in documentary films about the Vietnam War and the Iraq War: the images are provided with a narrative that acts as an organizing principle, and the resulting film is an "unplayed film" culled from several "played films." This is apparent in in Emile de Antonio's *In the Year of the Pig*, but it is how de Antonio selects his images that offers an interesting connection to a history of American photography in the late nineteenth and early twentieth century.

Four years after the release of *In the Year of the Pig*, de Antonio observed, "Power no longer resides in the universities, as it once may have, but in the television aerial."[4] The dispensing of information to the public, vital to the upkeep of a healthy democracy, had shifted to television news, he suggested, and was therefore highly susceptible to manipulation by powerful interests. De Antonio's *In the Year of the Pig* was a polemical challenge to the official discourse concerning the Vietnam War promoted through television. It relied heavily on the power of images not shown by the media, offering a competing set of images that provide a counterhistory to the distorted and sanitized one from the mainstream media. De Antonio rearranged and presented these images in a way that recalls the pathos formula of Civil War photography: preserving a graphic history of the war, condensed into micromoments, that could counter other forms of war reportage and serve as a cautionary tale for future generations.

The opening credit sequence of *In the Year of the Pig* immediately alerts the viewer to the film's legacy in the tradition of radical political filmmaking. The twenty-first-century viewer is advised that they are watching a film restored for DVD presentation by the UCLA Film and Television archive (Ross Lipman) and the Wisconsin Center for Film and Theater Research, with the original wear and tear kept intact, and with a preservation completion date of 2003—the year the Iraq War began. The first images are still photographs of Civil War monuments (notably the memorial to the 54th Massachusetts, the subject of Edward Zwick's *Glory*), cutting back and forth to black screens with vertical, static credit titles. On the audio track, as we watch these images, we hear a mechanical whirring noise that is difficult to identify (it is, according to de Antonio, the sound of twelve different helicopter blades electronically blended together to come out as one sound). The noise halts abruptly as an image of a tombstone appears on screen. The inscription reads: "As soon as I heard of American independence, my heart was enlisted—Joseph Angel, 1776." After this, the audience is treated to the film's first moving image shot, one that recontextualizes the mythology of a benevolent American military history. An elderly Vietnamese man, with children behind him, walks past the camera, which pans with him. The man makes a bow toward the camera, then continues walking, briefly glancing back at the camera with a fearful look in his eye. The sequence ends with a dose of irony—footage of a Washington official proclaiming, "I would remind you that scripture tells us 'Blessed are the peacemakers.'" Through this credit sequence, de Antonio casts his film as a historical documentary, but one that stands in stark contrast to the historical documentaries with which students of the time would have been familiar. This is a defamiliarizing, agitational documentary in which the "enemy" is recast as the American Revolutionary War soldier (or possibly a member of the 54th Massachusetts regiment), and the United States is recast as the British or the Confederacy.

As the film progresses, de Antonio's images continue to affect the spectator in a manner similar to the photographs of the Civil War— brutal images aimed at demythologizing American military exploits. The images de Antonio uses both illustrate and preserve a history of the war, with a particular emphasis on the decades preceding Johnson's escalation of the conflict in 1964. The manner in which de Antonio presents his images recalls the composition of Brady, Gardner, and O'Sullivan's photographs: still portraits of important figures, including a young Ho Chi Minh; group photographs of Viet Minh guerrillas proudly posing together; and corpses strewn about the battlefield. The camera pans across still images and newspaper articles, a tactic that documentary filmmaker Ken Burns would later use. Even when the images are not photographs but part of a motion picture shot, de Antonio often holds on the image in a single still life moment, placing emphasis on particular historical signifiers or reference within the frame.

After the opening credits, the film proceeds in the manner expected of a historical documentary film in setting the stage for the events of

1968: black and white colonial footage from French Indochina during the 1930s and 1940s (which de Antonio had procured from Paramount Studios) is shown ahead of the "talking head" segments—ambassadors, former French colonial officials, and a professor of Buddhism; people who had met Ho Chi Minh discussing Ho's connection with the Vietnamese people. These images, according to de Antonio, were intended to provide "a history without narration" (Green 1978). This segment of the film and many of the proceeding segments serve the narrative purpose of providing the audience with intellectual arguments to counter the administration's narrative. The power of the image to arouse sentiment without the assistance of narration, however, is critical to de Antonio's use of the film form to create his "historical/intellectual perspective." When we see footage of Senator Thurston B. Morton (of Kentucky, a Republican) stating that Ho Chi Minh "is considered by the North Vietnamese and a considerable portion of the South Vietnamese as the George Washington of their country," the recasting of Ho Chi Minh against the caricature presented by Washington and the press is made even more persuasive through the images presented in this segment of the film—those of Ho Chi Minh and his followers taken before American involvement in the conflict.

The connection de Antonio makes between the Vietnam War and earlier American conflicts can be illustrated by two images discussed in the previous chapter: an American GI dying in a Vietnamese forest during the final segment of *In the Year of the Pig* and a dead Union soldier at Cold Harbor, Virginia, in 1864. Despite being culled from a film reel, the shot from de Antonio's film—either slowed down in editing or overcranked during filming—possesses a similar evocative power as the Cold Harbor image. Even though we know (or have a rough estimate of) when both images were photographed, in both images it is time that is "out of place," in the words of Roland Barthes (Barthes 1981, 96). Both wars are humanized because the suffering and tragedy are transmitted through the face in the image. Images such as these are, according to Hermann Kappelhoff, "endlessly condensed micro-episode[s] occurring as affect" (Kappelhoff 2011, 2). The images of these soldiers invite us to relive war's savagery with us in their place.

Robert Hariman and John Louis Lucaites assert, "Just as emotions are construed as the outward expression of internal forces, the photo creates its own emotional power by situating an outcry within its compositional structure that compresses as it channels what is not otherwise being expressed in the scene" (Hairman and Lucaites 2007, 145). An image, still or moving, possesses the power to tell a story beyond what is simply captured in the frame. De Antonio's images of Vietnam are not used to complement the testimonies of scholars, such as Yale Professor of Buddhism Paul Mus and French historian Jean Lacouture, who are featured in the film, or to contrast the archival footage of Lyndon Johnson, John Foster Dulles, or Senator Joseph McCarthy justifying aggression in Indochina, a tactic employed in war documentaries such as Michael Moore's *Fahrenheit 9/11* (2004)—owing to their expressive potentials, the images themselves *are* the history.

De Antonio's artistic education coincided with the Golden Age of Photography, discussed in the previous chapter, of the 1930s, when, as described by Sharon Corwin and Ron Tyler, a new generation of photographers "embraced it and reinvented" advances in photographic technology in order to establish documentary photography (and by extension, documentary motion pictures) as a national tradition in preserving and projecting history (Corwin 2010, 3). Photography as historiography, therefore, was a reliable "national tradition" that enabled de Antonio to connect the audience to a history that was largely hidden from them. De Antonio would combine Brady's use of image-as-historical-document with established cinematic techniques for manipulating these images to conform to a historical narrative. One sequence roughly twenty minutes into his film employs the montage technique to counter the official historical narrative, to provide a history of what "is far away . . . hidden from view" and acts as a "social investigation [of a] vexed issue." Images of the gravestones of the French dead from Dien Bien Phu and footage of coffins, draped with the French flag and hoisted onto departing ships, are shown in a slow montage to the sound of *La Marseillaise* played on a đàn nguyệt (Southeast Asian stringed instrument). At the end of the sequence, de Antonio shows footage of a Viet Minh soldier playing a flute for French soldiers departing Vietnam. De Antonio abruptly jump cuts to a still image of the flutist (zoomed in to a closer shot), and then holds on the image as the soundtrack plays the last few notes of the anthem. Then de Antonio cuts to footage of a boat leaving Vietnam. The purpose of the sequence is to signify Dien Bien Phu as the end of one era and the start of another, but the singling out of the image of the flutist provides an explicit interpretation from de Antonio on this particular history: the Vietnamese left standing at the end become the masters of their own destiny.

In the Year of the Pig presents its images as found footage; de Antonio acts as a detective-filmmaker, presenting visual evidence to both complement and illustrate the written dissent of Noam Chomsky, Abbie Hoffman, and Allen Ginsberg. The ending of de Antonio's film circles back on itself, both stylistically and narratively. Just before the end credits roll, the image of a statue from Gettysburg National Military Park, first seen during the film's opening credits, is shown again as a still frame, this time in the form of a photo negative, accompanied by the *Battle Hymn of the Republic*. The outcry within the photo's compositional structure is that the viewer is witnessing a vicious cycle in history, from the defeat of the French early in the film to the defeat of the American military in an unwritten epilogue to the film. The final image is the payoff of Stella Bruzzi's characterization of the film's opening sequence. The use of a photo negative, rather than a developed one, foreshadows that many more will die before this is all over (Bruzzi 2000, 27).

Clint Eastwood's *Flags of Our Fathers* and "The Right Picture"

In an interview for the British Film Institute, Eastwood was asked, "How vital was it to deconstruct the hero myth?" Eastwood responded: "Very important . . . because in the era we're in now everyone is being considered a hero."[5] One way in which *Flags of Our Fathers* performs this deconstruction is by reconsidering the legacy of Ira Hayes, a Native American belonging to Arizona's Pima tribe and one of the Mount Suribachi flag raisers, within the context of a nation reconfiguring its own identity in the midst of warfare some sixty years after the Battle of Iwo Jima. Eastwood's film is clearly aware of the mythology surrounding Hayes, one that arose in the form of songs, books, and poetry after his death in 1955. Eastwood distinguishes his film from Allan Dwan's *Sands of Iwo Jima* (1949) or Delbert Mann's *The Outsider* (1961), the latter a film solely about the life of Ira Hayes (portrayed by Tony Curtis), by moving Hayes's story beyond the traditional hero narrative and instead focusing on how the concept of American heroism was manu-factured in World War II. I argue that *Flags of Our Fathers* critiques both sides of the American exceptionalism debate by using Ira Hayes's story to deconstruct both the notion of heroism and the defining dis-tinctions of race.

Anthony Smith argues that historical films specialize in "the recon-struction of ethnographs," citing, as an example, the famous Odessa steps sequence from Eisenstein's *Battleship Potemkin* as a scene that projects a national myth in a way "that is poetic and popular rather than strictly factual" (Smith 2000, 55). *Flags of Our Fathers* is a film that seeks to perform this task in reverse; Eastwood is critical of a national mythology that is "poetic and popular" and presents in its place a demystification of nationalism and patriotism.[6] The mythol-ogy surrounding Joe Rosenthal's iconic flag-raising photograph is chal-lenged alongside competing notions of a national identity forged by a nation at war. The lives of those present in Rosenthal's photograph, and the haunting memories these individuals experience, are used in Eastwood's film to bring into relief a post-9/11 discourse on war and national identity that seeks to affirm certain aspects of American excep-tionalism while at the same time offering a criticism of other aspects. The Native American character of Ira Hayes serves as perhaps the film's most potent critique of an American war hero mythology resurrected in the wake of 9/11, a hero mythology constructed by the media and popular cultural memory.

First, consider how Eastwood's film explicitly references two iconic photographs and the ensuing public response: Rosenthal's *Raising the Flag on Iwo Jima*, and Adams's *The Saigon Execution*. At the beginning of *Flags of Our Fathers*, an elderly John Bradley reflects on the impor-tance of the Rosenthal photo: "Now, the right picture can win or lose a war. Look at Vietnam. That picture of that South Vietnamese offi-cer blowing that fella's brains out the side of his head . . . That was it. The war was lost." Just as Rosenthal's photograph embodied what the American public—through Office of War Information (OWI) war pro-paganda and Hollywood films—had long imaged war heroism to be, Adam's photograph embodied the gruesome brutality that the Vietnam War became, signaling a sharp disconnect between mythology and real-ity. In light of this, we can say that Adams's photograph demythologizes and Rosenthal's photograph mythologizes, but Rosenthal's photograph involves the creation of a very specific element of national mythology that is relevant to the discussion of the mythology of Ira Hayes. In their analysis of *Raising the Flag on Iwo Jima*, Robert Hariman and John Louis Lucaites argue that the photograph provides "a coordinated visual transcription of three powerful discourses in America: egalitarianism, nationalism, and civic republicanism" (Hairman and Lucaites, 2007, 94–95). The egalitarianism expressed in Rosenthal's photo underscores the Hayes mythology and the mythology that is contested in Eastwood's film. This egalitarianism is identified by the fact that we see no faces, the uniforms are identical, and there is no brass or indication of rank present—"they are equal to the task because they are equal alongside each other" (Hairman and Lucaites, 2007, 98). *Flags of Our Fathers*, however, challenges the collective identity expressed in the photograph by drawing out the complex individual stories of those depicted there.

Perhaps one of the primary reasons that Eastwood's film contends with the hero mythology stemming from Rosenthal's photograph is that the memory contained in the photograph has been so absorbed by American culture, through the photograph's ubiquitous presence in popular culture, that it has become a memory believed to be shared by all. This form of memory is what Alison Landsberg calls "prosthetic memory," memories that are experienced as "a result of an engagement with a wide range of cultural technologies" and "become part of one's personal archive of experience" even though that memory does not actually belong to that person (Landsberg 2004, 26). When memory embeds itself into cultural artifacts in such a way, it can be difficult to challenge or dislodge. However, *Flags of Our Fathers* demonstrates that film, especially the historical film (war films and other historical films), is an effective tool for providing a counter narrative to the mythology that underscores these memories. Part of the mythology surrounding the flag raising photograph involves a mythology of Ira Hayes himself, promoted through film and song. To examine how Eastwood contends with the previous mythology of Ira Hayes, in service of his overall critique of previous American war myths, let us compare previous treatments of Ira Hayes as an American mythic figure in relation to the portrayal in *Flags of Our Fathers*.

Jacquelyn Kilpatrick has written, "American Indian heroism during the war made it more difficult to think of native peoples . . . as
the savages of the traditional Western" (Kirkpatrick 1999, 87). The
mythology of Ira Hayes confirms Kilpatrick's observations, serving
as a Civil Rights–era rebuttal to the mythologized America of the late
nineteenth and early twentieth century. The mythology surrounding
Ira Hayes developed after his death in 1955 and played the dual role
of redefining the postwar image of the American hero and contesting
America's earlier image of the traditional hero. Clint Eastwood draws
upon this mythology, however, in order to make a far-reaching critique
of the construction of the hero myth. The Ira Hayes of *Flags of Our
Fathers* is not merely the victim of racism, he is the victim of a socially
constructed hero myth—one that conveyed a new meaning after 9/11.
The post-9/11 hero mythology is deconstructed in Eastwood's film by
drawing a parallel with a hero mythology from the past, and the story
of Ira Hayes provides Eastwood with the essential tools with which to
perform this deconstruction.

In 1959, William Bradford Huie published *The Outsider*, detailing
the postwar life of Ira Hayes. Huie's story was later made into a film of
the same name with Tony Curtis in the role of Hayes. Delbert Mann's
film of *The Outsider* establishes the character of Ira Hayes through a
reversal of the veteran trope discussed in the previous chapter. The
film begins with Ira Hayes collecting his friend Jay, a serviceman and
fellow Pima Indian, from a bus stop. On the drive home, Ira asks Jay
whether the men he served with "are friendly." Jay's response is "Sure,"
and Ira then reveals to Jay that he has enlisted in the Marine Corps.
Their drive through Arizona's Gila River Pima Indian Reservation is
framed by cinematographer Joseph LaShelle to suggest isolation; both
men are about to embark on journeys that will become testimonies of
their individuality.

The Ira Hayes of Eastwood's film contrasts with Mann's Ira Hayes
on two levels. The first concerns Ira's hero image. Mann's film positions
Ira as a rebel hero who falls as Icarus, whereas Eastwood's Hayes refuses
to acknowledge his own heroism and is emotionally burdened by the
loss of his friends. The second difference concerns race. Burt Cardullo
writes that the fate of Curtis's Hayes centers on "bad luck at not being
born Caucasian" (Cardullo 2010, 53). *The Outsider*'s Hayes is portrayed

by a Jewish-American actor of Hungarian descent, and plays Ira as a man determined to contest the image of the savage Indian, proving that the Indian has equal status in American society alongside the white man. The Ira Hayes of *Flags of Our Fathers*, portrayed by Adam Beach (a Saulteaux Indian of Alberta), by contrast, finds himself a victim of negative stereotypes and is haunted by memories of his lost comrades.

Mann's film contributed to a mythology surrounding Ira Hayes, one that Eastwood's film would both acknowledge and critique in order to feed into a larger examination of the American hero mythology. The most salient feature of this mythology is the song *The Ballad of Ira Hayes*, written by Peter LaFarge (an Algonquin and Korean War veteran) in response to Mann's film and made famous through Johnny Cash, Bob Dylan, and Kris Kristofferson's cover versions. The song first appeared on LaFarge's album *As Long as the Grass Will Grow* (1963), a collection of protest songs regarding the treatment of the American Indian, which LaFarge subsequently introduced to Johnny Cash. The lyrics position Hayes's heroism around the notion that he was a figure to be contained by both American and Pima society; he is a "brave young Indian" that we "should remember well," but after the war he "started drinking hard" and "jail was often his home." LaFarge's Hayes (and Mann's) is one whom we should remember as a hero, as society had turned its back on him ("they'd let him raise the flag and lower it like you throw a dog a bone").[7]

Andrew J. Bacevich writes that the mythology of war in post-9/11 America is presented as a "seamless historical narrative ... with Operation Iraqi Freedom as a sequel to Operation Overlord" (Bacevich 2005, 98). Eastwood's film appears to entertain this idea in order to criticize an industry of myth making present during World War II and resurrected after 9/11. "Americans seem to concoct stories to make [the truths about war] more palatable," argues Bacevich, and the characters of *Flags of Our Fathers* contest these "stories" with stories of their own (97). A scene near the end of *Flags of Our Fathers*'s first act reveals Hayes's attitude toward the hero myth, as well as Eastwood's post-9/11 critique. When fellow flag raiser René Gagnon informs Ira that they were both in Rosenthal's photograph, Ira threatens him with a bayonet. "I wasn't there," he screams. In the following scene, Gagnon returns to the Marine base at Enewetak Atoll, where the superior officer who greets him informs him, "If I'm going to give up my seat to a hero then you had better have a good goddamn story to tell." Gagnon replies, "No, sir," to which the superior responds, "Enjoy it because they'll forget about you before Christmas." These two scenes suggest a counterargument to the post-9/11 hero myth. Eastwood explained this in his BFI interview in support of the film: "Growing up, I tried to think who's heroic, and with the war there was Patton, Eisenhower . . . literally a handful . . . of names . . . Now you have to decipher everything: everyone's a star." Ira's "heroism" in Eastwood's film contrasts with *The Outsider* and the ensuing mythology of Ira Hayes on the grounds that Eastwood acknowledges that the hero has become a social construct. *Flags of Our Fathers*, by contrast, engages with an earlier view of heroism, the "reluctant hero" from the work of mythologist Joseph Campbell, in which the hero "does not want to take on the burdens of the world" (Segal 2000, 187).

The third act of *Flags of Our Fathers* features a scene in which Ira, retired from military life, digs a drainage ditch with his fellow Pima. The sequence is introduced by James Bradley's narration: "But life had other plans for him." As he is digging, Ira is approached by a vacationing family passing through the area and asked by the father if he would pose for a picture with the wife and children. "You're him, aren't you? You're the hero, right?" the father asks. Ira merely smiles and produces a miniature flag and then poses for the picture. As the family leaves, the father tells his children, "That's a hero, kids." This scene punctuates Eastwood's critique of socially constructed hero myths, as Ira, despite being recognized as "the hero," will be defined for the rest of his life by a single photograph (Burgoyne 2010, 173).

Cultural memory, according to Marita Sturken, is different than personal memory and history in that it is "memory that is shared outside the avenues of formal discourse yet is entangled with cultural products and imbued with cultural meaning" (Sturken 1997, 7). Eastwood contends with the cultural memory of Iwo Jima, and World War II era notions of heroism, through his use of Bakhtin's notion of double-voicing. From a post-9/11 vantage point, he evokes the forms of pre-9/11 World War II representation and the remembrance of "the Greatest Generation" in order to challenge cultural memory, embodied in Rosenthal's photograph, with arguments put forward in the post-9/11

American exceptionalism debate. *Flags of Our Fathers* engages with a cultural memory of World War II provided by films ranging from the World War II–era combat films to Steven Spielberg's seminal film *Saving Private Ryan*. The storming of the beach at Iwo Jima in *Flags of Our Fathers* (and the combat scenes that follow) recalls the combat sequences in Spielberg's film: desaturated colors, a montage of varying camera speeds, and sudden and graphic violence. Notions of heroism present in earlier World War II combat films, and Spielberg's film, are also addressed and critiqued. *Flags of Our Fathers*, through these visual codes and through the story of Ira Hayes, engages with generational memory, cultural memory, and genre memory; the double-voicing in Eastwood's film is used for the purpose of bridging earlier ideas of war and national identities through the voice of a post-9/11 America attempting to reconfigure its own ideas of American exceptionalism in the wake of war abroad and an increased diversity at home that far exceeds that of both the World War II and Vietnam eras.

Digital Fatigue and the New Logistics of Perception

Around the same time as *Flags of Our Fathers*'s release, films about the Iraq War began to emerge. Brian De Palma's *Redacted* (2007) and Paul Haggis's *In the Valley of Elah* (2007) were among the earliest in the crop of fictional Iraq War films, and were also constructed in explicit relation to the Vietnam War films, while still emphasizing a contemporary media culture. *In the Valley of Elah* recalls Vietnam veteran films, such as Michael Cimino's *The Deer Hunter* (1978) and Hal Ashby's *Coming Home* (1978), to highlight the similarities between the Vietnam War and the Iraq War and the impact these wars had on the American social order. *Redacted* can be read as an Iraq War remake of De Palma's Vietnam War film *Casualties of War* (1989). Both films contain similar stories and characters, though *Redacted* uses its citations of *Casualties of War* to provide not only an antiwar film but also a critique of the war film form.

The Iraq War films, and other War on Terror films, that appeared during the latter half of the last decade represent a shift away from the overarching ideology of the war films that appeared at the end of the 1990s and at the start of the twenty-first century. The war films that appeared shortly after 9/11 and the launching of the War in Afghanistan were, according to Guy Westwell, largely prowar, with the World War II combat film, exemplified by *Saving Private Ryan*, providing a template for these films (*Hart's War*, *Black Hawk Down*, and *We Were Soldiers*, for example; Westwell 2006, 2). War films depicting the Iraq War, by contrast, were more critical in their depictions of US militarism, although, as Westwell observed, these films also conformed to post-9/11 heroic rescue fantasy, echoing Susan Faludi's view of "bravery absorbed into post-9/11 jingoism" (Westwell 2013, 393; Faludi 2007, 46–64). As mentioned in the introduction, there appeared to be a lateness of films that addressed the Iraq War and the Afghanistan War. There are, however, the following crucial differences between the Iraq War films and the Vietnam War films that account for the time between the initiation of both wars and the release of films about these wars: (1) Iraq War films ultimately began to appear while that war was still in progress whereas, for the most part, this cannot be said of the Vietnam War films, and (2) the visual and narrative codes that were in place during the Vietnam War were seen as insufficient to depict the conflict in a meaningful way, whereas pre–Iraq War films depicting urban combat and surveillance films laid the groundwork for the audiovisual codes that would come to dominate War on Terror films.

Redacted (2007) is an exemplar of these new genre codes. The narration in De Palma's film oscillates among the soldiers' points of view through digital video and helmet cameras, a documentary film, streaming web videos, and online video chat. These new visual modes are essential to other contemporary war films. *In the Valley of Elah* reveals an important plot twist through a digital video recovered from a dead soldier's cell phone; a Taliban propaganda video captures a critical moment in Jim Sheridan's *Brothers* (2009); a music video, featuring footage of soldiers in action and edited to hip hop music, commemorates fallen comrades in Kimberly Pierce's Iraq War veteran film *Stop Loss* (2008); Paul Greengrass's *Green Zone* (2010) weaves handheld camera footage into his Iraq War speculative fiction. This new visual language stands in stark contrast to the Vietnam War films. In his film review of *Redacted*, A. O. Scott writes, "The [Samarra] rape also recalls *Casualties of War*, Mr. De Palma's grievously misunderstood 1989 film about a similar incident in Vietnam. Both films walk a delicate line between moral investigation and exploitative sensationalism, and in both cases the measure of Mr. De Palma's artistic seriousness is his will-ingness to ask not only what it means to take part in an act of murder-ous sexual violence, but also what it means to represent it and to watch the representation" (Scott 2007).

At a press conference during the 2007 New York Film Festival, Brian De Palma characterized his approach to his Iraq War film *Redacted* as being driven by the fact that the "[Iraq War] has been so misrep-resented in the major media . . . I keep on saying all the time 'where are the pictures?' . . . The pictures that I saw [of] Vietnam got me out into the streets."[8] In *Redacted*, a film depicting a war crime akin to the Haditha massacre—the murder of more than twenty Iraqi civilians by American soldiers as "revenge" for the death of one of their comrades by an improvised explosive device (IED)—De Palma provides *us* with "the pictures," both real pictures and ones of his own creation, as an act of protest. The backlash against the film by right-wing critics, notably *FOX News*'s Bill O'Reilly, before the film was even released confirms the effectiveness of the film's blunt antiwar message and its existence outside the parameters of an "acceptable narrative" of the Iraq War experience.[9]

Redacted is an explicit acknowledgement of how war representation has changed radically in response to a period dominated by media tech-nology and digital photography, a technology that tends to work hand in hand with military strategies of disappearance and obscurity. Three prominent characteristics separate *Redacted* from Vietnam War films, including De Palma's own *Casualties of War*: first, the different modes of representation, one accessible to the Vietnam War generation and the other to the Iraq War generation; second, character transformation to underscore antiwar themes; and third, the overall narrative structure of the screenplay. I argue that in *Redacted*, De Palma rehearses the same narrative topic and themes as in *Casualties* based on his argument that the Iraq War generation is repeating the errors of the Vietnam War. I also argue that he has radically revised the structuring of the narra-tive, diminishing the role of his characters, and that he has radically shifted his visual approach. This shift in direction constitutes a revision or rejection of the "New Hollywood" narrative and visual approach. Furthermore, *Redacted* can be read as an acknowledgement that a graphic, *cinéma vérité* approach to "combat realism"—as embodied in

Causalities and other war films (*Full Metal Jacket* and *Saving Private Ryan*)—is insufficient to project combat realism in any meaningful sense and cannot, at present, provide an explicit antiwar critique. J. David Slocum notes that the visual language of the war film evolves alongside the evolution of technology since "increasingly impersonal technologies and the distant gaze through which one sees images of destruction empty those very images of meaning" (Slocum 2001, 16). This observation appears to update Paul Virilio's view that there is a direct correlation between a "way of seeing" in war and the development of cinematic vocabularies (Virilio 1989, 29). With this idea in mind, we can begin to analyze De Palma's stylistic departure from the earlier form. De Palma and his New Hollywood colleagues developed their own standards for realistically portraying graphic violence, a standard feature of the American New Wave cinema of the late 1960s through 1970—films for which Arthur Penn's *Bonnie and Clyde* (1967), Peckinpah's *The Wild Bunch* (1969), and Coppola's *Godfather* (1972) set a tone. The aim was to show personal and unsanitized violence in ways that removed the audience from its "comfort zone." De Palma, while unrelenting in his approach to graphic violence in *Redacted*, abandoned his previous, stylized approach to violence in favor of something more suitable to the post-9/11 world. The observation often attributed to François Truffaut that there could never be an antiwar film, as the violence in such a film would inevitably excite the viewer to the point of siding with one group over the other, appeared to be validated by such films as *Black Hawk Down* (2001), *We Were Soldiers* (2002), and *Saving Private Ryan*, graphically violent war films rendering the New Hollywood antiwar motive increasingly archaic and irrelevant.[10] *Redacted*'s juggling of representational modes and digital images attempts to correct this by critique the war film genre itself.

In one of its opening scenes, Private Angel Salazar (Izzy Diaz) sets the precedent for the visual style of *Redacted*. The film, according to Salazar, will not be a "Hollywood action flick—no smash cuts, no adrenaline pumping soundtrack, [and] no logical narrative to help make sense of it." This line not only establishes the representation register of *Redacted* but also reminds the viewer that the film is a repudiation of the visuals of earlier war films. In this sequence, Salazar is not only filming but also being filmed himself by Sargent Lawyer McCoy (Rob Devaney), establishing the fact that both characters are the subjects of a web of multilayered stories; neither one is the central hero of a single, logical narrative. De Palma places this narrative as the central focal point of the story, but he by no means treats it as the most vital portion of the overall narrative. Here, De Palma is addressing a critical representational issue plaguing post-9/11 war films, regardless of their implied stance on the war, which is also a continuation of an older, post–World War II theme: how the mechanization of war (in this case the digitization of war) contributes to the impersonal and disconnected nature of modern combat. In *Redacted*, De Palma exhibits what Garret Stewart refers to as "digital fatigue" in that "storytelling is among the casualties of . . . 'improvised' devices . . . Gone are the choreographed and the panoramic . . . We get instead random checkpoint suicides . . . all of it saturated by video" (Stewart 2009, 45). The intertwining of contemporary combat technology and cinematic strategies, what Virilio argues is the by-product of war and representation, has ultimately diminished notions of individual sacrifice and personal drama inherent to the traditional war film.

Digital fatigue is not the product of digital imaging in contemporary war cinema, as the use of digital images is part of much broader stylistic innovations in global cinema that emerged toward the end of the 1990s. Rather, digital fatigue is the product of a "political symptom" that underscores how this technology operates in both the war film and in actual warfare (47). The managing and strategizing of war through satellite imagery, live reconnaissance video feeds, and cell phones has placed a cold, impersonal distance from the death and destruction occurring at ground level. The result is that the use of digital technology, in both waging contemporary warfare and in representing it, overwhelms plot and narrative with the visuals, diminishing the drama that the spectator is accustomed to from earlier war films. In the case of *Redacted*, Stewart observes that the film relies so heavily handheld digital cameras, night-vision lenses, and surveillance equipment that "the only mission with any focus has become transmission itself" (51). Though drama and narrative may be overwhelmed by digital technology in *Redacted*, it is the use of this technology as "docudrama" that serves a particular antiwar aim of De Palma—a critique of past modes of visualizing war carnage in antiwar films.

De Palma's use of these various media modes to service his critique of the Iraq War and the use of both the internal and external perspectives supports Patricia Pisters's view that *Redacted* and other Iraq War films constitute a new logistics of perception, what she refers to as "Logistics of Perception 2.0." A coherent narrative is present in *Redacted*, one that is forwarded by multiple screens and acknowledges contemporary warfare's multimediated face, a literal "battle of the screens" (Pisters 2010, 241). De Palma's film acknowledges Jean Baudrillard's view of the relationship between war and media coverage while at the same time asserting that multiple perspectives (and multiple screens) are necessary when depicting a brought to the American public by cable news networks.[11] *Redacted* fills Baudrillard's "empty images" with actual death and destruction occurring at ground level in a way echoes the reasons his New Hollywood cohorts changed their approach to violence during the Vietnam War (241). The difference in the visual approaches to war violence in *Redacted* and *Casualties of War*, however, is part of the changes to the visual form in contemporary war films and indicative of a new logistics of perception.

The presentation of battlefield death helps to illustrate the logic behind De Palma's departure from earlier form. *Casualties of War* begins with the death of Sargent Brown (Erik King), the squad's paternal figure. From the moment Brown's body is struck by a sniper's bullet, the camera, lens stained with his blood, never strays from him, operating in slow motion as he falls to the ground. De Palma forces the viewer to absorb every detail of the process of life slowly fading from this "casualty of war." Editor Bill Pankow (*The Untouchables* and *Body Double*) does not cut away until after Browning has landed on the ground, screaming, at death's door. The visual construction of the scene borrows from war films of the previous two decades (an aesthetic tool made popular by New Hollywood icons Sam Peckinpah and Arthur Penn). A specific echo can be found in Stanley Kubrick's *Full Metal Jacket* with the death of Cowboy (Arliss Howard), sniped during the film's final showdown sequence. Kubrick sharpens the intensity of the moment, allowing the viewer to focus on every graphic moment of becoming a war casualty, achieving what Stephen Prince calls a "reaction against . . . movie traditions, misleading and grossly out of step with the times" (Prince 2000, 176).

If the aesthetic of slow-motion violence in *Full Metal Jacket* and *Casualties* can be seen as a "reaction against movie traditions," so too can the absence of slow motion in *Redacted*. Sargent Sweet (Ty Jones) is *Redacted*'s stand-in for *Casualties of War*'s Sargent Brown, the unit's leader whose death sets the film's central event in motion. Sweet's death, filmed through Angel Salazar's helmet camera, is witnessed at the speed as if the audience were actually in Salazar's boots. Sweet's death in slow motion would have been an illogical interruption to the chosen representational mode and would also have drawn attention to itself as a Hollywood device, inciting mistrust from the viewer. In *Redacted*, De Palma assumes the role of an "invisible director" in order to improve his approach to graphic violence as a tool for conveying an antiwar message, avoiding a distinct style that would call attention to itself, make his antiwar aims suspect, and suggest manipulation.

For Friedrich Kittler, the invasion by media and "serial photography" in war was intended to "bring about new bodies" (Kittler 1999, 128). In contemporary war films, these "new bodies" are brought to the attention of noncombatants via the digital technologies that shape our perception of modern combat—namely, Internet videos. Web technology contributes to the visual score of *Redacted* on two levels: first, in simultaneous support of both the external perspective and the internal perspective and, second, in support of the film's broader, antiwar message. The first level can be detailed without much difficulty. The YouTube videos and Skype chat dialogue further the overall narrative, either by enabling the central characters the space for private confession or by enabling noncharacters to provide a commentary on the general narrative. Web technology in support of an antiwar message identifies the role of an online culture of opposition since the outbreak of the Iraq War.

On April 5, 2010, WikiLeaks released cockpit footage from an Apache helicopter of the shooting of Reuters journalists in Baghdad on July 12, 2007, footage previously suppressed by the State Department and dubbed on YouTube the "WikiLeak Iraq Collateral Murder Video." The incident, coupled with a concurrent bombing in Afghanistan that killed innocent civilians, sparked a massive string of YouTube responses from across the globe. De Palma's use of this visual medium is an attempt to highlight both the role the Internet plays in the antiwar movement and the fact that candid, principled opposition is absent from conspicuous forms of mass media (e.g., the 24-hour cable news cycle).

De Palma also highlights the role of the Internet in the jihadist movement, videos used to shock and terrify the West and to highlight the exploits of jihadists in Iraq and elsewhere. The videotaped beheading of Angel Salazar at the hands of Al Qaeda later in the film is similar to videos of beheadings at the hands of Al Qaeda in Iraq's former leader Abu Musab Al-Zarqawi—notably the beheading of Nicholas Berg. These videos have not only been exploited by jihadists but also used by right-wing talk-show hosts and provocateurs (most notably Michael Savage) as a militaristic rallying cry, deliberately emphasizing otherness and drawing a clear, Manichean "us and them" narrative. Through the similarities between the video of the beheading of Nicholas Berg and the video of Salazar's death, De Palma illustrates that the Internet videos from Iraq are not merely a tool of the American antiwar left or mere documentaries used to enlighten American civilians in the comfort of their own homes.

Kevin Provencher's *Film Quarterly* review of *Redacted* opens with a suggestion that a possible reaction to the film would question its authenticity, and "*Redacted*, in many ways, conditions that reaction" (Provencher 2008, 32). Provencher is perhaps correct on the grounds that De Palma's film may invite such scrutiny, but De Palma's aim with this film is to invite dialogue and debate rather than to convey authenticity. One of the principle arguments, however, against authenticity and combat realism as the primary goal in De Palma's work, in my view, is based on how De Palma confronts both war and the war film. *Redacted* acknowledges the continued presence of the "cleansed image" in news media coverage of the Iraq war, what Baudrillard describes as "war enclosed in a glass coffin . . . purged of any carnal contamination or warrior's passion" (Baudrillard 2001, 65). In other words, Vietnam War films dramatized what audiences had witnessed on the nightly news coverage during the war, but Iraq War films, in order to deliver any meaningful antiwar message, are forced to dramatize these events in a unique visual register to de-dramatize them; American news coverage of warfare since the Gulf War has sanitized the presentation of warfare, and films such as *Redacted* and Iraq War documentaries are offering a counterrepresentation via their framing of conflict, depiction of bloodshed, and abandonment of—according to Angel Salazar—"logical narration to make sense of it all."

In the Valley of Elah

In an interview for *Creative Screenwriting*, Paul Haggis, when asked about what had inspired him to make *In the Valley of Elah*, stated that the idea of an Iraq War film came to him in 2003 after the war was launched. Haggis, frustrated with the way the cable news networks reported on the conflict, turned to online video diaries posted by soldiers serving in Iraq. One video struck a terrifying chord—made by an 18-year-old and edited to a rock anthem. In the video, the young soldier and his friends pose in front of the charred corpse of a dead Iraqi. The soldier lifts up the severed hand and waves it at the camera. Haggis's response was, "My God, what's happening? Because I know these to be good men and women . . . they go for all the right reasons most of them . . . it's late 2003 and this is happening already." This response, I argue, informs the sense of social urgency contained in *In the Valley of Elah* and films like Brian De Palma's *Redacted*, an urgency reinforced by a recognition of the delayed response of the Vietnam War films, which, by the time they were released, addressed not living history but memory. Haggis's viewing of these Internet videos also presents an interesting insight into the role of the new logistics of perception (digital fatigue) in shaping contemporary war cinema. That digital videos appear in Haggis's film is also a testimony to the influence of mass digital media on both war films and war reportage.

The film, set in the American Southwest, follows Hank Deerfield (Tommy Lee Jones), a Vietnam War veteran, investigating the murder of his Iraq War veteran son, Mike (Jonathan Tucker). During the his investigation, Hank recovers his son's cell phone from the military barracks and hires a technician to recover the data from the phone in the hope that it may generate a lead. A video recovered from the phone details an incident based on a true story that Boal recounted in an interview for *Playboy*: Mike and a fellow serviceman Gordon Bonner (Jake McLaughlin) are on patrol in Iraq, filming passing goat herds and Iraqi civilians from their Humvee. Bonner swats the cell phone camera away from him once he realizes that he is being filmed, causing the phone, still recording, to fall to the seat. Mike, now filmed at a low, canted angle from the seat, spots something on the road ahead. Bonner orders Mike to speed up, as it a strict military procedure not to slow down for any on-road impediments, lest it be a decoy for an IED or ambush. The camera jolts upward as the Humvee runs over the obstruction in its wake, revealed later in the film to be an Iraqi child. The footage then pixilates, rendering the subjects inscrutable, and then ends. This video, capturing the source of Mike's war trauma, not only provides Hank with clues for his investigation, it also mimics the video diaries that prompted Haggis to tell a story about the Iraq War, acknowledging the importance of these visual testimonials to preserving a historical and cultural memory of the Iraq War experience.

In the Valley of Elah can be described as a police procedural whose genre conventions have been corrupted by the Iraq War context. The film's opening shot suggests this form and harks back to the new logistics of perception discussed in the previous chapter—a distorted, digital-video shot in Iraq on a cell phone later followed by a title over a black screen that reads "Inspired by True Events." This title sequence also announces the importance of the digital image in refashioning our understanding of war. The digital image and information technology dominate the narrative structure and determine the information the viewer is privy to, despite Hank's initial resistance to this mode of technology. Hank Deerfield applies an organic approach to his quest, removing himself from the technological tools used by others and instead relying on instincts and logical enquiry. As testimony to an altered nation, this approach ultimately fails him. Mike, by contrast, never appears onscreen except for flashbacks, communicating only through the digital image. Mike's fellow soldiers murder him in a violent argument fueled by shared trauma, but the source of Mike's trauma only becomes clear to Hank and the viewer at the end of the film.

During this investigation, Hank's past experience as a veteran provides him with the intuition and technical knowledge to follow leads as to his son's whereabouts. The film hints at Hank's past without enunciating it clearly. For example, while staying at roadside motels, Hank polishes his boots before sleeping and then makes his bed every morning using military-style folds and tucks. When passing a high school, Hank stops the car to demonstrate to the groundskeeper the proper way to raise the American flag. And while assisting Detective Emily Sanders (Charlize Theron) in a crime scene investigation, Hank uses his acute observations of the terrain to reveal evidence of a crime—the crime that turns out to be Mike's murder. What Haggis reveals through Hank is a set of common cultural references, a sense of the collective memory of the Vietnam War that has now been eclipsed by the terrorist attacks of September 11, 2001. Although Hank Deerfield indicates that he has left Vietnam behind him—the "specter of Vietnam . . . buried forever in the desert sands of the Arabian Peninsula" as George H. W. Bush famously declared at the end of the Persian Gulf War—his son's murder, and the evidence of atrocity through Mike's cell phone video resurrects this specter. A past once thought to be forgotten has acquired new meaning, one that may illuminate a larger, intertextual message.

The cell phone video in the film is what Isabelle McNeil describes as "the memory supplement" in that it is a "cultural object that elicits memory [interacting] . . . with shared individual memories" and supplements the "psycho-social operations of memory" (McNeil 2010, 32). The video shifts Hank's mental perception by acting as a supplement to his memory of his son. Mike's video is an artifact of the war, one that encapsulates one history within the broader set of histories, and one that also acts as the inverse of what Paul Cornish describes as the intentions of war souvenirs. For Cornish, trophies are "victory . . . plainly announced, civilian morale bolstered" (Cornish 2009, 12). Just as the doughboys of World War I returned with German helmets, so did Iraq War veterans return with now-worthless Iraqi currency with images of Saddam Hussein. Mike's video, in this regard, acts as a negative trophy, one that provides a critical account of the Iraq War on its own, without the need for any accompanying antiwar commentary track or insert shots to provide context. Here, the imagery contains the same form of condensed history found in Civil War photographs, only in this case it is delivered through the digital technology used in contemporary targeting, surveillance, and representation.

There is also an interesting connection between *In the Valley of Elah*'s use of new logistics of perception and the disruptions of panoramic vision in contemporary war films, and this can be seen through the film's approach to composition and orchestration of its images. Cinematographer Roger Deakins uses wide shots to allow the terrain to act in support of the narrative and traumatized characters. Deakins also frames the film's characters against these landscapes through wide-angle shots that allow the landscape to dwarf the characters. This approach is similar to the framing of Vietnam veterans against the romantic primal wilderness of rural Ohio in Michael Cimino's *The Deer Hunter* (1978)—filmed by famed cinematographer Vilmos Zsigmond. Deakins, however, departs from Zsigmond's approach by way of technical adjustments to composition and camera movement. Deakins' camera lens, for example, is kept at 40mm or less, a technique that allows for the subjects, regardless of the frame composition, to always be kept at an uncomfortable distance. *In the Valley of Elah* also produces a change in social space by tampering with continuity and spatial consistency, specifically—through Jo Francis's shot matching—by crossing the 180-degree line, bringing the overall style of the film closer to the disruption of panoramic vision that would be realized over a year later in *The Hurt Locker*.

What is critical in the film is how the soldier videos (the film's digital fatigue) constitute evocative pathos scenes that can be tied back to early war photography, and this is well illustrated in the penultimate scene of the film. Hank, having solved the mystery behind his son's murder at the hands of other traumatized veterans, reimagines the

Figure 4.1   Mike Deerfield (Jonathan Tucker) photographs a war atrocity on his cell phone in Paul Haggis's *In the Valley of Elah* (2007).

incident captured on Mike's cell phone. In this scene, Hank sits in the driver's seat of his truck, parked outside the military base, filmed from outside of his truck in a medium shot. Editor Jo Francis cuts to Mike's video footage shown earlier in the film (a goat herd on the side of the road). We cut back to Hank behind the wheel, the framing tighter than before, and he turns his head toward the passenger seat. Then we cut to Bonner swatting the camera away, the same point of view shot from before, only this time it is filmed on 35mm and framed as a reaction shot to Hank turning his head. Bonner looks forward, spots the Iraqi child on the road ahead, and reacts to it. The film then cuts back to Hank, the framing even tighter, turning his head to look forward. It is as if Hank is reexperiencing war trauma, long suppressed in the decades that followed Vietnam, by putting himself in Mike's place. The cutting between Hank and Mike becomes quicker as Bonner tells Mike to not to stop. The film briefly returns to the cell phone footage after Mike has run over the child—the low, canted angle shot of Mike from the passenger seat. In this shot, the screen does not pixilate as seen before. The viewer sees Mike's hand reach for the camera. The film finally cuts back to 35mm, showing Mike rush out of the vehicle with his camera in hand. Ignoring Bonner's instructions to get back into the vehicle, Mike walks toward the body of the child, stops, then pulls out his camera and takes a picture. The scene ends on a close shot of Hank behind the wheel of his truck, recalling his final phone conversation with his son, heard at the beginning of the film. Up until this point, Hank, and the spectator, only viewed Iraq through digital video. After traveling through an America reshaped by war trauma, Hank and the film's viewer have arrived at a new understanding of suffering and war's consequences and, with this clarity, can detect something of themselves in Mike's video.

As I have discussed earlier, scenes of pathos, according to the Berlin Mobilization of Emotions in War Films, situate the spectator in world of shared sentiments in order to mobilize emotions through audiovisual strategies. When looking at the different categories of pathos scenes "assigned to different realms of affect," there is one category in particular that I see exhibited in both Civil War photography, *In the Valley of Elah*, and in other contemporary war films: the appearance of authenticity used to create a sense of shared memory and shared suffering. In this mode, the factualness implied by Civil War photography and digital videos in contemporary war cinema elicits an emotional involvement. During the Civil War, photography was seen as more accomplished at generating both support for the war and outrage in response to its atrocities than sketch illustrations (Thompson 1960, 69). Brady's camera, according to Jeff Rosenheim, was not merely a tool for documentary but rather a "corrector of poetics"; Civil War photography addressed the indulgence of painters and sketch artists, and at the same time it deepened their poetic potential with the promise of truthfulness (Rosenheim 2013). In contemporary war films, such as *In the Valley of Elah*, visual nods to the use of small-scale digital imaging in combat zones are used to strengthen the spectator's emotional investment in the war story. These films acknowledge viewer familiarity with an online video community, performing a generational revision of the war film form that seeks to correct the inadequacies of earlier modes. The soldier videos in these films not only elicit spectatorial engagement, they acknowledge the roles that "rage, panic, and automatic reflex" play in combat situations—identifiable human emotions that are rendered more subjective through small-scale digital modes (Pisters 2010, 243). On the one hand, this can be read as a generational improvement over Civil War photography, one that has repeated itself numerous times throughout the history of cinema. On the other hand, there is still the retention of a pathos formula and the ability to render history into fragments.

"Seeing the Elephant" in Contemporary War Films

As Jeff Rosenheim notes, a striking difference between soldier photographs taken at the beginning and at the end of the Civil War resides in how their faces transmit a series of signs that tell a story of war through emptiness. There is little pain or fear on their faces but rather a sense of hollowness; the soldiers at the time described this as having "seen the elephant" (Rosenheim 2013). As discussed in Chapter 3, these photographs constitute a photographic genre and pathos scene with a persistent presence in war cinema, and how these scenes play out in contemporary war films is very revealing. By the end of *Redacted*, the surviving soldiers, filming themselves at a homecoming party, break the fourth wall with the look of someone who has "seen the elephant." The elephant is also seen in *In the Valley of Elah* as demonstrated in the scene where Hank imagines Mike's traumatic encounter and stopping to photograph it—both have seen the elephant in this sequence. It is in the final scene from Kathryn Bigelow's *Zero Dark Thirty* (2012), however, where this influence of this photography genre can be clearly felt. The film's main character has "see the elephant" as well (Figure 4.2). Bigelow's film, chronicling the hunt for Osama Bin Laden in a style that many critics have characterized as a semidocumentary approach, ends with the film's protagonist, Maya, boarding a plane to leave Afghanistan after the Navy Seal Team Six operation on May 2, 2011. The pilot asks Maya where she wants to go. She gives no response and looks straight into the camera in the film's final shot, exuding the emptiness found at the end of a decade-long manhunt. Here, Bigelow summarizes an experience of the War on Terror in a single shot, inviting the spectator to partake in a shared suffering, much like the photographs of the Civil War soldiers who had "seen the elephant." The shot also writes a history of contemporary conflict that can act independently of exterior commentary or a linkage to the broader chain of events. Maya's near-death experiences, loss of loved ones, and the feeling of emptiness after years of obsession are written on her face in a single shot where only

Figure 4.2   The shell-shocked face of the War on Terror: Maya (Jessica Chastain) in the final shot of Kathryn Bigelow's *Zero Dark Thirty* (2012).

Alexandre Desplat's soft, delicate score can be heard. This finale shot can be read as a touchstone of contemporary war cinema retention of the representational principles that the Civil War photographers left to history: the combining of pathos with a small, yet emotive, stand-alone moment in history.

5

The Soldier Diary

"Civil war . . . What did those words mean? Was there any such thing as a 'foreign war?' Was not all warfare between men warfare between brothers?"

—Victor Hugo

By the end of 1862, English translations of Victor Hugo's *Les Misérables* began to appear in North America. Though the novel, released in five volumes, received mixed reviews in the North, Southern critics were very receptive, ironic given Hugo's staunch antislavery views (Masur 2013). John Esten Cooke, an aid to the maverick Confederate cavalry general J. E. B. Stuart, wrote, "[The novel] had been translated and published by a house in Richmond; the soldiers, in the great dearth of reading matter, had seized upon it . . . The soldiers, less familiar with the Gallic pronunciation, called the book 'Lee's Miserables!' Then another step was taken. It was no longer the book, but themselves whom they referred to by that name" (Cooke, 1864). This appears to be a recognition that a narration of war requires what Elisabeth Bronfen describes as individuals (troops) standing in "for political ideas and nation . . . individuals whose personal involvement renders abstract conflicts concrete" (Bronfen 2012, 4). The personal war narratives found in Civil War epistolary forms were similar to the way that the characters in *Les Misérables* were stand-ins for the larger moral questions Hugo posed for a post-Napoleonic/post-Revolutionary France, as in both cases a narrative of nationhood (on a large stage) is infused with pathos by being transmitted by human participants (on a small stage).

Historical memory of past conflicts plays an important role in framing the events of Hugo's novel (The French Revolution, Waterloo, and the July Revolution of 1830), which may, in part, explain the fascination with the novel by soldiers on both sides of the Civil War; a cultural memory of the American Revolution and, in the case of many commanders, a real memory of the Mexican-American War (1846–48) informed the attitudes of soldiers as they entered the conflict. Sixty years after the war, Henri Fescourt's 1925 silent adaptation of Hugo's novel featured the aftermath of the Battle of Waterloo, a scene from the novel seldom featured in other screen versions. The sequence is reminiscent of the haunting battlefield landscapes in Abel Gance's World War I film, *J'accuse* (1919). A large bird, hand painted onto the film strip, glides through a sky that is thick with smoke and dark rain clouds before it is eventually brought down by a lightning bolt. The film cuts to an immense wide shot of the battlefield littered with corpses. We soon see the crafty and unscrupulous M. Thenardier looting these corpses, eventually encountering and "saving" Colonel Pontmercy, establishing major plot developments that are to come. The imagery is reminiscent of photographed scenes from the American Civil War—Mathew Brady's images of corpse harvests and blood-stained battlefields. This scene, however, also contains a key element found in both Hugo's novel and in the diaries of the soldiers who carried the novel: memories of a real past are infused with a poetic narration, providing a story of war's trauma with pathos.

This chapter will look at the ways soldier-witnesses during the Civil War, in their writings of diaries, letters, and postwar memoirs, foregrounded the conflict in historical memory and employed formulas of pathos to provide the narration of war with human agency. The primary texts considered here are writings of Horace Porter and Elisha Hunt Rhodes, though other notable examples from both sides will also be examined. Central to my reading of these texts are the concepts of generational memory, the process by which historical memory is repurposed by successive generations and, according to David Thelen, reconnected with "its origins in the narrative form" (Thelen 1989, 1118). Both the writings of Civil War veterans and the war films that followed find their strength in a graphic rendering of the somatic experience of war coupled with what Robert Burgoyne describes as "a collective rethinking of the past" (Burgoyne 2013, 349). The writings of Civil War soldiers and generals, I argue, can be read as an anticipation of the narrative strategies that would be employed by filmmakers from the early twentieth century onwards. These written records infused the war story with formulas of pathos that invite future generations to take part in an emotionally charged remembrance, a vantage point from which to navigate the chaos of combat.

In his 1978 collection of essays, *Tropics of Discourse*, Hayden White lamented the way history books were being written—like nineteenth-century novels—and yet they mirrored fictional writing on the grounds that both were rooted in narrative, only in this case it is a narration of past events in a way that ostensibly reveals the truth (1978). This observation is seen by many theorists and historians to be the origins for critical, scholarly examinations of the way history is presented on film; the historical film, of which the war film is a subgenre, uses its audiovisual language and narrative strategies as a corrective to the shortcomings of historical writing, providing an alternative dialogue with the past. The work of historian James M. McPherson, however, provides a rejoinder to White's observation, one that incorporates the strategies of fictional writing and cinema with Civil War historiography. He interweaves quotations—from soldiers, politicians, and civilians—to breathe life into his historical writing.

Consider the following passage from his book *Battle Cry of Freedom* (1988), which recounts a campaign by General Patrick Cleburne (Army of Tennessee) to arm and train slaves in defense of the Confederacy: "At the time of Cleburne's proposal, however, such opinions still seemed dangerous. Most generals in the Army of Tennessee disapproved of Cleburne's action, some of them vehemently. This 'monstrous proposition,' wrote a division commander, was 'revolting to Southern sentiment, Southern pride, and Southern honor.' A corps commander abhorred it as 'at war with my social, moral, and political principles.' A shocked and angry brigadier insisted that 'we are not whipped cannot be whipped. Our situation requires resort to no such remedy . . . Its propositions contravene the principles upon which we fight" (McPherson 1988, 833).

Here, McPherson does more than weave famous quotage from well-known historical figures. The division commander, corps commander, and brigadier are kept anonymous, their words sounding naturalistic rather than iconic. If this paragraph were a sequence of a film, these soldier's responses to Cleburne could play as a montage—snippets of monologues from loosely associated people, yet orchestrated in a way that suggest an overarching cultural sentiment. McPherson's story of the Civil War is provided with dialogue and voiceover narration. McPherson, who served as a consultant on Ken Burns' *The Civil War*, demonstrates the narrative power of soldier voices in the cultural memory of the Civil War. Most importantly, this approach provides history with a pathos formula that has a distinct presence in war films—the soldier's words place human bodies at the center of chaotic events.

As I have shown with American landscape painting in Chapter 1, understanding the philosophy of the great literary minds of the time is crucial to understanding the development of the scenes of pathos that soldier writings would contain. As Randall Fuller points out, Hawthorne, Emerson, Melville, Thoreau, Alcott, and others predicted the Civil War in terms of a fulfillment of an American promise; they "seemed to view the impending conflict between North and South as the consummation of millennial reform, the fulfillment of America's destiny to lead the world in moral perfection. Emerson in particular seemed to relish the possibility of war, which he believed would purge the nation of the blot upon the citizens' souls, the moral stain preventing it from achieving its promise as the New Canaan" (Fuller 2011, 38). While the American landscape painters, fueled by these words, conveyed this notion of an American destiny to life in visual metaphors, soldiers who sought to encapsulate their own experience drew upon similar notions of what their national service meant and also fused this presentation of soldiering life with their particular brand of nineteenth-century American religiosity.

An important text to consider when discussing soldier diaries is *The Rules and Exercises of Holy Living and Holy Dying: Together with Prayers, Containing the Whole Duty of a Christian, and the Parts of Devotion Fitted to All Occasions, and Furnished for All Necessities*. Published in 1857 and adapting the work of the seventeenth-century English cleric Jeremy Taylor, this book served as a guide for coping with both life and death and informed the mid-nineteenth-century American attitudes toward death that would find their way into soldier writings about battlefield carnage and its aftermath. A striking difference between Americans in twenty-first century and nineteenth century, according to Drew Gilpin Faust, are their attitudes about death. In the nineteenth century, death "was seen as something that needed to be thought about constantly in order to live well and ultimately to die well." Faust also notes that the Civil War forced the United States to "embark on a new relationship with death because its survival would be assured . . . by the deaths of thousands of people." Thus the United States embarked on a new relationship with death on national level (revising the pension system, reburial system, and the bureaucracy of death; Burns 2012). Additionally, Mark S. Schantz observes that the Civil War did little to disrupt the commonly held American notions of death, one that involved a "more corporeal vision of heaven" with the idea that all bodies will be reunited in heaven accompanied by recognizable loved ones (ibid.). When one considers the letter by Union soldier Sullivan Ballou, written to his wife on the eve of the First Battle of Bull Run (July 1861) in which he would meet his end, the notion of a corporeal heaven comes into focus: "But, O Sarah, if the dead can come back to this earth, and flit unseen around those they loved, I shall always be near you in the garish day, and darkest night amidst your happiest scenes and gloomiest hours always, always, and if the soft breeze fans your cheek, it shall be my breath; or the cool air cools your throbbing temples, it shall be my spirit passing by. Sarah, do not mourn me dear; think I am gone, and wait for me, for we shall meet again" (Ballou 1861).

Ballou's letter also recalls the issue of haunting in war memories, discussed in earlier chapters. The idea that his spirit will always be near her "in the garish day, and darkest night" combines the notion of war as a haunted site in cultural memory with the fine line between the world of the living and dead in the mid-nineteenth-century American imaginary. The letter, propelled to prominence in cultural memory of the Civil War by the Ken Burns documentary, hints at some of the elements to be found in soldier writings of wars that followed, and touches upon a pathos formula present in these writings: the intensity of a traumatic war experience is crystalized into a narrative accessible to those who have not experienced it because these notions about death are culturally familiar signposts.

In addition to ideas of spiritual or religious transcendentalism woven into the national consciousness, written documentation of the

Civil War is also awash with allegory. Horace Porter's *Campaigning with Grant* (1897) strikes a balance between baring witness and literary flourish, critical to understanding the influence of soldier epistolary testimony on the development of war cinema's narrative modes. Porter's description of the events leading up to Lee's surrender at Appomattox Court House are peppered with antiquarian references; General Phil Sheridan is described as riding into battle with "the ingenuity of Hannibal," leading "unconquerable columns . . . with all the confidence of Caesar's Tenth Legion" (Porter 1992, 469). The use of allegory in this context can been seen in war cinema, notably in George C. Scott's iconic Patton performance in Franklin J. Schaffner's 1970 film ("The Carthaginians were proud and brave but they couldn't hold," as Patton famously states). In Terrance Malick's World War II film *The Thin Red Line*, Lieutenant Colonel Gordon Tall (Nick Nolte) quotes, in Greek, Homer's *Iliad*, drawing a comparison between the assault on Troy and the invasion of Guadalcanal (1942–43). If much of the public perception of war at the outset of the Civil War was tied to paintings that celebrated the exploits of American Revolutionary War figures (in the paintings of John Trumbull, for example), then evoking the epic battles of the *Iliad* and Roman conquests in war journals can be seen as providing a traumatic and chaotic experience with pathos, as it was a process by which an unfamiliar experience can be made relatable. The reader can experience Civil War combat on the page through a recasting of its history makers as the larger-than-life history makers from the ancient world—a world far removed from a young America and whose generals were undoubtedly the focus of study at the West Point academy.

Just as it has been argued that the visual form of the early war film drew upon the panorama paintings of the nineteenth century, I am also arguing that the Civil War soldier diaries and letters have contributed to the visual construction of battlefields, as they provide clear, first-person vantage points around which to build representations. A sense of topography and movement is also an essential component of Civil War epistolary, providing history with pathos scenes of troop mobilization and carnage. In Porter's book, for example, troop movements at the Battle of Cold Harbor (1864) are clearly described without the aid of maps, yet the inclusion of quotes from General Grant, deeply lamenting the human loss, provides the overview with pathos and human agency.

A very illustrative example, however, is when Porter later describes the exploding of the Petersburg mine, the event that opens Anthony Minghella's *Cold Mountain*, in which the Union army dug a mine underneath the Confederate lines and packed it with explosives (the Union attack that followed the explosion was a costly failure). He describes the dimensions of the "gallery" (511 feet long and 4.5 feet wide) and the weight of the explosives ("8,000 pounds of powder"). Relating the disaster that followed, Porter recounts the delay in the time that the fuse was lit to the actual explosion, a suspenseful period where he began to doubt that the plan would work. When it was discovered that the fuse was broken, a second attempt resulted in a deafening explosion. Porter writes, "The general had been looking at his watch, and had just returned it to his pocket when suddenly there was a shock like that of an earthquake, accompanied by a dull, muffled roar; then there rose two hundred feet in the air great volumes of earth in the shape of a mighty inverted cone, with forked tongues of flame darting through it like lightning played through the clouds" (Porter 1992, 263).

Porter follows with yet another description of dimensions and scope, this time the size of the crater ("30 feet deep, 60 feet wide, and 170 feet long"). The attack that followed was marked by "fatal errors in carrying out the orders," and the crater was soon filled with "disorganized men . . . mixed up with the dead and dying of the enemy, and tumbling aimlessly about, or attempting to scramble up the other side." This fatal error allowed for reorganized Confederate troops to shoot down upon Union soldiers fumbling in a crater they had created. In this episode, Porter's writing exemplifies one of the primary aims of pathos formulas in war representation: allowing the spectator (reader in this case) to successfully navigate the chaos of battle without being overwhelmed by it. This harkens back to the formulas afforded by the panoramic vision of battle, or what Virilio referred to as "panoramic telemetry."

Perhaps one of the most memorable soldier characters from Ken Burns's *The Civil War* is Elisha Hunt Rhodes (1842–1917), whose diary provides the film with some of its most memorable narration. Rhodes joined the Second Rhode Island Volunteer Infantry as a private at the start of the war and, having survived all five years of the war and participating in the some of the most famous battles fought by the Army of the Potomac, left the army at the end of the war with the rank of colonel. His diary and letters were preserved by his family and published in 1984 by his great grandson Robert H. Rhodes as *All for the Union: The Civil War Diaries and Letters of Elisha Hunt Rhodes*. His diary and letters exhibit many of representational principles of Civil War epistolary for providing the war story with pathos, and the Rhodes's status in Civil War cultural memory is a testimony to the immensely important role Civil War epistolary has in shaping a cultural understanding of the Civil War.

Let us consider a passage on Pickett's Charge on the third day of the Battle of Gettysburg, July 4, 1863, in Rhodes's diary:

> We could not see the enemy, and we could only cover ourselves the best we could behind rocks and trees. About 30 men of our Brigade were killed or wounded by this fire. Soon the Rebel yell was heard, and we have found since that the Rebel General Pickett made a charge with his Division and was repulsed after reaching some of our batteries. Our lines of Infantry in front of us rose up and poured in terrible fire. As we were only a few yards in rear of our lines we saw all the fight. The firing gradually died away, and but for an occasional shot all was still. But what a scene it was. Oh the dead and the dying on this bloody field. (Rhodes 1992)

In his description, notice how Rhodes provides a sense of topography and sense of battlefield vision. *The Gettysburg Cyclorama* depicts the same event and provides the spectator with multiple angels and ways of seeing—Civil War combat becomes a graspable reality through a pathos-laden visual reenactment. Rhodes's description, by contrast, turns Pickett's Charge into a pathos scene by first emphasizing an obstructed vision, tapping into an easily identifiable fear of not being able to see (what would later be known in the horror genre as "terror," a narrative strategy carrying a higher level of frisson than "horror" and the "gruesome").[1] What we hear ("soon the Rebel yell was heard") becomes an equally important component of the evocative power of Rhodes's words. As mentioned before, the *Gettysburg Cyclorama* (and other war panoramas) are accompanied by sound effects, and as evidenced by the award-winning sound design of *Saving Private Ryan* and *Apocalypse Now*'s famous advancement in surround sound technology (Dolby Stereo), sound and the sensations they provide are critical to understanding how Civil War epistolary contributes to a panoramic imagination of battle. Additionally, the battle is given dimensions

(Rhodes and his fellow Rhode Islanders were positioned "a few yards in the rear" and "30 men" die in a hail storm of fire), providing the imagination with the deep focus that can be also be seen in Philippoteaux's painting. How Rhodes ends this passage, however, is a pathos formula in stark form: proclaiming "the dead and dying on the battle field" as a grand "scene" offers a sensation of exultation at the end of a description of brutal combat, in which Rhodes and the Union army were the victors. The passage begins with an overwhelming and disorienting battle experience, a feeling alien to someone who never took part, and ends with a familiar consciousness that seems to organize the chaos in the mind of the reader—something that filmmakers would later attempt to replicate (and later disrupt).

Earlier in Rhodes's diary—in particular the first year—we see the appearance of a different set of pathos scenes, and these moments can be read as a precinematic rehearsal for war films where these scenes have a strong presence. The pathos scenes of "transition between two social systems" (scenes that emphasize the differences between civilian life and soldiering life and the journey the soldier makes from one to the other), scenes of the forming of the group body (the relationship between the individual soldier, his military unit, and military institution), and scenes of "battle and technology" (scenes that place technology at the center of the war story; MEWFP) can be found in moments before First Bull Run. On his way to Washington on June 21, 1861, Rhodes describes the ammunition his unit was issued:

> We were given three rounds each which were placed in our cartridge bags. It being the first warlike ammunition I had ever seen I examined mine with much interest. A few percussion caps were also handed to each of us . . . Our muskets are old fashioned smooth bore flint lock guns altered over to percussion locks, and the cartridge contains one round ball and three buck shot. We arrived in Baltimore after dark and disembarked from the cars to march through the city to the Washington Depot. Immense crowds met us at the Depot and the streets were lined with people who shouted for Jeff Davis and abused us roundly. But we said not a word and plodded on. (Rhodes 1992)

Here, Rhodes describes a moment that provides his war story with a moral message: the fight to reunite a divided nation. In April of 1861, Confederate sympathizers in Baltimore attacked Union troops on their way to way to Washington in an incident that was sketched by accompanying news illustrators. When Rhodes's company marched through the city, he found that tensions had not completely cooled since the incident in April, and this moment serves as a pathos scene of transition between two social systems—Baltimore presented as a different environment and frame of mind than his native Pawtuxet, Rhode Island—and at the same time the formation of a military body by showing that they "said not a word and plodded on in response." The description of the cartridges, rifles, and firing mechanism provides the war story with a sense of tactility. The issuing of ammunition and weaponry is shown, long before cinema, as a coming of age scene where soldier boys become soldier men, a seen that is so recognizable in war films.

If Elisha Rhodes's diary reads like a real life war film yet to be filmed, then naturally the final moments turn toward pathos scenes of "shared suffering" and "moral self-assertion." Let us contrast Rhodes's reaction to the surrender of Lee at Appomattox Court House on April 9, 1865, and his reaction to Lincoln's assassination later on April 14:

> Glory to God in the highest. Peace on earth, good will to men. Thank God Lee has surrendered and the war will soon end. How can I record the events of this day? . . . Rumors of intended surrender were heard [around 11 A.M.], but we did not feel sure . . . Some time in the afternoon we heard loud cheering at the front, and soon Major General Meade commanding the Army of the Potomac rode like mad down the road with his hat off shouting: "The war is over, and we are going home!" Such a scene only happens once in centuries. The Batteries began to fire blank cartridges, while the Infantry fired their muskets in the air. The men threw their knapsacks and canteens into the air and howled like mad.
>
> —April 9, 1865

> Bad news has just arrived. Corporal Thomas Parker has just told Mr. Miller that President Lincoln was dead, murdered. I sent for Parker and told him not to repeat the story, but in a short time a staff officer rode up and told me the sad sad news. He handed me a circular from General Meade announcing the terrible fact and giving the particulars as far as it is known. . . . The sad news received in grief and silence, for we all feel that we have lost a personal friend. We saw President Lincoln only a day or two before we captured Petersburg . . . We cannot realize the fact that our President is dead. May God help his family and our distracted country. I trust that good will come out of even this sad calamity.
>
> —April 15, 1865

In the first passage, Rhodes hints at a reversal of the "transition between two social systems" and "battle and technology" pathos scenes from the war's early days. An identifiable feeling of release is infused with a distinct American religiosity ("Glory to God in the highest"), providing this scene with corporeal sensations. Blank cartridges are fired, muskets are fired in the air, and knapsacks and canteens are thrown into the air in jubilation, a reversal of the "battle and technology" scenes from Rhodes's initial deployment. The second passage, by contrast, turns the story toward scenes of "shared suffering" and "injustice and humiliation/moral self-assertion." The "sad sad news" and "terrible fact" skewers the sense of triumphalism felt in the first passage, suggesting that although Rhodes and his fellow soldiers may have been finished with the war, the war will never be finished with them. Though this progression of scenes reads like a scripted, narrative war story, the fact that Rhodes was documenting his response to events beyond his control provides an even more teachable moment about how scenes of pathos operate in written accounts of war. War is an incommunicable experience, as Oliver Wendell Holmes once wrote, and yet the experience demands documentation to preserve its memory. The mere fact that war leaves behind battlefield ghosts that will inevitably stalk the present and future in the form of historical haunting attributes to the need to provide these haunted sites with safe and meaningful navigation. This is what Philippoteaux did, what Brady did, and what Rhodes did, though in the case of the latter, it was done subconsciously.

Lastly, as with photography and paintings, it is important to consider Civil War epistolary as a particular response to journalistic war correspondence, as war correspondence is a salient feature of both modern and premodern warfare and studies of war reportage and intended audiences are revealing. Elbert N. S. Thompson writes, "[At the start of World War I,] the newspapers . . . were more ready than any other for the demands placed upon them." The military and the citizenry had to be mobilized but the apparatus for war journalism was already in place (Thompson 1920, 93). Thompson cites the coverage of the English Civil War (1642–51) as one of the earliest examples of war journalism in human history, as "the public, bitterly partisan for one cause or another, was eager to be informed" (ibid.). Reports from the battlefield were doctored to garner support for a particular faction, written out in document form on tablets, and read aloud in town squares by appointed officials. Phillip Knightley's study of American Civil War journalism found that bitter partisanship was the rule: the *New York Times* and *Harper's Weekly* were pro-Lincoln (hence prowar/ pro-Federal) publications and the *Pittsburgh Gazette* and the *Chicago Times* were "Copperhead newspapers," anti-Lincoln and pro–Stephan Douglas (later pro–George McClellan in the 1864 election). Yet despite figures of as many as five hundred Northern correspondents in the field (the *New York Herald* spent one million dollars over the course of the war), correspondents were not interested in accounts of the war from a soldier's perspective (Knightey 1975, 20). Journals were preoccupied with military strategy and "cowed by censorship, determined to maintain morale, and poorly serviced by the majority of [their] correspondents" (Knightey 1975, 25). Cultural depictions of the Civil War in the postwar period, however, and indeed much of America's cultural memory of the war, were instead formed by first-person narrative accounts that began appearing in published form within ten years of the conclusion of the war. Letter anthologies, diaries, and oral histories pertaining to the Civil War contended with the record left behind by journalists, and were regarded as providing verisimilitude and an authoritative, if still partial, account of the conflict that shaped the cultural memory of the war.

Writing after the Civil War

David Thomson writes, "So many [World War I] films seem like ghosts from a 19th century twilight" (Thomson 2014, 41). The haunting elements in Civil War narratives appear to come into full form in World War I narratives, leaving a scar on its veterans with near-apocalyptic qualities. The ghostly texture of World War I memories is effectively rendered cinematically in films such as Abel Gance's *J'accuse* (1919), Robert Reinert's early German Expressionist film *Nerven/Nerves* (1919), and Lewis Milestone's iconic 1930 adaptation of Erich Maria Remarque's *All Quiet on the Western Front* (1929). Remarque was a veteran of the Great War, and after having served in the German army on the Western Front during the latter half of the war, left the conflict with both physical and mental scars that would inform the ghostly texture of his novel. The American novelist and journalist Thomas Boyd also served in World War I. His novel *Through the Wheat* (1923) is loosely based on his experiences fighting at the Battle of Belleau Wood (1918), during which William Hicks, the novel's central character, experiences friendly fire, machine gun assaults, and mustard gas (mirroring Boyd's own encounter with chemical warfare). The following passage recalls the aftermath of such a gas attack:

> For a distance of two miles, from the ravine to the village where the supply wagons were stationed, men lay dead and dying. In the woods and particularly in the gulley that ran through the woods to the village, the thick yellow gas clung to the ground. Whenever the gas had touched the skin of the men dark, flaming blisters appeared. Like acid, the yellow gas ate into the flesh and blinded the eyes. The ground was a dump-heap of bodies, limbs of trees, legs and arms independent of bodies, and pieces of equipment . . . Where yesterday's crosses had been erected, a shell had churned a body out of its shallow grave, separating from the torso the limbs. The crosses themselves had been blown flat, as if by a terrific wind. (Boyd 1923, 153)

What is striking about this passage from Boyd is the sense of topography that provides a mental panoramic vision of battle. Yet through poetic language and similes, this mental panoramic vision is distorted, mimicking the chaos and trauma of a chemical attack. This appears to be a reversal of Elisha Hunt Rhodes's description of Pickett's Charge, in which chaos and restricted vision is made navigable by tapping into a sensation of victory, though there are other elements of Civil War epistolary that seem to anticipate scenes of pathos in Boyd's World War I narrative. Consider Private David L. Thompson's account of Union commander Ambrose Burnside's offensive at Antietam (September 1862), which would later feature in *Battles and Leaders of the Civil War*, the inspiration for Stephen Crane's novel *The Red Badge of Courage*:

> Human nature was on the rack, and there burst forth from it the most vehement, terrible swearing I have ever heard. Certainly the joy of conflict was not ours that day. The suspense was only for a moment, however, for the order to charge came just after. Whether the regiment was thrown into disorder or not, I never knew. I only remember that as we rose and started all the fire that had been held back so long was loosed. In a second the air was full of the hiss of bullets and the hurtle of grape-shot. The mental strain was so great that I saw at that moment the singular effect mentioned, I think, in

the life of Goethe on a similar occasion—the whole landscape for an instant turned slightly red. (Sears 2012, 500)

Thompson attempts to articulate battle trauma by invoking the memory of Romantic poetry and its expressive capabilities, much like Porter's antiquarian allegories. Like Boyd, however, Thompson also uses images of scorched earth, recalling the scenes of pathos from similar photographs and paintings of the war but provided with a narration aimed at leaving the reader with a near encounter with an unimaginable chaos. Though World War I narratives turn sharply away from the sense of heroism and national triumph contained in Civil War writings and cultural memory, there is a retention of a pathos formula that aims to simultaneously involve the spectator and keep them at a distance, which is achieved through providing the reader with a sense of panoramic vision and (often poetic) disruptions to it.

In 2014, artist and screenwriter Phillipe Glogowski released his graphic novel *Ypres Memories* for the centennial of World War I. The book is broken down into three stories of British soldiers fighting in the trenches along the Western Front. One soldier recounts, "Nothing changes. War is a chronic disease of humanity and there is no remedy" (13). The book's cover features a gas mask–wearing soldier breaking the fourth wall, pointing at and directly confronting the reader as if to implicate him in this "disease," much in the same way the ending to Milestone's *All Quiet on the Western Front* does. This breaking of the fourth wall reoccurs at several points throughout the novel. "If life had been fairer," proclaims a soldier remembering guarding prisoners of war, "we would all have been friends. No matter what side you are on, no cause on earth is worth such a great sacrifice." On the one hand, *Ypres Memories* highlights a thematic shift away from the cultural remembrance of sacrifice contained in Civil War writings. This shift, exhibited strongly in World War I literature and expanded in World War II and Vietnam War writings in varying ways, anticipates the form for narrating what many described as postheroic warfare. On the other hand, *Ypres Memories* retains a pathos formula of placing the spectator in the midst of a seemingly unrelatable experience that is contained through emotions that are at the same time familiar. The combination of testimony with images that recall iconic war photography creates a narration of war that has persisted through different wars and different representational cycles.

World War II narratives offer a very interesting case study about how much cinema shapes our understanding of war. On the one hand, the writings of World War II veterans retain the key pathos formula present in Civil War soldier writings: an experience outside the everyday consciousness is simultaneously rendered imaginable and unimaginable through poetics and descriptions of scorched landscapes. The mosquito-infested tropical labyrinths of the South Pacific, the sulfuric, dusty terrain of Iwo Jima, and the shelled ghost towns of France and Belgium are the haunted sites from World War II novels made familiar through World War II combat films—the anticipation and aftermath of carnage uncannily foreshadowed in Civil War soldier diaries. On the other hand, the politics and war critique of World War II stories are tied to an understanding of war through cinema and other post–World War II conflicts. To illustrate this, let us contrast James Jones's novel *The Thin Red Line* (1962) with James Bradley's *Flags of Our Fathers* (2000). Both works have been adapted to film—Jones's novel twice (Andrew Morton's 1964 film and Terrance Malick's 1998 film) and Bradley's book as Clint Eastwood's 2006 film of the same name—and both books are quite graphic in their descriptions of combat. The differences, however, are tied to their era and how cinema informed their writing and reception. *The Thin Red Line* was written after the Korean War ended in stalemate on the eve of the Vietnam War, a conflict that would essentially shatter an American war mythology of invincibility. *Flags of Our Fathers*, by contrast, was released just before the events of September 11, 2001, and just after Spielberg's *Saving Private Ryan* helped fuel an end-of-the-century cultural remembrance of the Greatest Generation. Though written by flag raiser John Bradley's son, an aversion to Hollywood war representation is clearly reflected in James Bradley's presentation of veteran accounts. The book features, for example, John Bradley's response to the involvement of the real flag raisers in Allan Dwan's *Sands of Iwo Jima* (1949):

> They didn't get us out to California to help make the picture. All that was a cheap trick to get a little free advertising for the movie. Republic Studios

is making the movie, we were out there only two days and most of the time was spent fooling around. I think they only took about two shots of the flag-raising and that only took about ten minutes. If you think you will see real action like Iwo Jima by seeing the picture, I think you will be sadly disappointed. Chief [Ira] Hayes says they have the picture so fucked up he isn't even going to see the movie. (Bradley 2000, 322)

This testimony echoes Jones's 1963 article for *The Saturday Evening Post* titled "Phony War Films," in which he vents his frustration at Hollywood for distorting the experience of soldiers in World War II—jingoist propaganda with no regard for the mental damage endured by those who survived.

Technical squabbling about the grenade? I don't think so. Such a basically different viewpoint of infantry techniques from my own conveyed to me that the makers of this film had chosen to approach my war via an attitude of antiquated individual heroism which, by my experience, no longer pertained. Either because they had been ordered not to or had cynically decided to play to sentiment for the box office, those filmmakers had not even attempted to show—perhaps had no concept of—the random quality of cipherdom, the totally arbitrary, numerical killings upon which I knew modern warfare to be built. (Jones 1963)

Descriptions of combat in World War II narratives further the revised notions of war while at the same time retain some of the principles for providing the combat experience with pathos. In describing an assault on Japanese hillside fortified positions on Guadalcanal (1942), *The Thin Red Line* reads:

So [Pfc.] Doll had killed his first Japanese. For that matter, his first human being of any kind. Doll had hunted quite a lot, and he could remember his first deer. But this was an experience which required extra tasting. Like getting screwed for the first time, it was too complex to be classed solely as pride of accomplishment. Shooting well, at anything was always a pleasure . . . Just then a mortar shell sighed down for a half-second and ten yards away exploded a fountain of terror and dirt, and Doll discovered his confidence hadn't been helped so much after all. Before he could think he had jerked himself and his rifle down onto the floor of his little depression and curled up there, fear running like heavy threads of quicksilver through all his arteries and veins as if they were glass thermometers. (Jones 1962, 184–85)

The initial assault on the beaches of Iwo Jima is described thus in *Flags of Our Fathers*:

Death became demystified, an occupational hazard. The Marines quickly saw that even heroes could die. Sergeant John Basilone, the Medal of Honor winner who had helped change the course of the Guadalcanal battle, was leading a rifle unit along the beach toward a Japanese emplacement. "Come on, you guys, we gotta get these guns off the beach," he called to his men, and then was obliterated by a mortar shell. Moments of valor proliferated. Among the heroes were men sent to give solace. Corpsman Emery yelled "keep down!" to a fellow medic sitting upright in the sand. Crawling closer, he saw that the man was struggling to tie a tourniquet around the stump of his leg. "Take care of the others, I'll be OK," the injured medic called out. When Emery crawled back past the corpsman several minutes later, he was dead. (Bradley 2000, 161)

What is interesting about both of these passages is that killing is presented as matter of fact. Death is an "occupational hazard" for Bradley, and for Doll in *The Thin Red Line*, shooting is akin to hunting. In both episodes, a mortar shell disrupts what at first appears to be a clean narrative of events, plunging them into chaos, which is similar to the firsthand descriptions of Gettysburg and Antietam. There is a clash between a clear navigation through events as they unfolded (rendering them familiar) and a fog of war that, by contrast, renders the event beyond comprehension—the variables in the pathos formula of the war panorama are rearranged and accomplish the same effect. Scenes of death and sacrifice, battlefield technology, and battle and nature combine in both passages to unite in a pathos scene of shared suffering. The war narratives are provided with tactile, somatic sensations ("like getting screwed for the first time" and "fear running like heavy threads of quicksilver") and a moral meaning attached to cultural memory ("even heroes could die").

As discussed earlier, "The Vietnam War," according to William Hagen, "was an intimate, loosely framed, on-the-run *cinéma vérité* experience," and representations of the war can be seen as a competition of "war narrators," challenging the mainstream media's account of the war in more viscerally compelling ways (Hagen 1983, 230). Among the most compelling written accounts of the war from veterans, alongside works such as Tim O'Brien's *The Things They Carried* (1990) and

Gustav Hasford's *The Short Timers* (1979), is Michael Herr's *Dispatches* (1977), an autobiographical account that first appeared in *Rolling Stone* magazine in serialized form. The novel's prose is more hard boiled, lending itself for a perfect adaptation in Coppola's *Apocalypse Now* and Kubrick's *Full Metal Jacket* (Michael Herr contributed to the scripts of both).

> When I think of it quickly, just seeing the name somewhere or being asked what it was like, I see a flat, dun stretch of ground running out in an even plane until the rime of the middle distance takes on the shapes and colors of the jungle hills. I had the strangest, most thrilling kind of illusion there, looking at those hills and thinking about the death and mystery that was in them. I would see the thing I knew I actually saw: the base from the ground where I stood, figures moving across it, choppers rising from the pad by the strip, and the hills above. But at the same time I would see the other, too; the ground, the troops and even myself, all from the vantage of the hills. It was a double vision that came to me more than once there. And in my head, sounding over and over, were the incredibly sinister words of the song we had all heard for the first time only days before: "The Magical Mystery Tour is waiting to take you away." (Herr 1977, 109)

Herr's testimony is very revealing about the differences between war culture during the Vietnam War versus that of the Civil War, and it hints at how depictions of the war will employ the notion of genre memory. Herr's book (and those of other veterans) acknowledges how their initial impression of warfare upon enlisting was informed by popular war movies, a theme that would reoccur in later war movies like Sam Mendes's *Jarhead*. Though a sense of topography ("all from the vantage of the hills") and battle technology ("choppers rising from the pad"), manifest in Civil War epistolary and written accounts of other wars, is present in Herr's passage and aimed at providing pathos to his war story, it lends itself at the same time to a disruption of the panoramic vision in war that can also be found in Vietnam War films (as I have shown with *Apocalypse Now*) and, by extension, many contemporary war films. The passage describes the "colors of the jungle hills" in a way that anticipates how David Batchelor's concept of "chromophobia"—a fear and sense of otherness evoked by brilliant colors (Batchelor 2000, 52)—would operate in Coppola's film. Herr also acknowledges the role of music in the cultural memory of war (rock music providing a soundtrack to the war), and such musical cues would later service Vietnam War films with a means for dispensing with the traditional panoramic vision acoustically. In short, pathos scenes present in Civil War narratives are repurposed to provide yet another incommunicable experience with the narration that cultural memory demands.

War Movies and War Epistolary

Private First Class Robert Leckie. Corporal Eugene "Sledgehammer" Sledge. Gunner Sergeant John Basilone. Prior to the release of the HBO miniseries *The Pacific* (2010), these names were largely unknown to most Americans. In the series, the viewer experiences World War II through these men and many others, a cultural memory of America's involvement in the Pacific theater layered with shared experience and war trauma. Throughout the series, Leckie reads aloud his letters home to Vera, a woman he met only once while leaving church on a cold winter morning before shipping off to war. Sledge's story begins at his home in Mobile, Alabama, where he disobeys the wishes of his family and joins the marines even after a stern reminder from his father that the veterans of the Great War that he treated had "their souls torn out." Basilone receives the Medal of Honor for bravery on Guadalcanal, and the film cuts between his bond drives on US soil and the horrific combat faced by his comrades in the Pacific before he eventually rejoins them on Iwo Jima where he would meet his end. This narrative strategy in *The Pacific* is clearly informed by emotive power of soldier diaries and the previous war film narrations that draw upon these written testimonies. This is a direct acknowledgement that war epistolary connects the soldiering experience with a transformation of the landscape of the home front, situating both the soldiers and the civilians watching the war from afar in a united world of shared suffering—a crystallization of the emotive power of all pathos scenes (MEWFP).

War films draw their narrative strength on pathos provided by firsthand accounts combined with the representational principles and emotional content contained in war photography, the vision of combat found in panoramic depictions. As we will see in the following chapter, the narrators of war films provide war stories with what Jonna Eagle calls "strenuous spectatorship, a privileged vantage point on action alongside a fantasy of assault" (Eagle 2012, 19). A corporeal sense of battlefield death, strongly felt in Civil War epistolary traditions, is also retained in war films, as are allusions to history. A critical element of contemporary war films is that the agency provided by soldier witnesses is often disrupted by the new logistics of perception (or digital fatigue) that inform the visual language of these films; the soldier characters become patients rather than agents of the war narrative. In my exploration of *Restrepo*, however, we will see that although its presentation of war is guided by these new logistics of perception and the conventions of war correspondence, it still retains the influence of soldier diaries and letters: topography ("battle and nature" scenes), a "transition between two social systems," articulations of battlefield trauma, and a sense of war's unfinished business in the cultural imagination.

Civil War Epistolary and the Hollywood War Film

In 1895, the same year as the early film exhibitions from Edison and the Lumière brothers, and the reemergence of Brady's photographs from their hibernation period, Stephen Crane, a 22-year-old bohemian New Yorker—a man who had never witnessed combat in his life—published *The Red Badge of Courage*. The novel was heralded as a graphic and compelling account of the Civil War, told through the eyes of a young Union private and based largely on accounts from veterans, historians, and a popular postwar anthology, *Battles and Leaders of the Civil War*, a collection of essays and personal diary entries from both Union and Confederate veterans (Morris 2007, 137). Crane's novel, the story of Union private Henry Fleming's soldiering life, narrates the Civil War in first person and is informed by the emotive capacity and authoritativeness of first-person accounts of soldiers who fought the war. First-person testimonials, preserved in the letters and diaries of Civil War soldiers, evoked in Crane's novel, serve as competing histories to the ones written by historians and journalists. These competing histories can be read as counterhistories—alternative accounts that challenge the work of war journalists and even pictorial accounts—on the basis that a firsthand account serves as a more authoritative narrative of events.

More than a century later, in an early scene in *Saving Private Ryan*, General Marshall, while ordering the mission to find the missing James Ryan, reads aloud "The Bixby Letter," words of condolences written by Abraham Lincoln to bereaved mother Lydia Bixby:

I have been shown in the files of the War Department a statement of the Adjunct General of Massachusetts that you are the mother of five sons who have died gloriously on the field of battle. I feel how weak and fruitless must be any word of mine which should attempt to beguile you from the grief of loss so overwhelming. But I cannot refrain from tendering you the consolation that may be found in the thanks of the Republic they died to save. I pray that our Heavenly Father may assuage the anguish of your bereavement, and leave you only cherished memory of the loved and lost, and the solemn pride that must be yours to have laid so costly a sacrifice upon the alter of freedom.

Yours, very sincerely and respectfully,

A. Lincoln

The appearance of the Bixby letter in Spielberg's film provides the story with pathos twofold. In one sense, the letter provides the film with an invigorated sense of spiritual nationalism in contrast to the opening D-Day landing sequence in all its profane brutality (Burgoyne 2008, 62). Lincoln's words of comfort and invocation of shared sacrifice clash with images of soldiers searching the battlefield for their severed limbs or a Jewish-American soldier (Private Mellish, played by Adam Goldberg) enduring a slow, agonizing death at the hands of a German soldier's knife. In another sense, the Lincoln's words provide a direct acknowledgement of the role that Civil War epistolary has in informing both the narration and emotional content of war films. With this in mind, I would first like to explore how early cinema contains traces of this influence before turning to its appearance in other war films and concluding with how this influence is exhibited in *Restrepo*.

The soldier-as-witness and alternate historian also has a distinct presence in both twentieth- and twenty-first-century war films. Richard Beck writes, "Unless you or someone you know is a member of the American armed forces, chances are high that your Iraq War experience has been an experience of media reception" (Beck 2008, 8). What Beck suggests is that testimonials of soldiers, from firsthand experience, ranks high on the hierarchy of authoritative accounts of war, similar to David James and Rick Berg's argument that "almost all Hollywood films have proposed the experience of GIs . . . as the most authoritative guide to the war's meaning" (James and Berg 1989, 61). Soldier narration in these films is posited as a counternarration to the war reportage, a tradition exemplified by the epistolary traditions of the Civil War. As with Civil War photography, the diaries and letters of soldiers can be read as providing encapsulated microhistories as well as exhibiting various pathos formulas. Soldier testimonials, however, provided cinema with a different set of narrative strategies, ones designed to complement the visual coding of war.

Griffith's Civil War

What is interesting about the influence of epistolary traditions in war films is how quickly the writings of the Civil War informed the stories and narrative strategies used in early cinema. The Civil War, as Robert Eberwein notes, easily overtook the Spanish-American War as a subject of early war cinema due, in part, to the memory of the war still in the minds of a few surviving veterans and a Civil War mythology that was still young (Eberwein 2010, 14). Though Eberwein cites both *Drummer of the Eight* (1913) and *Grand-dad* (1913) as early examples of the Civil War film, the films of D. W. Griffith, in particular his controversial *The Birth of a Nation* (1915), provide a good starting point for scholarship on American Civil War films.

The memory of the Civil War had a profound impact on the life of D. W. Griffith. His father, Jacob ("Jake"), served in the Confederate army and fought in many notable battles in the Western campaign and served for a period under the famed cavalry commander Nathan Bedford Forrest. What is so fascinating about Jake's military career is that he was a Kentuckian. As Richard Schickel notes, Kentucky, though a slave state, was not secessionist, and the plantation system was never able to gain a foothold; Kentuckians who defected to the Confederate army were seen by many of their fellow statesmen as embarking on a quixotic fool's errand (Schickel 1984, 21). The stories of the Civil War had a profound influence on Griffith's life. He would listen to his father's stories, as well as those from old-timers, "fighting the Civil War over again-with ever increasing victories," as he recalled (27). He was an avid reader of Civil War history, alongside Tolstoy and Dickens, would visit battlefields, once attend a lecture by the widow of George Pickett (41), and adorned his bedroom with a Confederate war map (43). In additional to the oral histories he encountered, Griffith would draw on

Horace Porter's *Campaigning with Grant* (1897) to provide authenticity to the battle scenes in his Civil War films (Wills 2007, 12).

One of his first Civil War films was *In Old Kentucky*, a film that, like *The Birth of a Nation*, contains a story of brothers who fought on opposite sides (Schickel 1984, 137). In his 1911 film *His Trust* (serialized into two films, the second titled *His Trust Fulfilled*), also touches upon a family's reduction of circumstances as a result of the war, a theme also present in *The Birth of a Nation* and *In Old Kentucky*. All three films project a "tragic vision of war's effect on innocent victims, and perhaps even in the expansiveness that contemplation of the Civil War typical engendered in him" (155). In these films we have an equal concern for those off the battlefield and for those on it, a product of a pathos formulas contained in the Civil War soldier writing. In one of the opening scenes of *His Trust*, a Confederate officer leaves his family to fight for the Southern cause. The focal point of this scene are his embraces and fond farewells to his loved ones—his wife, his daughter, and his house slaves. The battle sequence that follows depicts an exchange of fire between soldiers entrenched behind a stone wall, a standard fortified position during the war. The camera is placed behind the Confederate soldiers, their backs to the camera, with a clear view of the Union soldiers (and the American flag in the distance). The film's main soldier character is easily identifiable, as the hat he wore in the previous sequence stands out. The film then crosscuts between the battle and the soldier's home, where the head slave (played by Griffith's friend Wilfred Lucas in blackface) comforts the family by stepping into a stepfatherly role. The soldier then leads a fatal charge. After the news of the soldier's death reaches his family, the film shifts to a story of the heavy burden borne by Southern women in the absence of their husbands and in the wake of a land scorched by war. It is in this film that we get an early, pre–*Birth of A Nation* view of the technique of tying the domestic with the horrors of battle, itself a type of pathos formula.

What prompted Griffith to adapt Thomas Dixon's novel *The Clansman* (1905) was that it was clear that the Civil War was a favorable subject matter for other filmmakers, notably from Griffith's rival Thomas Ince, who had produced the five reel *Battle of Gettysburg* in 1913 (207). *The Birth of a Nation* expanded the possibilities of intercutting in analytical editing through scenes that cross-cut between the battlefront and the home front (Figure 6.1). Before battle, Colonel Ben Cameron (Henry B. Walthall) receives a letter from his sister Flora (Mae Marsh) in a scene that provides pathos to the ensuing combat sequences by juxtaposing the memories of the home with the chaos of battle. Ben goes to battle knowing that his family is quite proud that he has "really grown a moustache—oh my!" and that Flora has grown into "such a big girl now" he would not even know her. Letter correspondence in Griffith's film constitutes an enduring genre code of the war film: the absence of loved ones and memories of home and prewar relations are evoked to enhance a sense of sacrifice in battlefield death. Seventy-eight years later, Ronald Maxwell's epic *Gettysburg* (1993) would feature as a subplot the real-life story of friendship between General Winfield Scott Hancock (USA) and General Lewis Armistead (CSA), a detail

Figure 6.1 Correspondence of the Civil War: the Cameron family in D. W. Griffith's *The Birth of a Nation* (1915).

providing a vast story with pathos and presenting Armistead's death at the hands of Hancock's troops as an honorable sacrifice. As Robert Eberwein notes, the war film is concerned with "the activities of the participants off the battlefield" and the "effects of war on human relationships" (Eberwein 2010, 45). The effect of war on human relationships, inscribed in soldier diaries and letters, is aesthetically rendered in war cinema to provide emotional depth to the celebration or critique of war.

The War Film Narrator

The advent of sound in cinema would bring epistolary forms to the war film in the form of voice-overs. Though a staple of 1940s film noir, this device was largely absent from the World War II combat films of the 1940s, usually appearing only as the voice of a war correspondent (notably Ernie Pyle) that was restricted to Office of War Information (OWI) talking points. Although the technique began to gain traction during the 1950s, with Stanley Kubrick's *Paths of Glory* (1957) as a notable example, it was in the Vietnam War films that the potential of this technique was realized. Michael Herr's *Dispatches* (1977), a war memoir that would provide the basis for the voice-over narration in *Apocalypse Now* and Stanley Kubrick's *Full Metal Jacket* (1987), exemplified the combining of art with the act of witnessing. In contrast to the "truths" presented by journalists and historians of the era, the soldier as the war's narrator would provide an emotional truth not far removed from the emotive capacity of Stephen Crane's novel. Even though nondiegetic narration in war cinema differs from the narration of war in novels, diaries, and letters—on the grounds that cinema audio narration alongside visual storytelling expands the range and possibilities of commentary—there is a commonality: the promise of verisimilitude and a contestation of the viewer's previous imagination of war. Looking beyond the novel-to-war-film paradigm, works such as John Huston's documentary *Let There Be Light* (1946), banned until 1981, use the soldier-as-witness perspective to add an extra layer of text to a history the public experienced through newspapers and newsreels. The construction of history and the shaping of cultural memory consist of layered histories that contribute to and complement the broader story.

Soldier testimony as voice-over narration would continue in war cinema after the 1970s and 1980s cycle of Vietnam War films. Terrence Malick's World War II film *The Thin Red Line* (1998), based on James Jones' eponymous 1962 novel, features a competing set of inner voices—dark insights that simultaneously engage and disorientate the viewer (Chion 2004, 55). What makes Malick's interpretation of the novel so interesting is how he connects the film to elements contained in Civil War epistolary and war photography in ways that Jones does not. According to Jon Hesk, vast, wide shots of landscapes are punctured by close shots of soldiers engaging in "the act of looking," the shell-shocked face of war photography is transferred to the role of an audible witness, combing the narrative strength of both (Hesk 2012, 1). The voice-overs in the film also make references to Homer, which is interesting as these allegories are neither in the novel nor the 1964 film, a testimony to their narrative power (3). The film does, however, uses multiple voice-overs in a way that challenges the traditional American war mythology present in previous war film cycles. Malick makes it "difficult for us to delineate and distinguish between the different members of C company," their voice-overs disembodied and freed from a sense of unity (2). The result is both a reliance on and a repudiation of previous war film conventions—genre memory performed in a uniquely Malickian way.

Voice-over narration is also a feature of contemporary war films depicting modern combat scenarios. Ridley Scott's *Black Hawk Down* (2001), for example, ends with a voice-over of a dead serviceman's letter to his loved ones: "So in closing, my love, tonight, tuck my children in to bed . . . tell them I love them . . . and give them a kiss from daddy," is played over the list of US Army Rangers and Delta Force operatives who died in the Battle of Mogadishu (1993), elevating their deaths to national sacrifice by evoking memories of the homeland. Sam Mendes's film *Jarhead* (2005) features a voice-over recounting a marine's experience in the Persian Gulf War, a narration that recalls Willard's from *Apocalypse Now* or Private Joker's from *Full Metal Jacket*. War films depicting twenty-first-century combat scenarios have also retained these narrative strategies by recoding soldier testimony through the digital technology that shaped our perception of that war: Mike Deerfield's cell phone video from *In the Valley of Elah*. In documentary cinema, the influence of Civil War soldier testimonials is evidenced through the use of long-standing documentary conventions. In the Afghanistan War documentary film *Restrepo*, it is the use of talking heads and the absence of an omniscient narrator that exemplifies the enduring influence of Civil War epistolary traditions. While the unrehearsed immediacy of soldiers' testimonies in *Restrepo* is distinct from the Civil War diaries and novels of war veterans, they nevertheless serve the same function. The testimonials in *Restrepo* leave behind a first-person history of the war that adds another layer of history to the distanced, third-person history currently being written by journalists and academics. The soldier-witness as a narrative device is both a documentary convention, the talking head, and a continuation of the soldier-as-alternative-historian approach in earlier war films.

I Lost *Restrepo*: The Soldier Diary and Contemporary War Cinema

Restrepo begins with a prologue sequence that echoes the naiveté of the Civil War soldiers who marched off to fight, a naiveté that contributed to their willingness to fight (Huddleston 2002, 4). The film opens on a train in Italy where young soldiers in civilian attire, heads shaved, are seated around a table in one of the coaches, engaged in manly banter and enjoying their last moments on Western soil before shipping out to Afghanistan. One soldier, Juan "Doc" Restrepo, turns to the camera, breaking the fourth wall, and says, "We're going to war." The diversity of this combat unit is a war film convention played out in the real world, and it will provide the film a different set of narrators competing to provide emotional truth to a story familiar through cable news coverage. The scenes of pathos familiar to the viewer through fictional war films are also orchestrated in *Restrepo* in similar ways, exhibiting the representational principles of the Civil War epistolary traditions.

Early in *Restrepo*, Specialist Misha "Pemple" Pemble-Belkin recounts the death of his comrade Juan "Doc" Restrepo: "The first friend I lost was Vimota [*sic*] . . . and then, a month after that, I lost Restrepo."

What is interesting in Pemble's testimony about Doc's death, described 12 minutes into the film, is that he states that "I" and not "we" lost Restrepo. The viewer is drawn inward from a story of a unit to the story of individuals with their own histories to impart. What is also revealing is the lighting and composition of the talking head segments. Each soldier is filmed against a black backdrop and lit with one key light from one side only (Figure 6.2). The witnesses are not provided with makeup or costumes. They appear as they choose to appear. The film's narrators appear to us cloaked in shadow, as if they are battlefield ghosts imparting a secret history not revealed through the news media. Talking head testimonials in *Restrepo*, such as Pemble's, provide the larger war story with pathos, a clear narrative thread for the spectator to navigate through the chaos of war. Through a comparison between the testimonials in *Restrepo* and the soldier testimonials in Civil War epistolary modes, we can see how formulas of pathos operate effectively across both narrative formats.

Captain Dan Kearney, the first of the film's talking heads, for example, states that he did not read up on the Korengal Valley before deployment, as he wanted a fresh perspective. Before leaving he was advised that posts in the Korengal take fire every day. On the one hand,

Figure 6.2 Specialist Misha "Pemble" Pemble-Belkin providing testimony in *Restrepo* (2010).

Kearney's testimony performs the same function as the traditional Hollywood first act: the character sets the scene, establishes the story's conflict, and proposes a solution ("just go out and kill them"). On the other hand, the spectator is drawn into the war as both an individual and as part of a collective experience. Kearney removes the spectator from their relationship with the limited, third-person narration of news media coverage.

Just as pathos is provided by the images of war—in Civil War photographs, narrative feature war films, and other documentaries like *In the Year of the Pig*, for example—soldier testimonials—the act of witnessing—provide war stories with pathos from a different angle. Grunt documentaries, like *Restrepo*, *Armadillo* (2010), and Deborah Scranton's Iraq War documentary *The War Tapes* (2006), for example, rely on their promise of authenticity and audience expectation of monstrous events (Pogodda 2012). The narration of the talking heads (witnesses) in these documentaries provides these stories with the pathos required to provide a clear narrative thread for audiences to navigate through the chaos of war. As in other fictional war films, some of which I will later discuss, we can see a sense of community formed by a diverse group of individuals, we can see the pain from the losses witnessed by the soldiers, and we can see the soldiers longing for their lives at home, which are all manifest in *Restrepo* as a result of the pathos provided by the testimonials. Through a comparison between the testimonials present in *Restrepo* and the soldier testimonials found in Civil War epistolary modes, we can see how formulas of pathos operate just as a effectively from first-person narration in war cinema as they do through the images of these films. Private Sam Watkins, Third Tennessee Infantry at the Battle of Shiloh, writes on April 6, 1862, "Advancing a little further on, we saw General Albert Sidney Johnston surrounded by his staff . . . We saw some little commotion among those who surrounded him, but we did not know at the time that he was dead. The fact was kept from the troops" (Burns 1990).

The death of Doc Restrepo was never captured on film. The death of General Albert Sidney Johnston was never photographed, although it was later sketched for Confederate newspapers. Their battlefield deaths are encapsulated mainly by the testimonies of those who were there. For Paul Virilio, war is a way of seeing, but war is also a way of hearing.

Restrepo's LaMonta Caldwell testifies that the shooting of Doc was "called in," and Miguel Cortez, Pemble, and Caldwell both recall seeing his injuries afterwards. Doc was alive when he was taken to a helicopter but bled to death in-flight. Despite never witnessing this scene, assuming that footage of it actually exists, the audience can easily reconstruct it in their minds from a memory bank filed with war film images. This moment in the film highlights a manifest difference between the speeds at which the news of death traveled in the Civil War and in contemporary combat theaters—the communication technology used in the field informs them of a soldier's death very quickly. Contemporary war films, including documentaries, use their soldier-witnesses to present the horrors of war as a shared experience, one that cannot be escaped by placement at opposite ends of a battlefield.

What becomes clear when reading Civil War soldier diaries, and indeed the diaries and novels of soldiers from other wars, is that inscribing the war experience was not a passive activity. When one's only mode for bearing witness is writing by hand, encamped off the battlefield, more time and thought is devoted to the prose. Consider, for instance, a letter from Samuel J. English, written to his mother after the First Battle of Bull Run, July 1861. Here he attempts to recreate, in his own words, the chaos of battle as Union troops fled the field: "The [Rhode Island] regiments . . . were drawn into a line to cover the retreat, but an officer galloped wildly into the column crying the enemy is upon us [*sic*], and off they started like a flock of sheep, every man for himself, and the devil take the hindermost; while the rebels' shot and shell fell like rain among our exhausted troops. As we gained the cover of woods the stampede became even more frightful, for the baggage wagons and ambulances became entangled with the artillery, and rendered every scene more dreadful than battle" (Simpson, Sears, and Sheehan-Dean 2011, 493–94).

In *Restrepo*, Pemble speaks about relaying his combat experience to his family: "To my family, I never really told them much until about half way into the deployment. I didn't tell them when . . . Restrepo got killed. When Restrepo got killed, it was a few days before my Mom's birthday also. So I had to suck it up. When I called my Mom on her birthday, [I had to] act like everything is OK, and say 'Hey, Mom, happy birthday.'"

There are two key differences between the two testimonies that can actually help us better understand their commonalities. First, Pemble's prose (or speech, rather) is quite informal, as speaking extemporaneously to the camera is more of a casual activity than writing a letter or diary entry. Second, Samuel English's mother would have had no other reference point for imagining a combat situation other than what her son had written. Pemble's mother may or may not have been alive at the time of the Vietnam War, when news coverage was more graphic than that of the Persian Gulf War or the Iraq War, but it may be safe to assume that she had seen Hollywood war films, providing a memory bank of images ready to be reedited to her son's war stories. Again, *Restrepo* returns to the idea that the connection between the genre memory of the narrative war film and the war documentary is inescapable, as war films have informed our imagining of combat.

In *Restrepo*, Aaron Hijar describes the constant fear of a Taliban ambush: "The fear is always there, especially at night when you can't see what is coming at you. When we started there, we only had maybe 14 guys up there. I mean, it doesn't take much. A few automatic weapons can keep a squad pinned down . . . [and] they can easily come up from a side and flank you and . . . basically clear house."

When we contrast this with a Civil War soldier's account of an ambush, we can draw connections between the prose and pathos formulas provided. John L. Collins of the Eighth Pennsylvania Calvary writes during the Battle of Chancellorsville in May 1863, "I now gave up hope of a mount, and seeing the Confederate lines coming near me, tried to save myself on foot. Once, when throwing myself down to escape the fury of the fire, I saw a member of my own regiment, whose horse had been shot, hiding in a pine top that had been cut down by a shell. He had thrown his arms that he might run faster and begged me to do the same. This I refused to do, and I got in safely, while he was never seen again" (Johnson 1956, vol. 3, 184).

The Battle of Chancellorsville and Grant's Wilderness Campaign, in roughly the same location a year later, were battles where confusion contributed to mass slaughter. The Army of Northern Virginia used the cover afforded by the dense forest of Spotsylvania County, Virginia, to mislead and ultimately ambush the Army of the Potomac in both instances. John L. Collins's account of his unit attempting to flee Stonewall Jackson's Corp attempts to recreate the sense of confusion and terror felt that day, while at the same time providing the reader with the means to navigate through the chaos. Aron Hijar's testimony conveys the same fear of an unseen enemy using the underbrush and rugged terrain of the Korengal Valley to screen their movements. By contrast, Hijar's testimony considers how events may unfold, whereas Collins remembers how events actually did unfold. Both testimonies, however, provide microhistories of the conflict that are laden with a pathos formula designed to provide the spectator with the tools to traverse the fog of war. The descriptions, accompanied by images in the case of *Restrepo*, allows the intensity of combat to be simultaneously overwhelming and contained. Elisabeth Bronfen states that this simultaneous overtaking by and containment of the spectacle of battle is in itself an aesthetic formulation (Bronfen 2012, 20). Consider, for example, the testimony of G. Norton Galloway (Army of the Potomac) at the Battle of Spotsylvania Court House (May 1864):

> The rain continued to fall and clouds of smoke hung over the scene. Like leeches we stuck to the work, determined by our fire to keep the enemy from rising up. Captain John D. Fish, of Upton's staff, who had until this moment preformed valuable service . . . fell, pierced by a bullet. The brave officer seemed to court death as he rode back and forth between caissons and cannoneers with stands of canister under his "gum" coat. "Give it to them, boys! I'll bring you the canister," said he; as he turned to cheer the gunners, he fell from his horse, mortally wounded. (Johnson 1956, vol. 4, 56)

Galloway sets his scene in the midst of a literal fog of war; the rain and smoke of rifle and cannon fire establishes the battle as a space where fear and chaos would overwhelm the reader who is now mentally engulfed in the fierce hand-to-hand combat taking place at a stone wall known thereafter as "the bloody angle." Galloway then brings Captain Fish to the scene, providing an almost palpable sense of moral rearmament. The description of Fish riding among his troops before his demise helps contain the chaos in the reader's imagination through the use of an identifiable emotion—courage in the face of death. This literary formula for reimagining combat would be retained for audiovisual renditions of battle in the war film, war turned into a cinematic spectacle where the viewer simultaneously feels overwhelmed and in control of the spectacle. In *Restrepo*, a film designed to provide a new set of histories on the war in Afghanistan, this formula is retained. The difference is that, rather than use a single narration, the war story is disseminated to multiple real-life soldier characters in order to convey a sense of shared suffering and sacrifice, a strong element of pathos present in the film.

To further illustrate how pathos scenes of "homeland" and "shared suffering" are repurposed in contemporary war films, let's look again at the Sullivan Ballou excerpt from Chapter 5. Written to his wife a week before his death at the Battle of Bull Run, the Ballou letter serves as a stellar example of how one's life off the battlefield heightens the memory of sacrifice on the battlefield, a common formula of pathos present in war cinema: "But, oh Sarah, if the dead can come back to this earth, and flit unseen around those they loved, I shall always be near you—in the garish day, and the darkest night—amidst your happiest scenes and gloomiest hours—always, always; and, if the soft breeze fans your cheek, it shall be my breath; or the cool air cools your throbbing temples, it shall be my spirit passing by. Sarah, do not mourn me dead; think I am gone and wait for thee, for we shall meet again" (Simpson, Sears, and Sheehan-Dean 2011, 453).

In contrast to this letter is a scene in *Restrepo* in which Specialist Sterling is on duty as a machine gunner, watching over the valley from Base Restrepo. He is communicating with another (unidentified) soldier through a walkie-talkie. To break the monotony of the moment, the other soldier enquires after Sterling's family:

> *Sterling*: Good, they're pretty good . . . It was a good time. We hung out at the ranch.
> *Other soldier*: Your family has a ranch?
> *Sterling*: Of course . . . A ranch just with land, you know, gates . . . some wildlife that you shoot at . . . like this [place].
> *Other soldier*: Yeah, but we're not hunting animals, just people.
> *Sterling*: Hearts and minds.
> *Other soldier*: Yeah, we'll take their hearts and we'll take their minds.

As mentioned earlier, the war film is concerned with "the activities of the participants off the battlefield" and the "effects of war on human relationships" (Eberwein 2010, 45). Sullivan Ballou's letter demonstrates that this war film criterion was present in the writings of Civil War soldiers, contextualizing his impending sacrifice in deeply spiritual terms and linking his potential demise to his role as a husband and father. Additionally, Sterling's conversation makes it clear that a soldier's family life informs his view of the battle zone. This point further illustrates how Hetherington and Jünger have crafted a documentary in the mold of the narrative war feature, as they are deeply concerned with the activities of the soldiers off the battlefield and the effects of their deployment on their relationships with those off the battlefield. Moments such as Sterling's scene, described above, and the talking head segments allow for these emotions to manifest despite being different in tone compared to Civil War diaries and letters. Pemble, for example, in one of his talking head segments, describes his upbringing in Eugene, Oregon, by a family with strong counterculture connections. He was not allowed to play with toy guns or violent video games as a child, and he finds it difficult to reconcile his chosen path of military service with his family history. These aspects of *Restrepo*'s testimonies are in service of the familiar war film trope that war's effects are never limited to the battlefield. William Wyler's *The Best Years of Our Lives* (1946), Michael Cimino's *The Deer Hunter* (1978), and Paul Haggis's *In the Valley of Elah* make this point blatantly clear, just as the soldiers of the Civil War were all too painfully aware of this fact and used their writings to make it known.

Coda

The Civil War, the American War Film, and Cultural Memory

In 2011, the Oklahoma-based punk rock group Red City Radio released the album *The Dangers of Standing Still*, featuring the break-up song "I'm Well, You're Poison." The song evokes the Battle of Gettysburg to frame the singer's feelings at the end of a failed relationship, an ill-fated last stand described as "my very own Gettysburg," proclaiming that "this battlefield is stained with blood." Here, in a different medium, we can see both a cultural and historical memory informing an aesthetic rendering of personal struggle: the experience of coming to grips with one's sense of self in the face of heartbreak is equated with battlefield defeat, a repurposing of the pathos formulas inherent in both written and visual depictions of the Civil War. That the listener can identify the intensity of the singer's emotional state through an evocation of a battle never experienced is a testimony to the residing power of this pathos formula in American culture.

A cultural memory of the Civil War remains an essential component in American generational renegotiations of national identity and a relationship with the past, a memory deeply felt in cultural artifacts. It becomes important, therefore, for scholars of history and media to consider the how early representations of the war contributed to an expressive visual and narrative language for maintaining this cultural memory and creating new artistic encapsulations of other moments of national trauma, wedded to an impulse to remember and confront the ghosts of history still haunting the present. The representational principles that can be gleaned from paintings, photography, and epistolary traditions informed the use of pathos scenes in early war cinema, and their presence continues to be felt in contemporary war films in spite of revisions to the genre through genre memory. There is a scene from Ken Burns's *The Civil War* that both acknowledges the pathos scenes of war cinema and, in retrospect, reveals something very telling about the nature of contemporary war films (and the contemporary wars that they depict). In the film's second episode, a voice-over actor portrays one soldier recounting the importance that photography played in the daily life of soldiers—portraits provided by photographers that traveled with the armies: "A man's conceit dwindles when he crawls into an un-teaseled shirt, trousers too short, coat too long, and a cap that is as shapeless as a feedbag. A photograph of anyone of them, covered with yellow dusts or mosaics of mud, could ornament any mantle, North or South, as a true picture of our boy" (Burns 1990).

The Civil War contains photographs of soldiers posing in groups in ways that exude camaraderie and fellowship and that are echoed in moments and promotion stills from films like *Hamburger Hill* (1987), *Memphis Bell* (1990), *Band of Brothers* (2001), and *Fury* (2014). In an odd way, these moments seem to disappear through the digital fatigue and the new logistics of perception in Iraq War films and other "War on Terror" films. I would like to pose the following three explanations for this shift: this is the product of (1) the search for new filmic languages and rhetorical containers as these films emerged, (2) the focus on the body of the individual soldier as a symbol of national sacrifice and a critique on what war does to the human psyche in films such as *The Hurt Locker* and Clint Eastwood's *American Sniper* (2014), and (3) a new consideration on violence in films like *American Sniper* and Kathryn Bigelow's *Zero Dark Thirty*. This is but one example of what can be deduced in war film scholarship that incorporates Civil War representations into a discussion on genre memory in war cinema.

I would like to turn briefly to two films—a Civil War film and a contemporary war film—to illustrate how, when all three Civil War representational modes are sutured, cinema can critically interrogate war mythology and the historical past. Edward Zwick's *Glory* (1989) brings together the emotive power contained in the Civil War panorama paintings, photography, and soldier diary to engage with the memory of the Civil War through the Emancipation Cause tradition and from an explicit post-Vietnam perspective. Sam Mendes's Persian Gulf War film *Jarhead* (2005) contains some traces of the influences these modes have had on war cinema and also critically engages with an American war mythology informed by war films themselves.

Glory

Robert Gould Shaw: "Dear mother: I hope you are keeping well and not worrying too much about me. You mustn't think that any of us are going to be killed, for they are collecting such a force here that an attack would be insane." So begins Edward's Zwick's *Glory*, a film chronicling the history of the ill-fated 54th Massachusetts regiment, the first black regiment of the Civil War, led by Colonel Robert Gould Shaw. A voice-over of Shaw reading a letter to his mother as the film's opening dialogue signals to the spectator that it will be Shaw who will narrate the Civil War; Kevin Jarre's screenplay is based on Colonel Robert Gould Shaw's personal letters, one of which describes his experience of the Battle of Antietam featured in the film's opening sequence (Canby 1989). The Battle of Antietam and the assault on Battery Wagner in the film's third act employ a panoramic vision of battle that appears to be lifted from the large-scale paintings and cycloramas of the era. The death harvests after these battles, fields and beaches strewn with corpses, eerily echo the photography of Brady and his cohorts. The film, like both Civil War photography and epistolary forms, offers a history within the history; the historical significance of the Civil War and the meaning its historical memory holds for Americans is compressed into an emotionally true story of a fraction of its participants. The sense of shared suffering and sacrifice and the use of character backstory, whether explicit or implied, operate as scenes of pathos, used to make a story of brutal combat in a distant past accessible to an audience generations removed.

An exchange between Shaw and former-slaved-turned-soldier Trip (Denzel Washington) in the film's third act, however, raises some interesting questions. In this scene, Trip declares to Shaw that he will not serve as color guard in the impending assault on Battery Wagner. "What's the point?" Trip asks Shaw, "Ain't nobody going to win. It's just going to go on and on." This appears to be an odd thing for a Civil War film character to say considering that films about the Civil War are generally cloaked in remembrance of the fallen and the celebration of a nation united. This line, however, does not feel out of place when one considers that the film remembers the Civil War from a post–Vietnam War vantage point, in sharp contrast to a film like John Houston's *The Red Badge of Courage*, released six years after the end of World War II. As Gary Gallagher notes, the Civil War received little to no direct attention between the release of *Shenandoah* (1965) and *Glory*, which he attributes to a "national repulsion" over the Vietnam War (Gallagher 2008, 54). It should be no surprise then that *Glory* appears to be informed not just by the Vietnam War but also by Vietnam War films (124). Robert Burgoyne also notes that the "moral chiaroscuro" of the character narratives, Shaw in particular, is more typical of a Vietnam War movie than a Civil War movie (Burgoyne 2010, 30).

The imagery of the film also brings to mind elements from other war films—notably, the construction of the combat units of World War II combat films. When death is confronted in the classic war film tradition, racial and ethnic identity completely blends into the idea of unified nationhood; when we bleed, the "blood [is] the same color" (Doherty 1993, 206). This idea is clearly felt in *Glory*; the death of Robert Gould Shaw alongside his regiment reaffirms what the Vietnam War film *Hamburger Hill* (1987), the classic World War II film *Bataan* (1943), and *Flags of Our Fathers* proposed in varying ways. The film is an "endorsement of a 'mystic nationhood' revealed only on the battlefield . . . reaffirming the dominant fiction at the site of its greatest potential harm" (Burgoyne 2010, 36). *Glory*, in turning to the influence of Civil War representations for its scenes of pathos, simultaneously disavows the Lost Cause tradition of *The Birth of a Nation*, affirms war's futility, and embraces liberal notions of national identity.

Jarhead

The Greatest Generation–remembrance films at the end of the 1990s, notably Spielberg's *Saving Private Ryan*, informed the tone of many of the war films that appeared at the start of the twenty-first century. Films such as *Black Hawk Down* (2001) and *We Were Soldiers* (2002) were viewed as "moral rearmament" films, encouraged by "a fin-de-siècle glance back at World War II" (Doherty 2005, 214). Other war films, such as *Behind Enemy Lines* (2001; the Bosnian Conflict) and *Wind-talkers* (2002; World War II), continued what Albert Auster describes as the 1990s reversal of the deglorification of war in cinema during the 1980s (Auster 2005, 205). The launching of the Iraq War, however, appeared to halt this trend in war cinema, as it was clear that the divisive nature of the conflict would place studio financiers in risky positions.[1] Although Michael Moore's polemic *Fahrenheit 9/11* (2004) was a highly successful interrogation of the Iraq War, its status as war cinema is questionable. Within a year of Moore's film, however, there appeared to be a shift away from "moral rearmament" in war films. Around 2005, war films began to appear that, while not directly confronting contemporary conflicts (such as the Iraq War or the broader War on Terror), seemed to address the issues surrounding these conflicts. Sam Mendes's *Jarhead* (2005) was one of these films—a film set during the Persian Gulf War yet reframed as a critique on the Iraq War. It is in how *Jarhead* performs this critique, however, that provides an important place to begin an examination of contemporary war cinema and the critical framework that I will use to examine other films in this book. Mendes's film draws upon previous war films and contemporaneous resources to provide the war film a new and distinct voice.

Based on Anthony Swofford's memoir of the same name, *Jarhead* recounts the experiences of a marine from basic training through the Persian Gulf War. The film's citation of Vietnam War films, and its presentation of the Persian Gulf War from a twenty-first-century vantage point, is very revealing. The film is narrated in Swofford's (Jake Gyllenhaal) voice-over, a familiar narrative strategy of many Vietnam War films. The film's opening scene, Swofford's introduction to basic training, is an explicit citation of the opening scenes from Stanley Kubrick's *Full Metal Jacket*—only in this case, Kubrick's steadicam shots have been replaced with Roger Deakins' handheld shots. Both *The Deer Hunter* and *Apocalypse Now* are literally featured in *Jarhead*, with soldier characters watching these films and responding to them as if they were, according to Swofford, war pornography (Rosenbaum 2005). In the film's Dessert Storm sequences, color is drained from the film stock, a technique used in *Saving Private Ryan* (1998) and later in Clint Eastwood's *Flags of our Fathers* and *Letters from Iwo Jima* (2006). Trauma in *Jarhead* is presented as the physical manifestation of battlefield haunting, shown through uncanny appearances and through Swofford's explicit acknowledgement of the battle zone as a haunted space (Swofford: "We are still in the desert")—battlefield haunting that is reminiscent of *Apocalypse Now*'s portrait of Vietnam or the no-man's-land of *All Quiet on the Western Front*. These are but a few examples of how *Jarhead* uses genre memory to create a new war cinema in dialogue previous war film cycles.

What Do War Films Teach Us?

War films teach us that representations of war are revised, generationally, through genre memory. Mikhail Bakhtin understood texts to have a genre memory, one that "communicates and accumulates a history" (Morson and Emerson 1990). The contemporary war films discussed in this book are both the sum of the parts of previous war films and the products of new representational modes. War cinema is always in dialogue with previous films and other art forms, even if the purpose of the dialogue is to critique these past forms in order to make a statement about recent events. Consideration of precinema representational modes when examining this dialogue is critical for understanding the larger picture. *The Hurt Locker*, for example, contains echoes of Stanley Kubrick's *Full Metal Jacket*, Francis Ford Coppola's *Apocalypse Now*, and the nineteenth-century moving panorama form, each providing a template for Bigelow to create a contemporary war film that distinguishes itself from previous war film cycles. *Restrepo*, by contrast, uses elements found in Civil War soldier diaries despite also sharing some characteristics with contemporary war documentaries and digital fatigue films.

War films also write a visceral history of war that can be tied to how Civil War painters, writers, and photographers viewed themselves as alternative historians. In the historical film, the filmmaker acts as a historian of sorts. Robert Rosenstone contests the notion previously put forward by historians that the historical film is simply a work of art and entertainment. Historical consciousness has risen alongside advancements in visual media (Rosenstone 2006, 12). The orientation of the war film and its narrative capacities have also expanded alongside advances in visual media, and this has influenced both how war films write history and the histories they write. One of the challenges facing contemporary war films, however, is that cinema is no longer the dominant medium for experiencing war images, whether re-staged or presented in unadulterated form. The rise of digital media and Internet videos has had implications for both the war film and cinema in general. New narrative forms and representational modes arisen and the means for inscribing history through film have changed as well. Filmmakers have, since early cinema, used film to bring audiences the war not written about in newspapers or books or seen on the nightly news. The war film finds its strength not in a quest for historical truth but in a quest for emotional truth, and the contemporary war film continues this tradition.

Notes

Introduction

1. Phil Gast, "150th Anniversary of Battle of Gettysburg Provides a Bigger Story," *CNN*, June 30, 2013, http://edition.cnn.com/2013/06/28/travel/gettysburg-anniversary.

2. Steve Vogel, "Gettysburg Address Remembered at Ceremony," *Washington Post*, November 19, 2013, http://www.washingtonpost.com/politics/gettysburg-address-remembered-at-ceremony/2013/11/19/3e5fd0c4-5150-11e3-9e2c-e1d01116fd98_story.html.

3. For more information, please visit the official website for The Lincoln Funeral Train, "Those Train People—The 2015 Lincoln Funeral Train," *Historic Railroad Equipment Association*, http://www.the2015lincolnfuneraltrain.com/2015-route.asp.

4. For further information, visit the "Mobilization of Emotions in War Films" project at http://www.empirische-medienaesthetik.fu-berlin.de/en/emaex-system/affektdatenmatrix/index.html.

5. For further reading on Linda William's notions of body genres, see "Film Bodies: Gender, Genre, and Excess," *Film Quarterly* 44, no. 4 (1991): 2–13.

6. Although *The Green Berets* (1968) was released as the war was still in progress (and directly dealt with the war), it was not received at the time as a serious-minded treatise on the war but rather as a jingoist call to arms and a condemnation of how the war was being reported, both seen as grossly out of step with what was increasingly becoming the national mood. Sidney J. Furie's *The Boys of Company C* (USA/Hong Kong, 1977) is generally seen as one of the first objective (nondocumentary) Vietnam War films.

7. For further reading on Bakhtin, see Gary Morson and Caryl Emerson's *Mikhail Bakhtin: Creation of Prosaics* (Redwood City: Stanford University Press, 1990).

8. As Robert Eberwein points out, Corliss was part of a chorus of a film critics and journalists (that included Adam B. Vary and Diane Garrett) who, between 2006 and 2007, argued that the box office failure of Iraq War films could be attributed to the contentious political nature of the debate surrounding the war; "Iraq had failed to sell" (Eberwein, 2010, 4). Eberwein also notes that part of this may have been a confusion about what they were seeing, a failure to notice the genre's in evolution, which I will discuss in detail in this book. Richard Corliss, "Where Are the War Films," *Time Magazine*, August 2006, http://www.time.com/time/arts/article/0,8599,1225667,00.html.

Chapter 1

1. Further reading on sketch illustrations and Civil War paintings can be found in the work of Peter Brownlee, Sarah Burns, Diane Dillon, and others in *Home Front: Daily Life in the Civil War North* (University of Chicago Press, 2013).

2 Wood engraving was a process developed in the late eighteenth century by English engraver and historian Thomas Bewick (1753–1828). He would use these engravings to illustrate his own history books, advertisements, and children's stories.

3. Perhaps the best examples of this can be found in Homer's first war painting *Sharpshooter* (1863; currently held in the Portland Museum of Art in Maine), *The Sutler's Tent* (1863; National Gallery of Art, Washington, DC), *Home Sweet Home* (1863; National Gallery of Art, Washington, DC), and in *Skirmish in the Wilderness* (1864; New Britain Museum of American Art, Connecticut), a depiction of the Battle of the Wilderness that bares many similarities to battlefield sketches.

4. My references to Eleanor Jones Harvey's work primarily draws on two important contributions to the field: "The Coming Storm: The Civil War and American Art" (lecture, Smithsonian Institution, Washington, DC, April 2013) and her book *The Civil War and American Art* (New Haven, CT: Yale University Press, 2012).

5. Eleanor Jones Harvey, interview with Tyler Green, *MAN Podcasts*, November 15, 2012, http://blogs.artinfo.com/modernartnotes/2012/11/the-man-podcast-american-art-the-civil-war.

6. For further information on the large scale paintings of the eighteenth century, see Ian Christie, "Kings of the Vast," *Tate Etc.* no. 23 (Autumn 2011), http://www.tate.org.uk/context-comment/articles/kings-vast.

7. Union General Gouverneur K. Warren is often credited with dispatching the 20th Maine to Little Round Top at the Battle of Gettysburg after spotting through his field binoculars an approaching Confederate assault. This is but one example of optical surveillance technology playing a crucial role in determining the outcome of a Civil War battle and arguably the war itself.

8. For further information on war technology and the advent of widescreen, see Giles Taylor, "Cinema: Training the Body through Immersive Media," *Velvet Light Trap: A Critical Journal of Film & Television*, no. 72 (Fall 2013): 17–32.

9. National Park Service, "The *Gettysburg Cyclorama*," http://www.nps.gov/gett/learn/historyculture/gettysburg-cyclorama.htm.

10. For further reading, see Peter C. Merril, "What Happened to the Panorama Painters," in *German-American Painters in Wisconsin*. Duestch-Amerikanische Studien Series (Stuttgart: Verlag Hans-Dieter Heinz, 1997).

11. Atlanta Cyclorama and Civil War Museum, "About Us," http://www.atlantacyclorama.org/history.php.

Chapter 2

1. For further reading on *Virtual Iraq*, see John J. Kruzel, "'Virtual Iraq' Combats Horrors of War for Troops with PTSD," *Department of Defense News*, September 25, 2008, http://www.defense.gov/news/newsarticle.aspx?id=51297.

2. For further reading on the October Panorama, see "October War Panorama," *Lonely Planet*, http://www.lonelyplanet.com/egypt/cairo/sights/museum/october-war-panorama.

3. Francis Ford *Coppola, Apocalypse Now*, director's audio commentary, Paramount Pictures, 2006 DVD release.

4. An article for MSNBC reported the use of Sophocles's plays at therapy for PTSD. In *Ajax*, for example, the titular character's wife, Tecmessa, describes her husband's postwar countenance as a "thousand-yard-stare." "Marines Turn to Greek Plays to Cope with Stress," *Associated Press*, August 14, 2008, http://www.msnbc.msn.com/id/26203463.

5. The traumatized soldier, according to the American Psychiatric Association, reexperiences [trauma] in "one (or more) of the following ways: 1) distressing recollections of the event, 2) distressing dreams of the event, 3) acting or feeling as if the event were re-occurring, 4) psychological distress at exposure to cues that symbolise or resemble the event, or 5) psychological reactivity to the cues that resemble an aspect of the event" (Glanz, 2008, 8–9).

6. The ending described can be found in *Apocalypse Now: Redux* and on DVD versions of the original theatrical release; they do not include images of Kurtz's compound exploding, which were contained in some of the original 35mm prints.

7. "'Apocalypse' Scribe Reveals Top Oscar War Films," *CNN*, March 9, 2010, http://articles.cnn.com/2010-03-05/opinion/milius.war.movies_1_hurt-locker-war-movies-apocalypse?_s=PM:OPINION.

8. See Jonathan Rosenbaum, review of *The Hurt Locker*, directed by Kathryn Bigelow, http://www.jonathanrosenbaum.com/?p=16094.

9. Martin Barker, *A "Toxic Genre": The Iraq War Films* (London: Pluto Press, 2011).

10. In the montage techniques outlined by Sergei Eisenstein in "A Dialectical Approach to Film Form," overtonal montage is described as a combination of other montage techniques (metric, rhythmic, and tonal) to produce a more complex or abstract effect. This approach is sometimes referred to as "associational montage."

11. For an example of *The Hunger Games* as an antiwar film disguised as a sci-fi adventure film, see Sarah Hall, "The True Story behind *The Hunger Games*," *Huffington Post*, March 28, 2012, http://www.huffingtonpost.com.

12. The concept of body genre was introduced through the work of Linda Williams, notably in her essay "Film Bodies: Gender, Genre, and Excess," *Film Quarterly* 44, no. 4 (Summer 1991), 2–13, in which she identifies pornography, horror films, and melodramas as genres that are constructed around somatic sensation. Additionally, we can discuss the war film as a body genre

as well, as I (and other scholars) argue that the war film draws its strength and iconic moments on its ability to graphically portray war as a somatic experience, one where the body in danger is an essential component.

13. Robert Burgoyne, "Embodiment in the War Film: *Paradise Now* and *The Hurt Locker*," *Journal of War and Cultural Studies* 5, no. 1 (2012).

14. One example to consider is Andrew O'Hehir, "'Restrepo' vs. 'The Hurt Locker,'" *Salon*, July 1, 2010, http://www.salon.com/2010/07/01/restrepo, an interesting, if often misguided, comparison of the two films.

Chapter 3

1. The collodion process, which overtook the original daguerreotype process by the 1850s, was a method for developing photographs in which a mixture of chemicals is poured onto a glass plate and then placed in a silver nitrate solution in a darkroom.

2. Jonny Weeks, "Ed Drew's Afghanistan: The First Wet-Plate Conflict Photos in 150 Years," *Guardian, photography blog,* http://www.theguardian.com/artanddesign/photography-blog/2013/jul/22/photography-art.

3. "Brady's Photographs: Pictures of the Dead at Antietam," *New York Times*, October 20, 1862, http://www.nytimes.com/1862/10/20/news/brady-s-photographs-pictures-of-the-dead-at-antietam.html.

4. Alfred Waud accompanied Brady during the first few months of the war and eventually forged a friendship with "death harvest" photographer Timothy H. O'Sullivan. O'Sullivan famously photographed Waud sketching the Battle of Gettysburg from Devil's Den as the battle was in progress.

5. Spirit photography, developed during the Civil War by a Bostonian photographer named William H. Mumler, used double exposure to make it appear as though the ghosts of dead soldiers were appearing behind their bereaved relatives. For further reading, see Louis Kaplan's *The Strange Case of William Mumler, Spirit Photographer* (Minneapolis: University of Minnesota Press, 2008).

6. For further reading on color in early cinema, I recommend Joshua Yumibe's *Moving Color: Early Film, Mass Culture, and Modernism* (New Brunswick, NJ: Rutgers, 2012).

7. Ted Widmer, "Cameristas," *New York Times*, Opinionator, May 2, 2013, http://opinionator.blogs.nytimes.com/2013/05/02/cameristas/?_php=true&_type=blogs&_r=0.

8. This classical structure is where the figures replicate the figures of portrait paintings from the late eighteenth century and early nineteenth century in varying ways. The paintings of Gilbert Stuart (1755–1828) contain prime examples of the classical structure.

9. For further reading, see Paul Virilio's *War and Cinema* (London: Verso, 1989) and Friedrich Kittler's *Gramophone, Film, Typewriter* (Redwood City: Stanford University Press, 1999).

10. For further reading on Muybridge, I recommend the work of Philip Brookman, Marta Braun, Corey Keller, and Rebecca Solnit (Steidl, 2010).

11. Carol Kino, "Battlefield Images, Taking No Prisoners," *New York Times*, November 8, 2012, http://www.nytimes.com/2012/11/11/arts/design/war-photography-at-the-museum-of-fine-arts-houston.html?emc=eta1&_r=0.

12. Eugene Atget (1857–1927) was known for photographing European city life before the rise of streetcars, electricity, and motion pictures. He was seen as a visual historian that preserved a memory of a premodern Europe through the images he created.

13. *Life Magazine*'s World War II artist and correspondent Tom Lea coined the "the two-thousand-yard stare" (Lea, 1945) later used in Vietnam—an extension of Sophocles's term "one-thousand-yard stare" (specifically from *Ajax* and *Philocetes*).

14. After the completion of *Rush to Judgment* (1967), a critical examination of the Warren Commission's investigation of the Kennedy assassination, de Antonio chose the modern-day plight of the Native Americans as his next documentary subject. If this film had been made, it is plausible that a similar style and narrative focus would have been employed as was seen in *In the Year of the Pig*. Nevertheless, de Antonio turned to the subject of Vietnam as, with a few notable exceptions, American television and documentary films supported the administration's position. In 1965, the Department of Defense released *Why Vietnam?*, required viewing for all GIs shipping out to Vietnam. With ten thousand prints of this film in circulation in a variety of other contexts, it became one of the first documentaries about Vietnam to be seen in American homes (Lewis, 2000, 79). In 1968, the Department of Defense, through the US Information Agency (a 1960s mimic of the OWI) released *Vietnam! Vietnam!* as a follow up to *Why Vietnam?* The film was directed by John Ford and narrated by Charlton Heston.

Chapter 4

1. The images in de Antonio's film predate the Tet Offensive and the publication of Eddie Adam's famous *Saigon Execution* photograph, two events that are credited as turning public opinion against the war.

2. For further information, see Walter Benjamin, "Little History of Photography," in *Selected Writings*, vol. 2, 1927–1934, by Walter Benjamin, ed. Michael W. Jennings, Howard Eiland, and Gary Smith, trans. Rodney Livingstone et al. (Cambridge: Harvard University Press, 1999), 507–29.

3. See Vertov's *Kino-Eye Manifesto* (originally published in 1919), found in Annette Michelson, "Kino Eye," in *Kino Eye: The Writings of Dziga Vertov*, trans. Kevin O'Brien (Los Angeles: University of California Press, 1984),

60–78. For further readings, see Ian Christie and Richard Taylor, *The Film Factory: Russian and Soviet Cinema in Documents, 1896–1939* (London: Routledge, 1994).

4. This 1972 interview with de Antonio features in Randolph Lewis, *Emile de Antonio: Radical Filmmaker in Cold War America* (Madison: University of Wisconsin Press, 2000), 17.

5. The rest of the interview can be found at "Flags Of Our Fathers: Interview with Clint Eastwood," compiled by Jack Foley, *IndieLondon*, http://www.indielondon .co.uk/Film-Review/flags-of-our-fathers-clint-eastwood-interview.

6. *Flags of Our Fathers*'s companion piece, *Letters from Iwo Jima* (Dream-Works, 2006), also directed by Eastwood, offers interesting insights into how post-9/11 war cinema addresses issues of national identity by demystifying nationalism and patriotism in ways that are both similar and different than *Flags of Our Fathers*. For further reading on *Letters from Iwo Jima*, see Robert Burgoyne, "Generational Memory and Affect in *Letters from Iwo Jima*," in *A Companion to the Historical Film*, ed. Robert Rosenstone (London: Wiley-Blackwell, 2013), 349–64, in which Burgoyne highlights how Eastwood's film engages with cultural memory to critique notions of nationalism and patriotism. Burgoyne's chapter "Haunting in the War Films: *Flags of Our Fathers* and *Letters from Iwo Jima*," is found in *Film Nation: Hollywood Looks at U.S. History* (Minneapolis: University of Minnesota Press, 2010).

7. In addition to Mann and Eastwood's films (and the real Ira Hayes's appearance in *Sands of Iwo Jima*), Ira Hayes was also played by Lee Marvin in the made-for-television film *The American* (1960), as part of the NBC Sunday Showcase series.

8. "Brian De Palma on His Critics," YouTube video from a Q&A session at the 2007 New York Film Festival Press Conference, posted by IFC News, October 9, 2007, https://www.youtube.com/watch?v=9zobBkH-aug.

9. Examples of right-wing outrage over *Redacted* are highlighted in "De Palma Flick Bombs," *New York Post*, November 25, 2007.

10. It is unclear where the quote attributed to Truffaut originally appeared, but this view has been echoed by film critics in discussions of both war films and nonwar films (see Roger Ebert's review of Mario Van Peeble's *New Jack City* [Warner Brothers, 1991], for example, at Roger Ebert, "New Jack City," *Chicago Sun Times*, May 1, 1991, http://www.rogerebert.com/reviews/new -jack-city-1991). Post-Vietnam antiwar films can be read as an attempt to contest Truffaut's view, and *Casualties of War* and *Redacted* appear to be such films.

11. During the Persian Gulf War (1990–91), Jean Baudrillard published a series of articles concerning the war in which he argued that the war may as well have not happened; the real war was never presented to Western audience, and what was seen instead was a clean war with no casualties produced by CNN.

Chapter 5

1. For further reading on horror concepts of "terror" versus "horror" and "the gruesome or the grotesque," see Stephen King's *Danse Macabre* (New York: Everest House, 1981).

Coda

1. In *A "Toxic Genre": The Iraq War Films*, Martin Barker details the history of an Iraq War film that never was: *No True Glory*. The film project was first announced in a December 16, 2004 issue of *Variety* under development by Universal Pictures. It was based on an optioned, yet unpublished, book by ex-marine Francis West about the assault on Fallujah, with rumors of Harrison Ford being attached to star in the film. Barker attributes the film's "nonappearance" to several factors, including fear of political backlash and changes in the relationship between major studios and independent film-makers (Barker, 2011, 17–26).

Chronology of Events

1775: Thomas Bewick pioneers the wood engraving process for newspaper, advertisement, and book illustrations.

1793: Etienne-Gaspard "Robertson" Robert attends magic lantern shows in Paris and develops his own version of a spectacle known as "phantasmagoria."

1825: English artist Thomas Cole, generally credited with founding the Hudson River School, paints his first American landscape in the Catskill Mountains of New York.

1837: Ralph Waldo Emerson delivers "The American Scholar" speech in Cambridge, Massachusetts.

1839: Louis Jacque-Mande Daguerre introduces his "daguerreotype" invention in Paris.

1844: Mathew Brady opens a photography study in New York City.

1851: Alexander Gardner encounters the photography of Mathew Brady (he would officially emigrate from his native Scotland to the United States in 1856).

1853–56: The Crimean War is fought.

1854: There are violent clashes between proslavery and antislavery forces in the Kansas territory.

1855:

- Frank Leslie creates *Frank Leslie's Illustrated Newspaper* in New York City.
- Roger Fenton's Crimean War photograph *The Valley of Death* is exhibited in London.

1857:

- The Harper and Brothers establish *Harper's Weekly*.
- Felice Beato's *Lucknow* photographs are the first to show battlefield death.

1859: John Brown's raid on Harpers Ferry fails.

1860:

- November: Abraham Lincoln is elected the sixteenth President of the United States of America.
- December: South Carolina secedes from the Union.

1861:

- February: Florida, Mississippi, Alabama, George, Louisiana, and Texas secede from the Union.
- April 12: Confederate forces attack a Federal garrison at Fort Sumter near Charleston, South Carolina. The Civil War begins.
- April 19: A mob of Confederate sympathizers attack Union troops in Baltimore, Maryland.
- May: Mathew Brady and illustrated news sketch artists arrive in Washington.
- June 5: Elisha Hunt Rhodes enlists in the Second Rhode Island Volunteer Infantry.
- July 21: The first major battle of the war at Manassas Junction in Virginia (also known as The First Battle of Bull Run) takes place.

1862:

- September 17: The Battle of Antietam is fought near Sharpsburg, Maryland.
- October: Mathew Brady opens *The Dead of Antietam* exhibition in New York City.

1863:

- June 7–8: The Battle of Chattanooga is fought.
- July 1–3: The Battle of Gettysburg is fought.
- November 19: Lincoln delivers his Gettysburg Address.

1864:

- May 5–7: The Battle of the Wilderness, near Chancellorsville, Virginia is fought.
- May 31‐June 12: The Battle of Cold Harbor, Virginia, is fought.
- June 9: The Siege of Petersburg, Virginia, begins.
- July 22: The Battle of Atlanta is fought.

1865:

- March 25: The Siege of Petersburg ends. Lee's Army of Northern Virginia flees westward.
- April 9: Lee surrenders to Grant at Appomattox Court House, Virginia.
- April 14: Abraham Lincoln is assassinated.

1866:   Winslow Homer's *Prisoners from the Front* is released.

1872:   Eadweard Muybridge (born Edward James Muggeridge) begins his motion photography experiments in Stanford, California.

1882:   Étienne-Jules Marey invents the chronophotographic gun.

1883:
- Paul Philippoteaux finishes his *Gettysburg Cyclorama*.
- The American Panorama Company is founded.

1886: *The Battle of Atlanta* cyclorama completed.

1895:
- The "hibernation period" ends and photographs of the Civil War are rediscovered.
- Stephen Crane's *The Red Badge of Courage* is published.
- The Lumière film exhibitions take place in Paris.

1897: Horace Porter writes *Campaigning with Grant*.

1898: The Spanish-American conflict in Cuba becomes the first war to be depicted through motion picture.

1904: The Russo-Japanese War, featuring the earliest use of searchlights used for targeting, takes place.

1905:
- Thomas Dixon publishes his novel *The Clansman*, the inspiration for D. W. Griffith's 1915 film *The Birth of a Nation*.
- Abraham Moritz "Aby" Warburg presents his concept of "pathos formula" at an academic congress in Hamburg.

1914: World War I begins.

1915: *The Birth of a Nation* (dir. D. W. Griffith) is released.

1919–40: This time period is considered "The Golden Era of Photography."

1930: Lewis Milestone's *All Quiet on the Western Front*, an adaptation of the Erich Maria Remarque novel of the same name, is released. Its German screenings are disrupted by members of the Nazi party and it is eventually banned in Germany.

1944: Robert Capra photographs the D-Day landing.

1945:
- Joe Rosenthal's *Raising the Flag on Iwo Jima* is published in *The New York Times* and elsewhere.
- Tom Lea's *Two Thousand Yard Stare* photograph is published in the June issue of *Life Magazine*.

1962: James Jones publishes his novel *The Thin Red Line*.

1968:
- Eddie Adams photographs *The Saigon Execution*.
- Emile de Antonio's *In the Year of the Pig* is released.

1978: Michael Cimino's *The Deer Hunter* is released.

1979: Francis Ford Coppola's *Apocalypse Now* is released.

1980: CNN, the first 24-hour cable news network, is launched.

1985: Robert H. Rhodes, great-grandson of Elisha Hunt Rhodes, publishes *All for the Union: The Civil War Diary and Letters of Elisha Hunt Rhodes*.

1987:   Stanley Kubrick's *Full Metal Jacket* is released.

1989:

- Edward Zwick's *Glory* is released.
- Brian De Palma's *Casualties of War* is released.

1990:   Ken Burns' *The Civil War* is released.

1993:   Ronald Maxwell's *Gettysburg* is released.

1998:

- Steven Spielberg's *Saving Private Ryan* is released.
- Terrance Malick's *The Thin Red Line* is released.

2003:

- March: The Iraq War is launched.
- Ronald Maxwell's *Gods and Generals* is released.
- Anthony Minghella's *Cold Mountain* is released.

2005:   YouTube is launched

2006:   Clint Eastwood's *Flags of Our Fathers* and *Letters from Iwo Jima* are released.

2007:   *Redacted* (dir. Brian De Palma) and *In the Valley of Elah* (dir. Paul Haggis) are released, some of the earliest narrative feature films to confront the Iraq War directly.

2008:   Kathryn Bigelow's *The Hurt Locker* premiers at the Venice Film Festival. The film is released theatrically the following year.

2010:   Tim Hetherington and Sebastian Jünger's Afghanistan War documentary *Restrepo* premiers at the Sundance film festival.

2011:   US and UK forces are withdrawn from Iraq.

2012:

- Kathryn Bigelow's *Zero Dark Thirty* is released.
- Steven Spielberg's *Lincoln* is released.

2013:   150-year anniversaries of the Battle of Gettysburg and Lincoln's Gettysburg Address, which included a live naturalization ceremony for sixteen new immigrants.

2015:   The Lincoln funeral train travels from Washington, DC, to Springfield, Illinois, traveling the same route as it did in 1865.

Filmography

Ashby, Hal. (1978). *Coming Home*. USA.

Bigelow, Kathryn. (2009). *The Hurt Locker*. USA.

———. (2009). *Zero Dark Thirty*. USA.

Burns, Ken. (1990). *The Civil War*. USA.

Chaplin, Charles. (1918). *Shoulder Arms*. USA.

Cimino, Michael. (1978). *The Deer Hunter*. USA.

Coppola, Francis Ford. (1979). *Apocalypse Now*. USA.

———. (1992). *Bram Stoker's Dracula*. USA.

———. (2001). *Apocalypse Now: Redux*. USA.

de Antonio, Emile. (1967). *Rush to Judgment*. USA.

———. (1968). *In the Year of the Pig*. USA.

De Palma, Brian. (1989). *Casualties of War*. USA.

———. (2007). *Redacted*. USA.

Dwan, Albert. (1949). *The Sands of Iwo Jima*. USA.

Eastwood, Clint. (2006). *Flags of Our Fathers*. USA.

———. (2006). *Letters from Iwo Jima*. USA.

———. (2014). *American Sniper*. USA.

Fleming, Victor. (1939). *Gone with the Wind*. USA.

Ford, John. (1954). *The Searchers*. USA.

Gance, Abel. (1919). *J'accuse*. France.

———. (1927). *Napoleon*. France.

Greengrass, Paul. (2006). *United 93*. USA/UK.

———. (2010). *Green Zone*. USA.

Griffith, D. W. (1915). *The Birth of a Nation*. USA.

———. (1918). *Hearts of the World*. USA.

Haggis, Paul. (2007). *In the Valley of Elah*. USA.

Hawks, Howard. (1930). *The Dawn Patrol*. USA.

Hetherington, Tim, and Sebastian Jünger. (2010). *Restrepo*. USA.

Hughes, Howard. (1930). *Hell's Angels*. USA.

Huston, John. (1946). *Let There Be Light*. USA.

———. (1951). *The Red Badge of Courage*. USA.

Irvin, John. (1987). *Hamburger Hill*. USA.

Iven, Joren. (1967). *Le 17e parallèle: La guerre du people/The Seventeenth Parallel: Vietnam in War*. France.

Jones, Eugene. (1968). *Faces of War*. USA.

Kubrick, Stanley. (1987). *Full Metal Jacket*. USA.

Lee, Spike. (2008). *The Miracle at St. Anna*. USA.

Longley, James. (2006). *Iraq in Fragments*. USA.

Malick, Terrance. (1998). *The Thin Red Line*. USA.

Mann, Delbert. (1961). *The Outsider*. USA.

Marker, Chris, Jean-Luc Godard, Alain Resnais, Agnes Varda, Claude Lelouch, William Klein, and Joris Ivens. (1967). *Loin de Vietnam/Far From Vietnam*. France.

Maxwell, Ronald. (1993). *Gettysburg*. USA.

McLaglen's, Andrew V. (1965). *Shenandoah*. USA.

Mendes, Sam. (2005). *Jarhead*. USA.

Metz, Janus. (2010). *Armadillo*. Denmark.

Milestone, Lewis. (1930). *All Quiet on the Western Front*. USA.

Minghella, Anthony. (2003). *Cold Mountain*. USA/UK.

Moore, Michael. (2004). *Fahrenheit 9/11*. USA.

Reinert, Robert. (1919). *Nerven/Nerves*. Germany.

Schoendorffer, Pierre. (1966). *The Anderson Platoon*. USA.

Scott, Ridley. (2001). *Black Hawk Down*. USA.

Sheridan, Jim. (2009). *Brothers*. USA.

Siegal, Don. (1971). *The Beguiled*. USA.

Spielberg, Steven. (1998). *Saving Private Ryan*. USA.

———. (2012). *Lincoln*. USA.

Stone, Oliver. (1986). *Platoon*. USA.

———. (1989). *Born on the Fourth of July*. USA.

Vidor, King. (1925). *The Big Parade*. USA.

Wallace, Randall. (2002). *We Were Soldiers*. USA.

Wyler, William. (1946). *The Best Years of Our Lives*. USA.

Zwick, Edward. (1989). *Glory*. USA.

Bibliography

Aaron, Michele. *Death and the Moving Image: Ideology, Iconography, and I*. Edinburgh: Edinburgh University Press, 2014.

Anderson, Duncan. *Glass Warriors: The Camera at War*. London: Collins, 2005.

Auster, Albert. "Saving Private Ryan and American Triumphalism." In *The War Film*, edited by Robert Eberwein, 205–13. London: Rutgers University Press, 2005.

Bacevich, Andrew J. *The New American Militarism: How Americans Are Seduced by War*. Oxford: Oxford University Press, 2005.

Ball, Edward. "Gone with the Myths." *New York Times*. Op-Ed. December 18, 2010.

Ballou, Sullivan. "Civil War Trust." Camp Clark, Washington, D.C., July 14, 1861. http://www.civilwar.org/education/history/primarysources/sullivan-ballou -letter.html.

Barker, Martin. *A "Toxic Genre": The Iraq War Films*. London: Pluto Press, 2011.

Barthes, Roland. *Camera Lucida*. New York: Hill & Wang, 1981.

Batchelor, David. *Chromophobia*. London: Reaktion Books, 2000.

Baudrillard, Jean. "The Gulf War: Is It Really Taking Place?" In *Postmodern Debates*, edited by Simon Malpas, 63–74. New York: Palgrave, 2001.

Bazin, André. *What Is Cinema?* Translated by Hugh Gray. Berkeley: University of California Press, 1967.

Biskind, Peter. "The Vietnam Oscars." *Vanity Fair*. March 2008.

Blight, David W. *Race and Reunion: The Civil War in American Memory*. Cambridge: Harvard University Press, 2002.

Blow, Charles M. "Lincoln, Liberty, and Two Americas." *New York Times*. Op-Ed. November 23, 2013.

Bolloch, Joelle. *War Photography*. Paris: Musée D'Orsay, 2004.

Boyd, Thomas. *Through the Wheat*. New York: Charles Scribner's Sons, 1923.

Bradley, James. *Flags of Our Fathers*. New York: Random House, 2000.

Bronfen, Elisabeth. *Spectres of War: Hollywood's Engagement with Military Conflict*. New Brunswick, NJ: Rutgers University Press, 2012.

Bruzzi, Stella. *New Documentary: A Critical Introduction*. New York: Routledge, 2000.

Burgoyne, Robert. "Abstraction and Embodiment in the War Film." *Journal of War and Cultural Studies* 5, no. 1 (2012): 7–19.

———. *Film Nation: Hollywood Looks at U.S. History*. 1997. Minneapolis: Minnesota University Press, 2010.

————. "Generational Memory and Affect in *Letters from Iwo Jima*." In *A Companion to the Historical Film*, edited by Robert Rosenstone, 349–65. London: Wiley-Blackwell, 2013.

————. *The Hollywood Historical Film*. London: Wiley-Blackwell, 2008.

————. "Stone's Alexander: The Epic as Phantasmagoria." Unpublished manuscript presented at the Film and History Conference, Milwaukee, Wisconsin, November 11–14, 2010.

Burgoyne, Robert, and John Trafton. "Haunting in the Historical Biopic: Lincoln." *Rethinking History* 19, no. 3 (2015): 525–35.

Burns, Ric. *The American Experience: Death and the Civil War*. PBS Original Broadcast: September 12, 2012.

Burns, Sarah, and Daniel Greene. "The Home at War, the War at Home: The Visual Culture of the Northern Home Front." In *Home Front: Daily Life in the Civil War North*, by Peter John Brownlee, Sarah Burns, Diane Dillon, Daniel Greene, and Scott Manning Stevens, 1–12. Chicago: University of Chicago Press, 2013.

Canby, Vincent. "*Glory* (1989): Black Combat Bravery in the Civil War." *New York Times*. December 14, 1989.

Cardullo, Bert. "Flags and Letters." In *Screen Writings: Genres, Classics, and Aesthetics*, vol. 1, by Bert Cardullo, 49–59. London: Anthem Press, 2010.

Childress, Heather M. "*The Gettysburg Cyclorama*: Chicago Edition." *International Panorama Council* (2010): 102–5.

Christie, Ian. "Kings of the Vast." *Tate Etc.* no. 23 (Autumn 2011). http://www.tate.org.uk/context-comment/articles/kings-vast.

————. *The Last Machine: Early Cinema and the Birth of the Modern World*. London: BFI, 1994.

————. "Seeing the Past: Film and Phantasmagoric Space." Paper presented at the Film and History Symposium with Robert Rosenstone, University of St. Andrews, October 10, 2010.

Comment, Bernard. *The Painted Panorama*. New York: Harry N. Abrams, 1999.

Corliss, Richard. "Where Are the War Films?" *Time Magazine*. August 2006.

Corwin, Sharon. *American Modern: Documentary Photography by Abbott, Evans, and Bourke-White*. Berkeley: University of California Press, 2010.

Cunningham, Douglas A. "Explosive Structure: Fragmenting the New Modernist War Narrative in *The Hurt Locker*." *Cineaction*, 81 (2010).

Deleuze, Giles. *Cinema 1: The Movement-Image*. 1983. Translated by Hugh Tomlinson and Barbara Habberjam. London: Athlone Press, 1986.

Dillon, Diane. "Nature, Nurture, Nation: Appetites for Apples and Autumn during the Civil War." In *Home Front: Daily Life in the Civil War North*, by Peter John Brownlee, Sarah Burns, Diane Dillon, Daniel Greene, and Scott Manning Stevens, 127–56. Chicago: University of Chicago Press, 2013.

Doherty, Stephen. "The New War Movies as Moral Rearmament." In *The War Film*, edited by Robert Eberwein, 214–22. London: Rutgers University Press, 2005.

Doherty, Thomas. "The Negro Soldier." In *Projections of War: Hollywood, American Culture and World War II*, by Thomas Doherty, 205–26. New York: Columbia University Press, 1993.

Eberwein, Robert. *The Hollywood War Film*. London: Wiley-Blackwell, 2010.

Efal, Adi. "Warburg's 'Pathos Formula' in Psychoanalytic and Benjaminian Contexts." *Art History Journal* (2001): 221–38. http://www5.tau.ac.il/arts/departments/images/stories/journals/arthistory/Assaph5/13adiefal.pdf.

Eisenman, Stephen F. *The Abu Ghraib Effect*. London: Reaktion Books, 2007.

Emerson, Ralph Waldo. "The American Scholar." Speech given at the Phi Beta Kappa Society, Harvard University, Cambridge, Massachusetts, August 31, 1837.

Faludi, Susan. *The Terror Dream: Fear and Fantasy in Post-9/11 America*. London: Scribe, 2007.

Faye, Dennis. "Bombs under Baghdad." *Writers Guild of America, West*. 2009. http://www.wga.org/content/default.aspx?id=3662.

Freud, Sigmund. "The Uncanny." 1919. In *Freud: The Complete Works*, edited by Ivan Smith, 3673–3700. West Lafayette, IN: Purdue University Press, 2000.

Fuller, Randall. *From Battlefields Rising: How the Civil War Transformed American Literature*. Oxford: Oxford University Press, 2011.

Gallagher, Gary W. *Causes Won, Lost and Forgotten: How Hollywood and Popular Art Shape What We Know about the Civil War*. Chapel Hill: University of North Carolina Press, 2008.

Geng, Veronica. "Mistuh Kurtz—He Dead." *New Yorker*. September 3, 1979: 70.

Goodheart, Adam. "Forward." In *Home Front: Daily Life in the Civil War North*, by Peter John Brownlee, Sarah Burns, Diane Dillon, Daniel Greene, and Scott Manning Stevens, xv–xx. Chicago: University of Chicago Press, 2013.

Green, Warren. "Emile De Anotonio: Interview with Warren Green." *State Historical Society of Wisconsin Journal*. July 1978. Madison: University of Wisconsin, 1978.

Gunning, Tom. *D. W. Griffith and the Origins of American Narrative Film*. Chicago: University of Illinois Press, 1991.

———. *Illusions of the Past: Phantasmagoria and Its Specters*. Chicago: University of Chicago Press, 2004. http://www.mediaarthistory.org/refresh/Programmatic%20key%20texts/pdfs/Gunning.pdf.

———. "Never Seen This Picture before: Muybridge in Multiplicity." In *Time Stands Still: Muybridge and the Instantaneous Photography Movement*, edited by Phillip Prodger, 222–57. Oxford: Oxford University Press, 2003.

Hagen, William H. "*Apocalypse Now*: Joseph Conrad and the Television War." In *Hollywood as Historian: American Film in a Cultural Context*, edited by Peter C. Rollins, 230–45. Louisville: University of Kentucky Press, 1983.

Hariman, Robert, and John Louis Lucaites. "Performing Civic Identity: Flag Raisings at Iwo Jima and Ground Zero." In *No Caption Needed: Iconic Photographs, Public Culture, and Liberal Democracy*, by Robert Hariman and John Louis Lucaites, 363–92. Chicago: University of Chicago Press, 2007.

Harvey, Eleanor Jones. *The Civil War and American Art*. New Haven, CT: Yale University Press, 2012.

———. "The Coming Storm: The Civil War and American Art." Lecture for The Effects of the Civil War on American Art series at the Smithsonian Institution, Washington, DC, April 2013.

Hellmann, John. *American Myth and the Legacy of Vietnam*. New York: Columbia University Press, 1986.

———. "Vietnam and the Hollywood Genre Film: Inversions of American Mythology in *The Deer Hunter* and *Apocalypse Now*." *American Quarterly* 34, no. 4 (Autumn 1982): 418–39.

Henderson, Robert M. *D. W. Griffith: His Life and Work*. Oxford: Oxford University Press, 1972.

Herr, Michael. *Dispatches*. New York: Alfred Knopf, 1977.

Hesk, Jon. "Homeric Spectacles of War in Terrence Malick's *The Thin Red Line*." Paper presented at the War as a Spectacle Colloquium, Open University, Milton Keynes, June 15, 2012.

Hicks, Robert. "Why the Civil War Still Matters." *New York Times*. Op-Ed. July 2, 2013.

Horan, James D. *Mathew Brady: Historian with a Camera*. New York: Crown, 1960.

Huddleston, John. *Killing Ground: Photographs of the Civil War and the Changing American Landscape*. Baltimore: Johns Hopkins University Press, 2002.

Huhtama, Erikka. *Illusions in Motion: Media Archeology of the Moving Panorama and Related Spectacles*. Boston: MIT Press, 2013.

Jameson, Fredric. "War and Representation." *PMLA* 124 (2009): 1532–47.

Johnson, Robert Underwood. *Battles and Leaders of the Civil War*. Edited by Ned Bradford. New York: Thomas Yoseloff, 1956.

Jones, James. "Phony War Movies." *Saturday Evening Post*. March 30, 1963.

———. *The Thin Red Line*. New York: Charles Scribner's Sons, 1962.

Jones, Jonathan. "Painting with Light." *Guardian*. Cultural Section. July 9, 2003.

Kappelhoff, Hermann. "For Love of Country: World War II in Hollywood Cinema at the Turn of the Century." Unpublished paper, Freie Universität Berlin, October 2012.

Katz, Harry. "Bringing the Civil War to Life." *National Geographic* 221, no. 5 (May 2012): 44–59.

Keough, Peter. *Kathryn Bigelow: Interviews*. Conversations with Filmmakers Series. Jackson: University of Mississippi Press, 2013.

Kilpatrick, Jacquelyn. *Celluloid Indians: Native Americans and Film*. Lincoln: University of Nebraska Press, 1999.

King, Geoff. "Seriously Spectacular: 'Authenticity' and 'Art' in the War Epic." In *Hollywood and the War: The Film Reader*, edited by J. David Slocum, 287–302. In Focus Series. New York: Routledge, 2006.

King, Martin Luther, Jr. "I Have a Dream." Speech given at the March on Washington for Jobs and Freedom, Washington, D.C., August 28, 1963.

Kittler, Friedrich A. *Gramaphone, Film, Typewriter*. Translated by Geoffry Winthrop-Young and Michael Wutz. Stanford: Stanford University Press, 1999. Original German publication, Berlin, 1986.

Klinsporn, Geoffrey. "War, Film, History: American Images of 'Real War.'" In *Hollywood and the War: The Film Reader*, edited by J. David Slocum, 33–44. New York: Routledge, 2006.

Knightley, Phillip. *The First Casualty: The War Correspondent as Hero, Propagandist, and Myth Maker from the Crimea to Vietnam*. London: Andre Deutsch, 1975.

Kroll, Jack. "Stanley Kubrick's Horror Show." *Newsweek*. June 2, 1980: 52–54. http://www.visual-memory.co.uk/amk/doc/0053.html.

Landsberg, Alison. *Prosthetic Memory: The Transformation of American Remembrance in the Age of Mass Culture*. New York: Columbia University Press, 2004.

Lea, Tom. "Peleliu: Tom Lea Paints Island Invasion." *Life Magazine*. June 11, 1945.

Lewis, Randolph. *Emile de Antonio: Radical Filmmaker in Cold War America*. Madison: University of Wisconsin Press, 2000.

Lieven, Anatol. *America: Right or Wrong*. London: Harper Perennial, 2005.

Lipset, Seymour Martin. *American Exceptionalism: A Double-Edged Sword*. New York: Norton, 1996.

Lowry, Rich. "Dead Bodies and a Standing President: Alexander Gardner's 'Terrible Reality.'" Paper presented at the Interdisciplinary Symposium on Violence/Crisis, University of St. Andrews, St. Andrews, United Kingdom, May 15–17, 2013.

Martin, Iain C. "Ties to the Past: Amos Humiston—The Unknown Soldier of Gettysburg." *Touched with Fire: The Writing Journal of Iain C. Martin* (blog). January 2, 2013. http://iaincmartin.blogspot.co.uk/2013/01/ties-to-past-amos-humiston-unknown.html.

Masur, Louis P. "In Camp, Reading *Les Misérables*." *New York Times*. Opinion Section. February 9, 2013. http://opinionator.blogs.nytimes.com/2013/02/09/in-camp-reading-les-miserables/?_php=true&_type=blogs&_r=0.

McNeil, Isabelle. *Memory and the Moving Image*. Edinburgh: Edinburgh University Press, 2010: 32.

McPherson, James M. *Battle Cry of Freedom*. Oxford: Oxford University Press, 1988.

Morris Jr., Roy. "One Whose Responsibility? The Historical and Literary Underpinnings of *The Red Badge of Courage*." In *Memory and Myth: The Civil War in Fiction and Film from* Uncle Tom's Cabin *to* Cold Mountain, edited by David B. Sachsman, S. Kittrell Rushing, and Roy Morris Jr., 137–52. West Lafayette, IN: Purdue University Press, 2007.

Morson, Gary Saul, and Caryl Emerson. *Mikhail Bakhtin: Creation of a Prosaics*. Amazon Kindle ed. Stanford: Stanford University Press, 1990.

Nelson, Dustin Luke. "A Modest Lens: An Interview with Roger Deakins." *InDigest*. November 2009. http://www.indigestmag.com/deakins1.htm.

Oettermann, Stephen. *The Panorama: History of a Mass Medium*. Translated by Deborah Lucas Schneider. New York: Urzone, 1997.

Ondaatje, Michael. *The Conversations: Walter Murch and the Art of Editing Films*. London: Bloomsbury, 2002.

"Paul Haggis Interview." *Creative Screen Writing Magazine*. May 16, 2008.

Pisters, Patricia. "Logistics of Perception 2.0: Multiple Screen Aesthetics in Iraq War Films." *Film Philosophy* 14, no. 1 (2010): 232–52.

Pogodda, Cilli. "Case Study: Genre Modality in Iraq War Documentaries—*The War Tapes*." 2006. Paper presented at the War as a Mediated Experience Workshop, Freie Universität, Berlin, Germany, October 18–19, 2012.

Porter, Horace. *Campaigning with Grant*. New York: Smithmark, 1992.

Primono, John W. *The Appomattox Generals: The Parallel Lives of Joshua L. Chamberlain, USA, and John B. Gordon, CSA, Commanders at the Surrender Ceremony of April 12, 1865*. New York: McFarland, 2013.

Prince, Stephen. "The Aesthetic of Slow-Motion Violence in the Films of Sam Peckinpah." In *Screening Violence*, edited by Stephen Prince, 177–204. London: Athlone Press, 2000.

Provencher, Ken. "Redacted's Double Vision." *Film Quarterly* 62 (Fall 2008): 32–38.

Rabinowitz, Paula. "Wreckage upon Wreckage: History, Documentary, and the Ruins of Memory." *History and Theory* 32, no. 2 (May 1993): 119–37.

Remarque, Erich Maria. *All Quiet on the Western Front*. 1929. New York: Random House, 1987.

Rhodes, Robert Hunt. *All for the Union: The Civil War Diary and Letters of Elisha Hunt Rhodes*. 1985. New York: Vintage Books, 1992.

Rosenbaum, Jonathan. "War Porn [Jarhead]." *Chicago Reader*. November 4, 2005. http://www.jonathanrosenbaum.net/2005/11/war-porn.

Rosenheim, Joe. "Seeing the Elephant: Photography and the Civil War." Effects of the Civil War and American Art Series. Washington, DC: The Smithsonian Institution, 2012.

Rosenstone, Robert. *History on Film/Film on History*. London: Longman Pearson, 2006.

Schickel, Richard. *D. W. Griffith*. London: Pavilion Books, 1984.

Scott, A. O. "Rage, Fear and Revulsion: At War with the War." *New York Times*. November 16, 2007.

Sears, Stephen W., ed. *The Civil War: The Second Year Told by Those Who Lived It*. New York: Penguin, 2012.

Segal, Robert. *Joseph Campbell: An Introduction*. 1987. London: Signet, 2000.

Simpson, Brooks D., Stephen W. Sears, and Aaron Sheehan-Dean, eds. *The Civil War: The First Year Told by Those Who Lived It*. New York: Library of America, 2011.

Slocum, J. David. *Violence and American Cinema*. London: Routledge, 2001.

Smith, Anthony D. "Images of Nation: Cinema, Art, and National Identity." In *Cinema and Nation*, edited by Mette Hjort and Scott Mackenzie, 45–52. London: Routledge, 2000.

———. *National Identity*. London: Penguin Books, 1991.

———. *Nationalism*. London: Blackwell, 2001.

Snyder, Joel. "Photographers and Photographs of the Civil War." In *The Documentary Photograph as a Work of Art: American Photographs 1860–1876*, edited by Joel Snyder and Doug Munson, 17–22. Chicago: University of Chicago Press, 1976.

Stewart, Garrett. "Coppola's Conrad: The Repetitions of Complicity." *Critical Inquiry* 7, no. 3 (Spring 1981): 455–74.

———. "Digital Fatigue: Imaging War in Recent American Film." *Film Quarterly* 62, no. 4 (Summer 2009): 45–55.

Storaro, Vittorio. *Scrivere con la luce/Writing with Light*. Rome: Accademia Dell' Immagine, 2001.

Sturken, Marita. *Tangled Memories: The Vietnam War, the AIDS Epidemic, and the Politics of Remembering.* Berkeley: University of California Press, 1997.

Taylor, Jeremy. *The Rules and Exercises of Holy Living and Holy Dying.* 1650–51. Oxford: Clarendon, 1989.

Thelen, David. "Memory and American History." *Journal of American History* 75, no. 4 (March 1989): 1117–29.

Thomson, David. "Grand Illusions: Cinema of the Great War." *Sight and Sound* (July 2014): 38–44.

Thompson, Elbert N. S. "War Journalism Three Hundred Years Ago." *PMLA* 35, no. 1 (1920): 93–115.

Thompson, Patricia. "Risk and Valor: *The Hurt Locker.*" *American Cinematographer* (July 2009). http://www.patriciathomson.net/AC-Hurt_Locker.html.

Thompson, W. Fletcher. *The Image of War: The Pictorial Reporting of the American Civil War.* New York: Thomas Yoseloff, 1960.

Toplin, Robert Brent. "Ken Burns *The Civil War* as an Interpretation of History." In *Ken Burns The Civil War: Historians Respond,* edited by Robert Brent Toplin. Kindle ed. Oxford: Oxford University Press, 1997.

Virilio, Paul. *War and Cinema.* Translated by Patrick Camiller. London: Verso, 1989.

Westwell, Guy. "In Country: Narrating the Iraq War in Contemporary US Cinema." In *A Companion to the Historical Film,* edited by Robert Rosenstone, 384–406. London: Wiley-Blackwell, 2013.

———. *War Cinema: Hollywood on the Front Line.* London: Wallflower Press, 2006.

Wilentz, Sean. "Lincoln in Hollywood: From Griffith to Spielberg." *New Republic.* December 2012. http://www.newrepublic.com/article/books-and-arts/magazine/111242/the-lost-cause-and-the-won-cause.

Wills, Brian Steel. *Gone with the Glory: The Civil War in Cinema.* New York: Rowman and Littlefield, 2007.

Wilson-Bareau, Juliet, and David C. Degener. *Manet and the American Civil War: The Battle of the U.S.S. Kearsarge and C.S.S. Alabama.* New York: Metropolitan Museum of Art, 2003.

Index

Ackroyd, Barry (cinematographer),
    61–62, 65, 93
Afghanistan War
    in cinema, 9, 16, 18, 22–23, 68, 106–7,
        150–57, 178
    in journalism, 155
    photography, 71, 170
    PTSD and, 49
    soldier video diaries and, 22, 78,
        89–90
Alcott, Louisa May, 31, 34, 126
allegory (in soldier writings), 25, 128,
    136, 149
All Quiet on the Western Front (1930),
    4, 14, 24, 47, 52, 134, 136, 164, 177
Al Qaeda, 113
ambrotypes, 77–78
American Revolutionary War, 32, 97,
    124, 128
American Sniper (2015), 160
Anderson Platoon, The (1966), 88
Antietam, Battle of, 4, 11, 21, 74, 76,
    79, 84, 135–36, 139, 161, 176
    depictions on film, 21, 161
    photographs of, 4, 11, 74, 79, 84, 176
    written depictions, 135–36, 139
Apocalypse Now (1979), 4, 6, 7–8, 13,
    47, 50–51, 53, 55–62, 66–68, 130,
    140, 177
    monkey sampan scene (deleted
        scene), 58
    sound technology, 130
    use of color, 57–58
Apocalypse Now: Redux (2001), 58–59
Appomattox Court House, 38, 128,
    132, 176

Bakhtin, Mikhail, 14, 15, 105, 164
    double voicing, 15, 105
    genre memory, 14, 164
Band of Brothers (2001), 160
Barnum, P. T., 29
Batchelor, David, 57, 140
Bazin, André, 9
Beato, Felice, 73, 79, 175
Ben Hur: A Tale of Christ (stage play), 40
Bierstadt, Albert, 33
Bigelow, Kathryn, 8, 13, 50, 51, 54,
    59–62, 66–68, 93, 120, 160, 164,
    178
Birth of a Nation, The (1915), 5, 20, 47,
    51–52, 145–47, 162, 177
Biskind, Peter, 15–16
Black Hawk Down (2001), 3, 107, 109,
    149, 162
body genre (concept of), 12, 61
Bonnie and Clyde (1967), 109
Brady, Mathew, 4, 5–6, 21, 36, 38, 71,
    74–76, 80, 83, 87, 91, 95, 97, 99,
    119, 124, 133, 143, 161, 175–76
Bronfen, Elisabeth, 4, 9, 18–19, 45–46,
    59, 62, 68, 81, 88, 92, 123, 155
Brothers (USA, 2009), 18, 107
Brown, John, 34, 175
Burgoyne, Robert, 12, 14, 18–19, 22,
    26, 40, 54, 61, 105, 124–25, 144,
    162, 170, 172
Burns, Ken, 1, 21–23, 26, 76, 82, 91, 97,
    126–27, 129, 152, 160, 178
Bush, George H. W. (US president), 116

Cameron, Simon (US secretary of war,
    1861–62), 74

carte-de-visite(s), 77–79, 85
Casualties of War (1989), 106–8, 110–12, 178
Chapman, Conrad Wise, 28, 30
chromophobia (concept of), 57, 140
Church, Frederic Edwin, 28–29, 33, 35–36
Civil War, The (1990 PBS documentary), 1, 21–23, 76, 82, 126–27, 129, 160, 178
Civil War films, 19–26, 53, 160–62
Cold Mountain (2003), 2, 24, 129, 178
Cole, Thomas, 33, 175
Coming Home (1978), 16, 18, 106
Coppola, Francis Ford, 4, 8, 13, 47, 50–51, 54–57, 59–61, 66–68, 109, 140, 164, 177
Crane, Stephen, 6, 20, 135, 143, 148, 177
Crimean War, 42, 72–73, 79, 175
photography of, 72–73

Daguerre, Louis Jacques-Mandé, 72, 175
daguerreotype, 72, 74, 77, 170
Dalí, Salvador, 54
De Antonio, Emile, 8, 59, 88, 93–100, 171–72, 177
Deer Hunter, The (1978), 16, 18, 47, 106, 117, 157, 163, 177
Deleuze, Giles, 65
digital fatigue, 89–91, 95, 106, 110–11, 114, 117, 142, 160, 164
in contemporary war films, 109–11
original conception, 89–90
and surveillance technology, 16, 89, 160, 164
Dispatches (1977 book), 4, 140, 148
Drew, Ed (photographic artist), 71
Dulles, John Foster, 99

Eastwood, Clint, 8, 94–95, 100–106, 137, 160, 163, 172, 178
Eisenstein, Sergei, 61, 100–101, 169
Emerson, Ralph Waldo, 31, 33–35, 46, 126, 175

concept of "New Canaan," 34–35, 126
epistolary (in war), 6–9, 11, 19, 21–22, 27, 31, 90, 123–40, 141–52, 151, 160–61

Far from Vietnam (1967), 88
Fenton, Roger (photographer), 72–73
Flags of Our Fathers (2000 James Bradley book), 137–39
Flags of Our Fathers (2006 film), 8, 94–95, 100–106, 137, 162–63, 172, 178
Foote, Shelby (historian), 1, 24, 26, 91
Fox News (cable news channel), 108
Frank Leslie's Illustrated News, 29, 75, 85, 175
Free State of Jones, The (2016), 2
Freud, Sigmund, 13, 58, 63
Full Metal Jacket (1987), 7, 54, 61, 68, 109, 111–12, 140, 148–49, 163–64, 178
Fury (2014), 160

Gangs of New York (2002), 25
Gardner, Alexander, 4, 25, 36, 38, 74, 76–80, 85, 97, 175
Gardner's studio (Washington, DC), 76–77, 85
Gattorno, Antonio, 54
Gaul, Gilbert, 30
genre memory, 7, 13–15, 17–19, 47, 60, 69, 91, 95, 106, 140, 149, 154, 160, 164
origins of concept, 14–15
in war films, 7, 15, 18–19, 47, 60, 69, 95, 106, 149, 154, 160, 164
Gettysburg (1993), 23–24, 53, 147, 178
Gettysburg (2011 television film), 3
Gettysburg, Battle of, 3, 5, 38, 43–47, 52, 130, 159, 167–68, 176, 178
in art, 5, 28, 38–39, 44–47, 52, 130, 177
on film, 3, 23–24, 53, 146, 147
in music, 159

photographs, 11, 38, 79–80, 170
written accounts, 3, 139
Gettysburg Address (speech), 1, 26, 35, 167, 176, 178
Gettysburg National Military Park, 2, 45, 100, 168
Gibson, James (photographer), 74
Gifford, Sanford Robinson (artist), 8, 28–29, 33, 38
Glory (1989), 11, 21, 23–24, 96, 160–62, 178
Godfather, The (1972), 109
Gods and Generals (2002), 24, 53, 178
Gone with the Wind (1939), 20, 24, 53
Go Tell the Spartans (1978), 16
Green Berets, The (1968), 16, 167
Greengrass, Paul, 65, 93, 107
Green Zone (2010), 93, 107
Griffith, David Llewelyn Wark "D. W.," 5, 14, 20, 47, 51–52, 145–47, 177
Gunner Palace (2004), 93
Gunning, Tom, 28, 43, 55, 84

Haggis, Paul, 8, 18, 95, 106, 114–16, 157, 178
Hamburger Hill (1987), 160, 162
Hancock, Winfield Scott, 44, 75, 147–48
Harpers Ferry Raid (1859), 34, 175
Harper's Weekly, 29, 30, 37–38, 74–75, 80–81, 134, 175
Harvey, Eleanor Jones, 32–33, 36, 38, 79, 168
hauntology, 19, 59, 62–64, 67–68, 71, 73–74, 76, 79, 86, 88, 101, 124, 127, 133–34, 159, 164, 172
Hawthorne, Nathaniel, 31, 36, 126
Hayes, Ira, 100–106, 138, 172
Heade, Martin Johnson, 35
Herr, Michael, 4, 140, 148
Hetherington, Tim (filmmaker/journalist), 7, 69, 157, 178
Homer, Winslow (artist), 8, 10, 28–31, 33, 37–39, 46
Battle of Bunker Hill, The, 30

Prisoners from the Front, 10, 37–38, 46
as a sketch artist, 29–30, 38
Hudson River School, 28, 33–35, 175
meteorological metaphors, 35
Hugo, Victor, 34, 123–24
Hunger Games, The (2012), 2, 61, 169
Hurt locker (meaning), 63–64
Hurt Locker, The (2008), 8, 13, 47, 50–51, 54, 59–69, 93, 117, 160, 164, 169, 170, 178

Innis, Chris (film editor), 61, 66
In the Valley of Elah (2007), 7–8, 18, 95, 106–7, 114–20, 150, 157, 178
In the Year of the Pig (1968), 8, 82, 88, 93–100, 152, 171, 177
Iraq War
in cinema, 2, 3, 7–8, 15, 18, 50, 60–61, 66–68, 89–91, 93, 95, 106–19, 152, 160, 163, 167, 173, 178
cultural memory of, 24, 59, 65
reportage, 144, 154
trauma, 18, 49, 67–68
Ivens, Joris, 88
ivory type (photographic technique), 77–78

Jameson, Fredric, 17–18
Jarhead (2005), 61, 140, 149, 161–64
Johnson, Eastman (artist), 29
Johnson, Lyndon B., 99
Jünger, Sebastian (filmmaker/journalist), 7, 69, 157, 178

Kappelhoff, Hermann, 4, 9, 33, 73, 79, 81, 98
King, Martin Luther, Jr., 35
"I Have a Dream Speech," 35
Kittler, Friedrich, 16–17, 84–85, 89, 112, 171
Kubrick, Stanley, 12, 25, 54, 111, 140, 148, 163–64, 178

Lacan, Ernest (photographer and art critic), 72

Langlois, Jean-Charles, 41, 73
Lea, Tom, 55, 87–88, 171, 177
Leslie, Frank, 29, 75, 85, 175
Les Misérables (novel), 123
Les Misérables (1925 film), 124
Lincoln (2012), 2, 25–26, 76, 78, 178
Lincoln, Abraham, 1–2, 25, 36, 74, 76, 132, 134, 143–44, 175–76
Lincoln Funeral Train, 2, 167, 178
Longest Day, The (1962), 5, 47, 50, 52

Malick, Terrance, 7, 128, 137, 149, 178
Manet, Èdouard, 39
   Battle of the Kearsarge and the Alabama, The (1864 painting), 39
Marey, Étienne-Jules, 16, 85, 176
   chronophotographic rifle, 16, 85, 176
   relationship with Eadweard Muybridge, 85
McCarthy, Joseph, 99
Méhédin, Léon-Eugène (photographer), 73
Méliès, Georges, 55
Melville, Herman, 31, 34, 126
Mobilization of Emotions in War Films Project (Freie Universtät Berlin), 9–10, 25, 46, 79, 131, 141
Moore, Michael, 99, 163
Murawski, Bob (film editor), 66
Murch, Walter (film editor), 55, 66–67
Muybridge, Eadweard, 79, 84–85, 171, 176

Napoleon (1927), 5, 52
national identity, 1, 13, 17–18, 94, 101, 159
Native Americans (in war), 100–101, 103, 171
New Hollywood (film historical period, circa 1967–80), 108–9, 111
New York Illustrated News, 29, 74

O'Sullivan, Timothy, 4, 27, 38, 76, 79–80, 97, 170

Outsider, The (1961), 100, 103–5

panorama paintings, 5, 40
   Atlanta Cyclorama, 45, 47, 53, 169, 177
   Gettysburg Cyclorama, 5, 28–29, 39, 45–47, 50, 52, 130, 161, 168, 177
   history of, 40–47
pathos formula
   in Civil War epistolary, 12, 123–30
   definitions, 4, 9, 12
   origin of the term, 9–10
   in panorama paintings, 12, 27, 31, 42, 52
   in photography, 12, 72–74, 79–82, 84–92, 95, 117–19, 121
   as a psychological process, 12
   scenes of, 10–11, 25, 33, 46, 79–80, 95, 117–19, 128, 130–33, 139, 141, 156, 160
   in war films, 4, 52
Paths of Glory (1957), 25, 50
Patton, George S. (general), 105, 128
Patton (1970), 128
Peale, Charles Willson, 32, 71
phantasmagoria, 53
   in Apocalypse Now, 53–58
   exhibition practices, 53–55
   history in Europe, 53–55
   other examples in cinema, 55
Philippoteaux, Paul, 5, 44–47
photography (in war)
   advent of, 72–74
   and the Civil War, 5–6, 94
   in contemporary media, 89–90
   death harvest photographs, 4, 11, 73–74, 79–80
   exhibition practices, 73
   photographic genres, 78–80
   and the Vietnam War, 81, 88–89
   and World War I, 86
   and World War II, 87–88
Pinkerton, Alan, 74
Pisters, Patricia, 89–90
Platoon (1986), 7

Porter, Horace
  Campaigning with Grant (1897), 124, 128–29, 136, 146, 177
PTSD, 18, 49, 55, 83, 87, 169

Radio City Radio (band), 159
Raising the Flag on Iwo Jima (1945 photograph), 81, 101–2, 138
Redacted (2007), 7, 95, 108–14
Red Badge of Courage, The (novel), 6, 135, 143, 177
Red Badge of Courage, The (1951 John Huston film), 20, 162
Restrepo (2010), 7–9, 23, 68–69, 142, 144, 150–58, 162, 170, 178
Rhodes, Elisha Hunt, 27, 124, 129–33, 135, 176
Russo-Japanese War, 43

Saving Private Ryan (1998), 4–5, 15, 25, 47, 50, 52, 61, 81, 87, 94, 106–7, 109, 130, 137, 143, 162–63, 178
Schindler's List (1993), 15
Seventeenth Parallel, The (1967), 88
sketch illustrations, 8, 27, 29, 39, 44, 74–76, 80, 83, 85, 87, 119, 132, 152, 168, 170, 176
  newspapers, 8, 28–30, 74–76, 80, 85, 132, 152, 176
  origins, 29, 168
Skype, 112
Southern Illustrated News, 30
Spielberg, Steven, 2, 4, 15, 23, 25, 76, 78, 94, 106, 137, 144, 162, 178
Stewart, Garrett, 56, 58, 89–91, 95, 110
Stop Loss (2008), 18
Storaro, Vittorio (cinematographer), 55, 57–58, 66–67
  use of color, 55, 57–58
strenuous spectatorship (concept of), 42, 49

Thin Red Line, The (1962 novel), 137–39, 177

Thin Red Line, The (1998 film), 7, 128, 137, 149, 178
Thoreau, Henry David, 31, 33–34, 126
True Blood (television series), 2, 18
Trumbull, John, 32, 71, 128

United 93 (2006), 65

Vietnam War
  activism against, 14, 20, 88–89, 94, 96, 99, 101, 108
  in cinema, 4, 7–9, 14–16, 18, 20, 47, 50, 54–56, 60–62, 66–69, 88, 93, 96, 99, 106–8, 111, 113–14, 140–41, 148–49, 171–72
  cultural memory of, 15–16, 23, 25, 56, 59–60, 83, 94, 98–99, 101, 106, 108, 114, 116, 136–37, 139–40, 154, 161–64, 167, 171
  photography, 88–89
  written narratives of, 140–41
Virilio, Paul, 5, 16–17, 42–43, 52, 68, 84–85, 89, 91, 109–10, 129, 152, 171
Virtual Iraq (therapeutic virtual program), 49–50, 54
virtual reality, 49, 54

Warburg, Abraham Moritz "Aby," 9, 177
war trauma. *See* PTSD
Waud, Alfred, 75, 170
Weir, John Ferguson, 29
We Were Soldiers (2002), 107, 109, 162
WikiLeaks, 112
Wild Bunch, The (1968), 109
Williams, Linda Ruth, 12, 169
World War I
  American Civil War as a precursor of, 24, 91
  in cinema, 14, 24, 50, 52, 124, 134
  cultural memory of, 24, 116
  journalism, 133

World War I (*continued*), photography,
    86–87, 91
  and trauma, 88
  written narratives of, 11, 134–37
World War II
  in cinema, 7–9, 14, 52, 94, 106–7,
      128, 137–41, 148–49, 162
  cultural memory of, 15, 94–95, 101,
      104–6, 110, 162–63

journalism, 55, 87–88, 171
photography, 87–88, 91, 177
trauma, 87–88, 171
written narratives of, 137–39

YouTube, 112, 178

Zero Dark Thirty (2012), 61, 89,
    120–21, 160, 178

CPSIA information can be obtained at www.ICGtesting.com
Printed in the USA
BVOW09*1331150416

444361BV00005B/14/P